READERS' GUIDES TO ESSENTIAL CRITICISM

CONSULTANT EDITOR: NICOLAS TREDELL

Published

Lucie Armitt	George Eliot: *Adam Bede – The Mill on the Floss – Middlemarch*
Richard Beynon	D.H. Lawrence: *The Rainbow – Women in Love*
Peter Boxall	Samuel Beckett: *Waiting for Godot – Endgame*
Claire Brennan	The Poetry of Sylvia Plath
Susan Bruce	Shakespeare: *King Lear*
Sandie Byrne	Jane Austen: *Mansfield Park*
Alison Chapman	Elizabeth Gaskell: *Mary Barton – North and South*
Peter Childs	The Fiction of Ian McEwan
Christine Clegg	Vladimir Nabokov: *Lolita*
John Coyle	James Joyce: *Ulysses – A Portrait of the Artist as a Young Man*
Martin Coyle	Shakespeare: *Richard II*
Michael Faherty	The Poetry of W.B. Yeats
Sarah Gamble	The Fiction of Angela Carter
Jodi-Anne George	Chaucer: The General Prologue to *The Canterbury Tales*
Jane Goldman	Virginia Woolf: *To the Lighthouse – The Waves*
Huw Griffiths	Shakespeare: *Hamlet*
Vanessa Guignery	The Fiction of Julian Barnes
Geoffrey Harvey	Thomas Hardy: *Tess of the d'Urbervilles*
Paul Hendon	The Poetry of W.H. Auden
Terry Hodgson	The Plays of Tom Stoppard for Stage, Radio, TV and Film
Stuart Hutchinson	Mark Twain: *Tom Sawyer – Huckleberry Finn*
Stuart Hutchinson	Edith Wharton: *The House of Mirth – The Custom of the Country*
Betty Jay	E.M. Forster: *A Passage to India*
Elmer Kennedy-Andrews	The Poetry of Seamus Heaney
Elmer Kennedy-Andrews	Nathaniel Hawthorne: *The Scarlet Letter*
Daniel Lea	George Orwell: *Animal Farm – Nineteen Eighty-Four*
Philippa Lyon	Twentieth-century War Poetry
Merja Makinen	The Novels of Jeanette Winterson
Carl Plasa	Tony Morrison: *Beloved*
Carl Plasa	Jean Rhys: *Wide Sargasso Sea*
Nicholas Potter	Shakespeare: *Antony and Cleopatra*
Nicholas Potter	Shakespeare: *Othello*
Berthold Schoene-Harwood	Mary Shelley: *Frankenstein*
Nick Selby	T.S. Eliot: *The Waste Land*
Nick Selby	Herman Melville: *Moby Dick*
Nick Selby	The Poetry of Walt Whitman
David Smale	Salman Rushdie: *Midnight's Children – The Satanic Verses*

Patsy Stoneman	Emily Brontë: *Wuthering Heights*
Susie Thomas	Hanif Kureishi
Nicolas Tredell	F. Scott Fitzgerald: *The Great Gatsby*
Nicolas Tredell	Joseph Conrad: *Heart of Darkness*
Nicolas Tredell	Charles Dickens: *Great Expectations*
Nicolas Tredell	William Faulkner: *The Sound and the Fury – As I Lay Dying*
Nicolas Tredell	Shakespeare: *Macbeth*
Nicolas Tredell	The Fiction of Martin Amis

Forthcoming

Pascale Aebischer	Jacobean Drama
Simon Avery	Thomas Hardy: *The Mayor of Casterbridge – Jude the Obscure*
Paul Baines	Daniel Defoe: *Robinson Crusoe – Moll Flanders*
Sandie Byrne	Contemporary British Poetry
Justine Edwards	Postcolonial Literature
Jodi-Anne George	*Beowulf*
William Hughes	Bram Stoker: *Dracula*
Matthew Jordan	Milton: *Paradise Lost*
Matthew McGuire	Contemporary Scottish Literature
Jago Morrison	The Fiction of Chinua Achebe
Stephen Regan	The Poetry of Philip Larkin
Mardi Stewart	Victorian Women's Poetry
Michael Whitworth	Virginia Woolf: *Mrs Dalloway*
Gina Wisker	The Fiction of Margaret Atwood
Matthew Woodcock	Shakespeare: *Henry V*
Angela Wright	Gothic Fiction

Palgrave Readers' Guides to Essential Criticism
Series Standing Order
ISBN 1–4039–0108–2
(outside North America only)

You can receive future titles in this series as they are published by placing a standing order. Please contact your bookseller or, in the case of difficulty, write to us at the address below with your name and address, the title of the series and the ISBN quoted above.

Customer Services Department, Macmillan Distribution Ltd, Houndmills, Basingstoke, Hampshire RG21 6XS, England

Shakespeare
Antony and Cleopatra

NICHOLAS POTTER

Consultant editor: Nicolas Tredell

First published 2007 by
PALGRAVE MACMILLAN
Houndmills, Basingstoke, Hampshire RG21 6XS and
175 Fifth Avenue, New York, N.Y. 10010
Companies and representatives throughout the world

PALGRAVE MACMILLAN is the global academic imprint of the Palgrave
Macmillan division of St. Martin's Press, LLC and of Palgrave Macmillan Ltd.
Macmillan® is a registered trademark in the United States, United Kingdom
and other countries. Palgrave is a registered trademark in the European
Union and other countries.

ISBN-13: 978–1–4039–9040–2 hardback
ISBN-10: 1–4039–9040–9 hardback
ISBN-13: 978–1–4039–9041–9 paperback
ISBN-10: 1–4039–9041–7 paperback

This book is printed on paper suitable for recycling and made from fully
managed and sustained forest sources.

A catalogue record for this book is available from the British Library.

A catalog record for this book is available from the Library of Congress.

10 9 8 7 6 5 4 3 2 1
16 15 14 13 12 11 10 09 08 07

Printed and bound in China.

To Ninon

CONTENTS

The Introduction discusses the place of *Antony and Cleopatra* among Shakespeare's works and summarises the chapters to follow.

'Let's do it after the high Roman fashion': Shakespeare's Classical World

The chapter outlines the debate over the extent of Shakespeare's classical education, which has continued ever since his friend Ben Jonson remarked that he had 'little Latin and less Greek', and asks why it should matter so much to some critics whether he had or had not had much direct contact with classical sources.

Shakespeare's World Well Lost? Theatre in England during the Interregnum and After

The chapter begins with the closure of the theatres during the Puritan parliamentary rule or 'Interregnum' during the seventeenth century and sets out the background for a consideration of Dryden's revision of *Antony and Cleopatra*. F.R. Leavis's contrast between Dryden's play and Shakespeare's introduces a consideration of some key early twentieth-century critical concerns.

Dryden's Revision of *Antony and Cleopatra*

The chapter discusses *All for Love* to bring out how Dryden's revision of Shakespeare's play throws light on the earlier work.

NOTE ON THE TEXT

All references to *Antony and Cleopatra* are standardised to Stanley Wells and Gary Taylor, eds, *William Shakespeare: The Complete Works* (Oxford: Oxford University Press, 1988); act, scene and line references are all given in Arabic numerals (for example '1.2.3–4').

Introduction: 'Like to a vagabond flag upon a stream': The Vagaries of Opinion Concerning *Antony and Cleopatra*

'Infinite variety', the phrase famously applied to Cleopatra by Antony's faithful follower, the professional soldier Enobarbus (2.2.242), may as well describe the responses to the play itself throughout its critical history. *Antony and Cleopatra* has rarely met with unqualified approval: argument has been dominated by disagreements about what kind of play it is: chronicle history or love story, political drama or romantic tragedy. This Guide will survey some of the most important tendencies in criticism and scholarship, closely discussing the most prominent or indicative of these. It will also, in the notes provided for each chapter, suggest further reading on particular topics, the titles of which are collected for convenience in a select bibliography at the end of the Guide. It cannot be stressed enough that nothing can be taken for granted in a discussion of this play. So various has opinion been and so divided in judgement that only the broadest summaries can hope to do justice to it.

When Shakespeare turned to subjects drawn from classical sources, he seemed to be joining a movement that had already begun as many plays, some popular, some decidedly not, had been written and sometimes performed on themes and subjects drawn from classical history, legend and mythology. One of the defining themes of the Renaissance as it spread across Europe from Italy was the enthusiastic rediscovery of parts of the heritage of the ancient world that had lain neglected throughout the Middle Ages. For Shakespeare to write about Rome and things Roman was not for him to do anything very new. *Titus Andronicus* (1594; perhaps earlier?) was his first attempt, the poem *The Rape of Lucrece* (1594) his next. *Julius Caesar* (1599) followed hot on the heels of *Henry V* (1599) and seems to indicate a turning away from subjects from English history, apart from conjectured contributions much later to *All is True*, also known as *Henry VIII* (1613). *Antony and Cleopatra* (1606) picks up the story of *Julius Caesar* some years after that play left it and may be seen as a companion piece. However, where the earlier play, although described as a tragedy, is also described as a chronicle (that is, like *Richard II* (1597), for example, it follows the narrative of events as they are retrieved from

1

history). *Antony and Cleopatra*, focusing as it does so strongly on the two lovers, has struck many critics as more tragic in its overall character, although few have shared the confidence of Samuel Taylor Coleridge (1772–1834) and ranked it as he did, with the 'big four': *Hamlet* (1602); *Othello* (1604); *King Lear* (1606); *Macbeth* (1606).

Chapter One considers a background question: what was the extent of Shakespeare's familiarity with the ancient world from which he derived the elements for his play? This is an important question for it leads on to a second question: what was the nature of his interest in that ancient world? Chapter One shows how the discussion began in Shakespeare's own day and has continued through to the present day. Some writers insist that Shakespeare could read at least Latin and was well read in classical literature; others that he relied wholly on translations. Some writers have used his supposed classical learning, or his equally supposed lack of it, to make arguments about whether he can be credited as the author of all the plays traditionally attributed to him, or indeed any of them. The chapter warns against those arguments that jump too quickly to the conclusions they wish to reach.

The first significant critical response to *Antony and Cleopatra* is in fact not a critical essay at all but a revision: *All for Love* (1678) by John Dryden (1631–1700) explicitly pays homage to its great original but rewrites it so thoroughly as to produce not so much an adaptation as a wholly new work. Adaptations of Shakespeare's plays to bring them up to date for the tastes of Restoration audiences were common, frequently displacing the original entirely: the *King Lear* (1681) of Nahum Tate (1652–1715) or *The Enchanted Island* (1667; based on *The Tempest*, 1611) of John Dryden and Sir William D'Avenant (1606–68) are two examples but many plays had additions made to them, such as D'Avenant's 1664 adaptation of *Macbeth*, or *A Midsummer Night's Dream* that became *The Fairy Queen* (1692) with music by Henry Purcell (1659–95). *All for Love* may be seen in this context of bringing Shakespeare up to date but must also be seen as a critical revision, revealing at once a reverence for Shakespeare and a recognition that his work belonged to another age. Therefore Chapter Two begins with an important moment in English theatrical history: the so-called 'Interregnum': the period from the execution of King Charles I (1600–49; reigned 1625–49) in 1649 to the Restoration of his son, Charles II (1630–85; reigned 1660–85), in 1660. During this period, Parliament, dominated by the 'Puritan' tendency in English Protestantism, implemented various regulations designed to order English life more in line with Puritan views: the closure of the theatres was one such measure. The reopening of the theatres shortly after the Restoration led to a revival of Shakespeare's work, at least partly because of the shortage of new plays. English theatre had, to a tremendous extent, to reinvent itself. It did so far more influenced by classical precept than had been the Elizabethan or Jacobean theatre. Continental theatre was dominated by classical precept and late seventeenth-century English theatre followed suit. Dryden's treatment of Shakespeare's play offers an insight into this moment.

This Guide takes *All for Love* as a key moment in the history of critical response to *Antony and Cleopatra*, not only because of the Interregnum and its consequences for English theatrical history but also because Dryden's play is the occasion of an essay by F.R. Leavis (1895–1978), who contrasted the two plays very much to Dryden's disadvantage and in so doing revealed much of what he thought was at stake in discussions of literature and criticism and, most importantly, literary history. This is significant because what he thought and what, for example, T.S. Eliot (1887–1965) thought on certain aspects of the discussion of literature and criticism throws much light on critical discussion in the first half of the twentieth century, the 'modernist' period. This, in turn, throws much light on the Romantics and Victorians who preceded them and the 'postmodernists' who followed them. The views that these critics have put forward can be seen to most advantage in the light of their context in literary history.

Chapter Three discusses *All for Love*, finding in it a fine play that clearly shows, in the very clarity of its outline, what Shakespeare did not do. By clarifying the dilemma with which Antony is faced and by purifying the conflicting motives that plague him, Dryden showed how Shakespeare had been doing something very different. By 'tidying up' Shakespeare, Dryden shows what a different kind of orderliness Shakespeare was attempting.

Chapter Four addresses the nineteenth century, starting with the Romantics: Augustus Wilhelm von Schlegel (1767–1845) claims of the lovers that 'As they die for each other, we forgive them for having lived for each other'; Coleridge saw in the play 'exhibitions of a giant power in its strength and vigour of maturity'; William Hazlitt (1778–1830) struggles to reconcile the world of 'known facts' with that of 'fancy' in a discussion of a play he regards as a history play (as did Dr Johnson (1709–84), and as does Schlegel), putting it, perhaps presciently, given later discussions, 'not in the first class of Shakespear's productions'. Among the Victorians, Anna Brownell Jameson (1794–1860) concentrates on Cleopatra, calling her 'a brilliant antithesis' and 'a glorious riddle'; Charles Bathurst (*Remarks on … Shakespeare's Versification*, 1857) thought the play 'carelessly written'; Edward Dowden (1843–1913) claimed that to contrast *Julius Caesar* and *Antony and Cleopatra* was like passing from 'a gallery of antique sculpture' into 'a room splendid with the colours of Titian [Venetian painter, *c.* 1487–1576] and Paul Veronese [Venetian painter, 1528–88]'; Algernon Charles Swinburne (1837–1909) contributes a sort of rhapsody; Arthur Symons (1865–1945) outdoes him. Georg Brandes (1842–1927), the great Danish critic, offers a measured and comprehensive discussion, claiming that 'the final picture is that which Shakespeare was bent on painting from the moment he felt himself attracted by this great theme – the picture of a world-catastrophe'. A.C. Bradley (1851–1934) discusses with great care his view that 'To regard this tragedy as a rival of the famous four, whether on the stage or in the study, is surely an error'. The chapter closes with the bracingly forthright denunciation by George Bernard Shaw (1865–1950) of the ideology of Romantic love and its depiction in *Antony and Cleopatra*, memorably describing the lovers as 'the soldier broken down by debauchery, and the typical wanton in whose arms such men perish'.

Chapter Five begins with Harley Granville-Barker (1877–1946) who is discussed as one of the vanguard of theatre practitioners whose revival of Elizabethan and Jacobean theatre was of such importance to the modern movement in literature and criticism; the bold intuition of John Middleton Murry (1889–1958) that Cleopatra may be seen as 'a child, lost in a dark forest, wavering and timorous: caught between her vision of a world made magnificent by Antony, and her knowledge of a world made dead by his death' is pursued as it follows a winding, sometimes tortuous, path; H.A. Mason offers an alternative view, reminiscent in its scepticism of Shaw; L.C. Knights (1908–91) is more positive and Franklin Dickey offers an interesting account of the play as a morality.

Chapter Six looks at some of the editions of the play in the twentieth century: at the form in which the play becomes familiar to most readers. The Arden, the New Cambridge, the Signet and the Penguin are discussed. The importance of the editions is that they bring together at one time both criticism and scholarship in the manner of the eighteenth-century editions, whereas critical essays isolated from scholarship often give the impression that what is being discussed is a text already established. Furthermore, it has become increasingly the practice of editors to include stage history and commentary on the significance of performance to understanding the play.

Chapters Seven and Eight discuss those critics who have looked at the play as one of a group of 'Roman' plays. Chapter Seven deals with Mungo MacCallum (1854–1942) (*Shakespeare's Roman Plays and their Background*, 1910), who may be credited as the first critic who argued extensively for the definition of the group, and Robert Miola (*Shakespeare's Rome*, 1983). Chapter Eight discusses Coppélia Kahn (*Roman Shakespeare: Warriors, Wounds and Women*, 1997) and Ania Loomba (*Race, Gender and Renaissance Drama*, 1992). As Kahn is heavily influenced by perspectives often collectively designated 'theory', her work provides a suitable bridge to Chapter Nine, which addresses a loose grouping called here 'postmodernists', distinguishing them from the modernists only very generally by chronology. Linda Fitz, Leonard Tennenhouse, Janet Adelman and Jonathan Dollimore are discussed, each offering a different view of the play from the others, united only perhaps by an interest in history and cultural practice, often informed by Marxism, psychoanalysis or both.

The Conclusion asks what the future holds for criticism of *Antony and Cleopatra*. Basing its view on the history it has surveyed, the Guide ends with the hope that the play will continue to provoke interesting reactions among playgoers, readers and critics for at least the foreseeable future.

CHAPTER ONE

'Let's do it after the high Roman fashion': Shakespeare's Classical World

The basic outlook that shapes this Guide is that Shakespeare, taking the story of Antony and Cleopatra as material for a play, was consciously making a contribution to a process of interpretation that had been going on for some time before he joined the discussion and which has continued long after he made his contribution. The story of Antony and Cleopatra had been told and retold already: his contribution complicated the discussion considerably, adding the task of interpreting that contribution to the already difficult business of interpretation to which he had contributed.

The context within which *Antony and Cleopatra* must be seen is classical in both its inspiration and the form in which the works are cast. Mary Sidney (1561–1621), who had become the Countess of Pembroke on her marriage to the Earl of Pembroke, translated, in 1590,[1] the play *Marc Antoine* by Robert Garnier (1534–90); Garnier's play was firmly based on classical dramatic precepts and was part of a conscious effort to recall the classical epoch.[2] The *Cleopatra* of Samuel Daniel (1562–1619), which owed its inspiration to the Countess's work, equally deliberately recalls the work of the ancient Roman dramatist Lucius Annaeus Seneca (c. 4 BC–AD 65), whose work was widely influential in Europe. The French stage was dominated by the Senecan school, of which Garnier's *Marc Antoine* is an example, but the English stage had been formed upon quite different models and they proved resistant to change.

In 1598, Samuel Brandon published *The Virtuous Octavia* and John Fletcher (1579–1625) and Philip Massinger (1583–1640) staged *The False One* in 1620 or thereabouts; the *Cleopatra* of Thomas May (1595–1650) was acted in 1626 and printed in 1639.[3] The *Antony and Cleopatra* of Sir Charles Sedley (?1639–1701) was acted at the Duke's Theatre in 1676 or 1677 with Betterton as Antony; it was printed in 1677 and reappears in 1702 as *Beauty the Conqueror* or *The Death of Marc Antony*.

In 1678, Dryden published *All for Love, Or, The World Well Lost*. In 1759, David Garrick (1717–79) put on a version of Shakespeare's play at Drury

Lane and the stage history of that play begins to eclipse that of any other play on the same theme. After 1759, Shakespeare's play becomes the established version of the story until Shaw's revision, *Caesar and Cleopatra* (1898).

Shakespeare drew heavily on the 'Life of Marcus Antonius' from *The Lives of the Noble Grecians and Romans* by Plutarch (Ploutarchos, *c.* AD 46–120), a work that had become, in French and then in English translations, one of the staples of Renaissance Europe's reading. Plutarch was a near contemporary of the satirical poet Juvenal (Decimus Junius Juvenalis, AD 60–140), and a native of Chaironeaia in Boiotia. He spent some time in Rome on public business, where he gave lectures on philosophical topics, learned some Latin and read some Roman authors. His *Parallel Lives,* as it is also sometimes known, is a set of parallel studies of Grecians and Romans on the principle that for every distinguished Roman there was a similar Grecian figure. Mark Antony (Marcus Antonius) is paired with Demetrios Poliorketes. Plutarch's interests were moralistic; he was, by all accounts, a pious man, a priest of Apollo. Jacques Amyot (1513–93) translated the work into French in 1559 and Sir Thomas North (?1535–1601) translated from Amyot's French into English in 1579. Verbal echoes establish North as Shakespeare's source.[4]

The fact that Shakespeare used an English translation from the French of a work written in Greek raises a question that is marginal to *Antony and Cleopatra* but of great significance to his work as a whole and especially to that portion of his work directly dealing with Graeco-Roman antiquity: what was the nature of his familiarity with that antiquity? How classically learned was Shakespeare?

It is important to get the measure of this question for it is not a merely scholarly question. It is in fact a question that cuts to the root of Shakespeare's place in the English cultural tradition and to the root of that tradition itself. It is one of the purposes of this Guide to raise the question of the English cultural tradition because that question is raised by discussion of the critical history of *Antony and Cleopatra,* so it is apposite to address this matter immediately and establish the theoretical framework with which this Guide will be working before proceeding much further.

It is almost a precept of modernist criticism that, in T.S. Eliot's famous phrase, 'in the seventeenth century a dissociation of sensibility set in, from which we have never recovered'.[5] It was important to the development of Eliot's poetry that he fashion a theory of literary history that would enable him to define a tradition that would circumvent and describe a period whose own tradition had resulted in the production of work against which Eliot wanted to delineate his own work with the utmost sharpness. He wanted to see his work as redressing an imbalance. He wanted to see the Romantics and their Victorian and late Victorian heirs as a reaction against a period that had lurched into imbalance and which was, hence, unbalanced itself. English literary history had stumbled, overbalanced the other way in order to right itself but was now, in his work especially, finding its feet again. It was an extremely bold venture, the success of which may still not be safely described as merely local and temporary.

The influence of modernist criticism has been significant, not least in the emergence of a post-modernist (or postmodernist) criticism as an antidote to some of its effects. The identification of the period of the civil wars as distinguishing the beginning of the seventeenth century (and thus the last part of Shakespeare's career) from the end of the seventeenth century (that may be identified with the work of John Dryden) will be further explored in an examination of F.R. Leavis's comparison of Dryden's *All For Love* with *Antony and Cleopatra*. For the time being it is enough to say that the emphasis introduced into literary studies, which has been widely influential, obscures another, equally important distinction between a period that conducted criticism as part and parcel of its ordinary activities and a period that began to identify a particular social role, that of the literary critic, and an activity associated with that role, literary criticism, that is, between the earlier and the later part of the late seventeenth century and the development of that later part of the late seventeenth century into the eighteenth century.

This period began also to develop serious scholarship in matters of English letters, producing editions of Shakespeare's works as well as biographical studies, and discussions of questions such as what knowledge did Shakespeare have directly of the work of the classical world about which he was writing plays. This question was first seriously discussed by Richard Farmer in *An Essay of the Learning of Shakespeare* published in 1767. Dr Farmer (1735–97) argued that Shakespeare's direct knowledge of the classics was as limited as his friend Ben Jonson (1572–1637) had said it was in his Memorial Verses: 'Thou hadst little Latine and Lesse Greeke'. Two enthusiastic rather than accurate works had suggested otherwise;[6] Dr Farmer was putting the record straight.

Dr Johnson thought Farmer was right and makes a characteristically judicious summary of the facts as they stood in his view:

■ There has always prevailed a tradition that Shakespeare wanted learning, that he had no regular education, nor much skill in the dead languages. *Johnson* his friend affirms, that *he had small Latin, and no Greek*; who besides that he had no imaginable temptation to falsehood, wrote at a time when the character and acquisitions of *Shakespeare* were known to multitudes. His evidence ought therefore to decide the controversy, unless some testimony of equal force could be opposed.[7] □

The 'testimony of equal force' that Johnson argued would be needed to refute that of Ben Jonson, if that is what it is, was supplied by John Aubrey (1626–97), who recorded in his *Brief Lives* (1681) that William Beeston, the son of Christopher Beeston who had been a member of

Shakespeare's company, told him that Shakespeare 'understood Latine pretty well: for he had been in his younger yeares a Schoolmaster in the Countrey'.

Other major contributions to the discussion in the eighteenth century that should be noted here include that of George Steevens (1736–1800), who appended an essay, 'Ancient Translations from the Classic Authors', to his 1773 edition of the plays, which argued that Shakespeare had copied from the translations, and that of Edmond Malone (1741–1812), who offered a more generous account of Shakespeare's education in his *Life*, published at last in *Boswell's Malone*.[8]

Jonson's commemorative verses set the tone for the seventeenth century: John Milton (1608–74) contrasts Jonson and Shakespeare in *L'Allegro* (1631?):

■ Then to the well-trod stage anon,
   If Jonson's learned sock be on,
   Or sweetest Shakespeare fancy's child,
   Warble his native wood-notes wild □

In 1668, John Dryden had written of Shakespeare in *An Essay of Dramatic Poesy*:

■ He was the man who, of all modern and perhaps ancient poets, had the largest and most comprehensive soul. All the images of nature were still present to him, and he drew them not laboriously, but luckily. When he describes anything, you more than see it, you feel it too. Those who accuse him to have wanted learning give him the greater commendation. He was naturally learned. He needed not the spectacles of books to read nature. He looked inwards, and found her there.

   I cannot say he is everywhere alike. Were he so, I should do him injury to compare him with the greatest of mankind. He is many times flat, insipid, his comic wit degenerating into clenches, his serious swelling into bombast. But he is always great when some great occasion is presented to him. No man can say he ever had a fit subject for his wit and did not then raise himself as high above the rest of poets,

   quantum lenta solent inter viburna cupressi [as cypresses often do among the bending osiers]

   The consideration of this made Mr Hales of Eton say that there was no subject of which any poet ever writ, but he would produce it much better treated of in Shakespeare.[9] □

The John Hales story was later told more fully by Nicholas Rowe (1674–1718):

■ In a Conversation between Sir *John Suckling* [1609–41], Sir William *D'Avenant*, *Endymion Porter*, Mr. *Hales of Eaton*, and *Ben Johnson*;

Sir *John Suckling*, who was a profess'd admirer of *Shakespear*, had undertaken his Defence against *Ben Johnson* with some warmth; Mr. *Hales*, who had sat still for some time, hearing *Ben* frequently reproaching him for want of Learning, and Ignorance of the *Antients*, told him at last, That if [though] Mr. *Shakespear* had not read the Antients, he had likewise not stollen any thing from 'em; (a Fault the other made no Conscience of) and that if he would produce any one Topick finely treated by any of them, he would undertake to shew something upon the same Subject at least as well written by *Shakespear*.[10] □

Rowe's own testimony is given in the Preface to his edition of 1709:

■ For those Plays which he has taken from the *English* or the *Roman* History, let any Man compare 'em and he will find the Character as exact in the Poet as the Historian.[11] □

Nahum Tate agreed:

■ I confess I cou'd never yet get a true account of his Learning, and am apt to think it more than Common Report allows him. I am sure he never touches on a Roman Story, but the Persons, the Passages, the Manners, the Circumstances, the Ceremonies, all are Roman. And what Relishes yet of a more exact Knowledge, you do not only see a Roman in his Heroe, but the particular Genius of the Man, without the least mistake of his Character, given him by their best Historians. You find his *Antony*, in all the Defects and Excellencies of his Mind, a Souldier, a reveller, Amorous, sometimes Rash, sometimes Considerate, with all the various Emotions of his Mind.[12] □

Dryden argues that this ability is not the result of learning:

■ Those who accuse him to have wanted learning give him the greater commendation. He was naturally learned. He needed not the spectacles of books to read nature. He looked inwards, and found her there.[13] □

On the other hand, Tate's observations raise an objection to Dryden's formulation. Tate argues that the closeness of Shakespeare's depictions to their originals in the histories shows a familiarity with those histories, which, on the face of it, is a strong argument. It is difficult to imagine how intuition could have arrived at the histories. Shakespeare is not imagining a man like Mark Antony, he is imagining Mark Antony.

The question is not whether Shakespeare had much of a classical education, but why it should matter either way. It is then a matter of observing in each contribution to the discussion whether or not it matters to the contributor if Shakespeare had or had not had a classical education. It does not seem to bother Samuel Johnson that he had not; it seems to have irritated Ben Jonson that he had not. Peter Whalley and John Upton wanted to ascribe one to him; Richard Farmer showed that they had failed to do so successfully. The question then is why they should have wanted him to have one.[14]

For some writers, it seems, the fact of Shakespeare's achievement is irreconcilable with the fact that he was not classically educated. They therefore seek to persuade themselves and others that he was classically educated, or that the plays are not as good as some think (a path taken, famously, by Thomas Rymer (1643–1713) in *A Short View of Tragedy* (1693) in which he ridicules *Othello*), or that the plays were written by someone who did have a classical education, that is, not by William Shakespeare. There are two main versions of this question: one is sometimes called 'disintegrationism'; the other is sometimes called 'anti-Stratfordianism'. The first is associated mainly with Frederick G. Fleay, whose *Shakespeare Manual* (1878) argued that Shakespeare could not have written the plays demanding classical knowledge as he had not had a classical education. The implication is that someone else did. This conclusion leads to the second version of the question, discussion of which is well summarised by John Fiske in 'Forty Years of Bacon-Shakespeare Folly' (1897).[15]

In the twentieth century, John Dover Wilson (1881–1969) summarised the 'small Latin' controversy and intervened in it rather testily. He relates the John Hales story and quotes Dryden and Johnson approvingly; he relates the Aubrey anecdote but holds that even were it accurate it would tell us little, as even if Shakespeare had been an 'usher' helping a schoolmaster with the junior boys, 'not much knowledge would be required for such instruction'.[16] He is especially irritated by T.W. Baldwin's study[17] and quotes J.A.K. Thomson:

> ■ Professor Baldwin tells us in very great detail what Shakespeare *could* have learned at school. But the hard fact is that we do not know what amount of schooling Shakespeare had ... moreover I cannot believe that Professor Baldwin has sufficiently considered that a practical man of letters is constantly picking up information – even information contained in books – from other people.[18] □

This last point is extremely important. A hypothesis demanding little stretch of the imagination and embracing the facts as they appear is that what Shakespeare did not know himself he took from other people. After all, much learning is acquired in much the same manner. Even verbal echoes can be explained by this hypothesis. There is no reason why a writer should have picked up a phrase in the course of his or her reading when it could have come from conversation or instruction. There is a further element to this discussion, however.

John Dover Wilson takes a dozen lines from *The Merchant of Venice* (5.1.1–14) and, having discussed the possible 'sources', he then says, 'It is absurd to think of Shakespeare digging that glorious stuff out of books'.[19] The force of this argument is to be found in the juxtaposition of 'digging' and 'glorious'. To dig something out is to go about something laboriously (Dryden had remarked that 'All the images of nature were still present to him, and he drew them not laboriously, but luckily'); 'glorious' is a word that may be glossed by a reference to Wordsworth's picture of the loss of childhood vision, 'there hath passed away a glory from the earth'. We are in the realm of the spiritual, certainly not the manual. Our delight would be vitiated should we come to believe that 'that glorious stuff' came about as the result of anything like mere spade-work. Dryden's 'luckily' makes the same point: such effects cannot have been striven after; they must have presented themselves.

This discussion raises several themes: that of nature versus civilisation as earlier identified is the controlling theme. Secondly, the theme of instinct versus deliberation in the creation of works of art is raised by Milton's picture of Shakespeare and Dryden's as well ('not laboriously, but luckily'). Sir Philip Sidney's Astrophil is admonished by his Muse for seeking inspiration for his poems in the work of other writers: 'Fool, said my Muse to me: Look in thy heart and write.' The theme of classical, or neoclassical, and Romantic is also raised, before the terms of the debate have even been invented. There is also a theme of native tongue versus the learned languages ('warble his *native* wood-notes wild'). This theme is connected with the emergence of the vernacular during the Renaissance period and in turn is connected with the development of the national consciousness that is such an important building block for the development of the ideology of the 'nation-state' during the nineteenth century. Finally, Dover Wilson's use of the word 'glorious' implies something about what art evokes, what art 'sees'. The impatience in his essay is not just with what he sees as an overfastidious classicism but also with a critical obtuseness that cannot or will not respond to 'that glorious stuff' but must rob it of its power by tracing it back to its sources.

The debate may be summarised by observing that the emergence of a national culture is never a straightforward business. A national culture is a specific formation within another culture (in the case of English culture within the classically dominated European tradition, the culture of the Catholic 'Christendom' of the Middle Ages) and it is an evolution first of all within that culture and then out from it into a specific and distinct tradition in its own right. It is never a clear-cut matter what it still owes to its parent and at what point it has become distinct in its own right. The status of Shakespeare, which derives of course from the power of his achievement, from the influence of his work over others, is central to the process of the evolution of a national culture for the

English people.[20] The picture is further complicated as the English language becomes, as it spreads through the world carried by English and later by British[21] colonial expansion, the property of peoples who begin to develop and then assert their own national cultures.

That passions ran high in the course of this discussion is evidenced by the treatment Dover Wilson's essay received in a work in connection with which no researcher in the field of Shakespeare's Roman plays may overlook the debt owed to John W. Velz, who patiently collected the material for what became the standard bibliographical survey of discussions of the plays. Velz is firmly on Baldwin's side. His comment on Baldwin's *William Shakespeare's Small Latine* is as follows:

■ This thorough study provides the groundwork of inductive probability on which criticism of [Shakespeare's] use of his cultural assets can be built.[22] □

He is severe to F.S. Boas:

■ Though he begins with the implication that he is familiar with the research of the 'thirties and 'forties in America on [Shakespeare's] classical education, Boas always clings tenaciously to what has come to be identified as the British view of [Shakespeare] as a semiliterate.[23] □

It must be supposed that any suggestion from this side of the Atlantic that 'the research of the 'thirties and 'forties in America on [Shakespeare's] classical education' might have been mistaken in its conclusions would only further reveal British narrowness. The same limitations will no doubt be assumed of anyone objecting to the description of someone who has small Latin and less Greek as 'a semiliterate'.

The situation is, however, a little more complicated than it might appear: British scholarship had not overlooked Elizabethan education[24] and the picture in America was not uniform.[25] Velz's reaction to Dover Wilson is not measured. He describes the essay as 'this strangely obtuse brief survey' and continues to say that Wilson:

■ shares with J.A.K. Thomson a patronizing attitude towards [Shakespeare's] use of [translation], suggesting that only inability to read Latin fluently would have driven him to Golding.[26] □

In fact, Wilson has not suggested this at all, saying instead that Shakespeare's evident familiarity with the Elizabethan translation

(1565–7) by Arthur Golding (?1536–1605) of the *Metamorphoses* of the ancient Roman poet Ovid (Publius Ovidius Naso, 43 BC–AD 18):

■ a familiarity so intimate that Golding's actual words, at times even his additions, recur to his mind and appear in his verse, is not easily accounted for if he read the original Ovid with facility. □

This is not to say that he was 'driven' to Golding, but that it is difficult to explain the presence of Golding if Shakespeare were acquainted with Ovid himself. The extent of Velz's annoyance with Dover Wilson may be judged by his statement that Wilson's dismissal of Baldwin's 'conclusive evidence' is not only 'cavalier' but also 'surprising, coming as it does from a normally responsible scholar'.[27] That this is not entirely a measured debate will now be obvious, but as a postscript it is worth noticing that Velz takes Thomson to task on another occasion,[28] accusing Thomson of ignoring 'in his argument for [Shakespeare] as Nature's child the conclusions of T.W. Baldwin, e.g., on [Shakespeare's] obvious competence in Latin'. The inclusion of the word 'obvious' raises a suspicion concerning the nature of the method Velz has styled 'inductive probability'. In a note on Baldwin's other major study,[29] Velz describes Terence as 'the preferred author for lower forms in [Shakespeare's] day'[30] and goes on to say of Udall's *Floures* that this was a translation 'which [Shakespeare] doubtless used as a pony [crib] in school for difficult passages'.[31] He adds that Shakespeare's 'school text of Terence was probably the Willinchins [edition]'.[32] This is all very well, but 'doubtless' is not an argument but an assertion for which there is not a shred of evidence beyond the very loosely circumstantial, and the question of which edition of Terence Shakespeare used at school begs the question whether he used any edition at all, for which, again, the evidence, if any, is only circumstantial.

In addressing himself to the classical world, it must be said that Shakespeare only invited such attention. If he was not a classicist himself (and there is no compelling evidence that he was, only suggestive indications), then he invited the critical attention of those who were and he invites the attention of those who are. The question of why he did so is a matter for speculation, although both MacCallum and Kahn address their attention to it.[33] The question that does not demand classical training is what he made of the world to which he addressed himself, and criticism of *Antony and Cleopatra* has largely concerned itself with this question. This Guide begins with a study of a work, not itself a critical work but a poetic drama, that brings into sharp focus some of the key critical and literary historical questions with which the play has been associated. John Dryden's play *All For Love* puts into perspective not only the drama before it and the drama after it, but the literature as a whole, and critical approaches to it have proved remarkably eloquent about some of the deepest questions with which English literary criticism is concerned.

Before examining Dryden's play, it will be useful to consider briefly the social, political and theatrical contexts within which it was produced. The seventeenth century is a period of deep and rapid change: Shakespeare's play comes at the beginning of that period of change and Dryden's comes towards the end of it. The next chapter sets the scene for a close look at Dryden's tribute to and version of Shakespeare's *Antony and Cleopatra*.

CHAPTER TWO

Shakespeare's World Well Lost? Theatre in England during the Interregnum and After

Shakespeare's theatre belongs to the end of an age as much as to the beginning of one. It belongs to the beginning of a 'modern' period as distinct from a 'medieval' period, in the sense that convincing continuities can be traced between our world and its world, and in the more precise sense that the modernist critics, especially T.S. Eliot and F.R. Leavis, drew heavily on Shakespeare's work to justify their critical practice and their theories. However, it belongs to the end of the medieval period in the important sense that the political and religious frameworks within which it operated are more directly continuous with that world out of which it grew than with that world into which it looked forward. The movement from *Antony and Cleopatra* to *All For Love* is a movement from that world out of which it grew into the world into which it looked forward, and a clear contrast between the two will help to bring out what Shakespeare was doing. In this sense, *All For Love*, although a poetic drama and not a critical essay, will perform the function of bringing the earlier play into critical focus.

This chapter will establish a background for a consideration of *All For Love*, particularly exploring Dryden's notions of 'imitation', as this concept lies behind much of the critical and creative practice of the period. The chapter will then discuss Leavis's essay on *All For Love* in order to set out the theoretical background that it is essential to appreciate in order to understand fully the extent to which modernist criticism revised, or attempted to revise, literary history in order to make its points.

The break between the two ages is most clearly visible in the years of parliamentary rule following the execution of Charles I in 1649. These years, sometimes called the 'Interregnum' (the 'between reign') are the years in which the English theatre of Shakespeare's time was systematically rooted out of English society. In 1633, William Prynne (1600–69) printed *Historiomastix*, the most notorious of the many attacks on the stage by Puritan agitators against what they saw as the immorality of their age. For being found guilty of making an insulting remark about Queen

for virtue: but, to draw forth out of the best, and choicest flowers, with the bee, and turn all into honey, work it into one relish, and savour: make our imitation sweet: observe how the best writers have imitated, and follow them. How Virgil, and Statius have imitated Homer; how Horace, Archilochus; how Alcaeus, and the other lyrics: and so of the rest.[6] [Virgil, Publius Vergilius Maro, ancient Roman poet, 70–19 BC; Statius, Publius Papinious, ancient Roman poet, c. AD 45–96; Homer, ancient Greek poet, supposed author of the *Illiad* and *Odyssey*; Archilochus, ancient Greek poet, mid seventh century BC; Alcaeus, ancient Greek poet, active about 600 BC] ☐

There is a theory of literary history implied in this: that of tradition as imitation in this richest of senses, that a poet be able 'to convert the substance ... of another poet, to his own use'. Such conversion must involve a transformation; the production of something new out of what already exists. Seneca makes use of the example of the bees that transform what they gather from the flowers they visit into honey in their hives.[7] Talk of originality merely confuses, especially when the idea of creation out of nothing is in the background: in this view originality arises out of a specific use to which the absorbed influence is put.

Dryden made some useful remarks on translation in his Preface to the edition of Ovid's *Epistles*, a set of translations by several hands, published in 1680 by Jacob Tonson (1656–1736), to which Dryden contributed three of the Epistles as well as the Preface:

■ All translation I suppose may be reduced to three heads.
First that of metaphrase, or turning an author word by word, and line by line, from one language into another. Thus, or near this manner, was Horace's *Art of Poetry* translated by Ben Jonson. The second way is that of paraphrase, or translation with latitude, where the author is kept in view by the translator, so as never to be lost, but his words are not so strictly followed as his sense, and that too is admitted to be amplified, but not altered. Such is Mr Waller's translation of Virgil's fourth *Aeneid* [this refers to the poet Edmund Waller, 1606–87]. The third way is that of imitation, where the translator (if now he has not lost that name) assumes the liberty not only to vary from the words and sense, but to forsake them both as he sees occasion: and taking only some general hints from the original, to run division on the groundwork, as he pleases. Such is Mr Cowley's practice [Abraham Cowley, 1618–67] in turning two odes of Pindar, and one of Horace into English.[8] ☐

Dryden later amplifies his definition of imitation:

■ I take imitation of an author in their [Cowley and Sir John Denham, 1615–69] sense to be an endeavour of a later poet to write like one who has written before him on the same subject: that is, not to translate his words, or to be confined to his sense, but only to set him as a pattern, and to write as he supposes that author would have done had he lived in our age, and in our country.[9] □

However, he decides against imitation as an extreme to be avoided as sedulously as what he calls 'verbal version':

■ To state it fairly, imitation of an author is the most advantageous way for a translator to show himself, but the greatest wrong which can be done to the memory and reputation of the dead.[10] □

It may be seen that what he deprecates in the translation of an author who has written in another tongue he has practised in the imitation of Shakespeare. Admiring the work of the earlier writer, Dryden set out to render it 'as he supposes that author would have done had he lived in our age'.

Dryden invited comparison of course by claiming that he was imitating Shakespeare and that comparison, in the spirit of Dryden's own discussion of imitation, is both eminently fair and not at all to Dryden's disadvantage. First we must remember that we are transposing comments to the detriment of imitation from one context, that of writers in a tongue other than English and from another age, to another, that of a writer in English from another age. The work of that writer is accessible to any reader; Dryden is discussing the work of writers in another tongue whose work is not accessible to any reader, as there are readers not conversant with the original tongue. Dryden's argument is that Denham's objection to literal translation is sound:

■ 'Poetry is of so subtle a spirit, that in pouring out of one language into another, it will all evaporate; and if a new spirit be not added in the transfusion, there will remain nothing but a *caput mortuum* [dead head].' I confess this argument holds good against a literal translation, but who defends it?[11] □

It is Dryden's view that 'thought, if it be translated truly, cannot be lost in another language' and 'The sense of an author, generally speaking, is to be sacred and inviolable'. What then of imitation in the author's own language? Surely Dryden was thinking of his own practice only three years earlier when he wrote that imitation of an author was the 'endeavour of a later poet to write like one who has written before him on the same subject: that is, not to translate his words, or to be confined to his sense, but only to set him as a pattern, and to write as he supposes that author would have done had he lived in our age'?[12] As it turns out, that is exactly what he has done in *All For Love*. What this work shows audiences today is precisely why *Antony and Cleopatra* would not have done for Dryden's own age; why it did so well for its own; and why the twentieth century, in such striking instances as Leavis's comparison between the two in *The Living Principle* (1975), embraced Shakespeare's play rather than Dryden's.

In this light, Dryden's work must be seen not only in prosodic terms, because then the reader will retire puzzled, as the relationship between Dryden's verse and Shakespeare's is far from immediately obvious, but primarily in conceptual terms. Dryden has recast Shakespeare's work (itself an imitation of Plutarch's through North) to suit his particular purpose, his vision of the story. This vision is made clear in the opening statements of his Preface:

■ The death of Antony and Cleopatra is a subject which has been treated by the greatest wits of our nation, after Shakespeare; and by all so variously, that their example has given me the confidence to try myself in this bow of Ulysses amongst the crowd of suitors; and, withal, to take my own measures, in aiming at the mark. I doubt not but that the same motive has prevailed with all of us in this attempt; I mean the excellency of the moral. For the chief persons represented were famous patterns of unlawful love; and their end accordingly was unfortunate. All reasonable men have long since concluded, that the hero of the poem ought not to be a character of perfect virtue, for then he could not, without injustice, be made unhappy; not yet altogether wicked, because he could not then be pitied. I have therefore steered the middle course; and have drawn the character of Antony as favourably as Plutarch, Appian [*c.* 1st–2nd AD], and Dion Cassius [AD 163–*c.* 235] would give me leave; the like I have observed in Cleopatra.[13] □

Dryden observes the defect of the story in tragic potential:

■ That which is wanting to work up the pity to a greater height, was not afforded me by the story; for the crimes of love, which they both committed, were not occasioned by any necessity, or fatal ignorance, but were wholly voluntary; since our passions are, or ought to be, within our power.[14] □

He is worried that he has distributed the audience's sympathies too much by introducing Octavia but notes that none of his critics noted this weakness. He devotes his attention to the objection that he has written a spirited exchange between Octavia and Cleopatra, which, he admits, French poets would not have done.

The significance of Dryden defending himself against the practice of French poets is that they modelled themselves so exactly upon Aristotelian principles. Ludovico Castelvetro (1505–71) had translated Aristotle's *On*

Poetry into Italian in 1570, and was copied by others, notably René Rapin (1621–87) and Jules des Mesnardière (1610–63) in France and Thomas Rymer in England. The effect of this was highly significant in France and highly controversial in England. French drama, indeed Continental drama, was fundamentally shaped by it, whereas English drama, which had had different origins and influences, was already shaped by, among others, Shakespeare.[15] Dryden feels the pressure of these principles but defends himself on the grounds of naturalness:

> ■ And it is not unlikely, that two exasperated rivals should use such satire as I have put into their mouths; for, after all, though the one were a Roman, and other a queen, they were both women.[16] □

However, he is also aware that the naturalness of things is no excuse by itself for their public representation and, to those who have accused him of impropriety, he says:

> ■ It is true, some actions, though natural, are not fit to be represented; and broad obscenities in words ought in good manners to be avoided: expressions thereof are a modest clothing of our thoughts, as breeches and petticoats are of our bodies. If I have kept myself within the bounds of modesty, all beyond it is but nicety and affectation; which is no more but modesty depraved into a vice.[17] □

He takes the advantage offered to go on the offensive against French poetry:

> ■ Yet, in this nicety of manners does the excellency of French poetry consist. Their heroes are the most civil people breathing; but their good breeding seldom extends to a word of sense; all their wit is in their ceremony; they want the genius which animates our stage; and therefore it is but necessary, when they cannot please, that they should take care not to offend.[18] □

Dryden has already quoted Montaigne (1533–92) and it is worth looking quickly at the passage:

> ■ Nous ne somme que cérémonie; la cérémonie nous emporte, et laissons la substance des choses. Nous nous tenons aux branches, et abandonnons le tronc et le corps. Nous avons appris aux dames de rougir, oyans seulement nommer ce qu'elles ne craignent aucunement à faire: Nous n'osons appeler à droit nos membres, et ne craignons pas de les employer à toute sorte de débauche. La cérémonie nous défend d'exprimer par paroles les choses licites et naturelles, et nous l'en croyons;

la raison nous défend de n'en faire point d'illicites et mauvaises, et personne ne l'en croit.[19]

[We are all convention; convention carries us away, and we neglect the substance of things. We hold on to the branches, and let go of the trunk and the body. We have taught ladies to blush at the mere mention of things they are not in the least afraid to do. We dare not call our parts by the right names, but we are not afraid to use them for all sorts of debauchery. Convention forbids us to express in words things that are lawful and natural; and we obey it. Reason forbids us to do what is unlawful and wicked, and no one obeys it.] □

Montaigne's objection is to what appears to be the most despicable form of hypocrisy: a carelessness about doing wrong so long as one does not speak about it. He objects to a concern with form over substance; to a triumph of manner over matter, appearance over reality. This will work as long as we are confident about substance and can make the distinction between form and substance and mark the contrast where it exists. If, however, we are told of the substance without being able to detect it, then we may suspect that only form exists. Montaigne's striking opening phase, 'Nous ne sommes que cérémonie' (which may be translated as 'we are nothing but ceremony') has a special relevance for a century that has become used to taking this sort of statement quite literally, where Montaigne means to surprise us by a paradoxical statement and shock us into making the opposite affirmation of 'the substance of things'.[20]

Dryden is sticking up for solid things such as what is natural and he is appealing to a common sense that the French have taken manners too far:

■ I should not have troubled myself thus far with French poets, but that I find our *Chedreux*[21] critics wholly form their judgements by them. But for my part, I desire to be tried by the laws of my own country; for it seems unjust to me, that the French should prescribe here, till they have conquered.[22] □

These are sturdy sentiments, especially in 1678, a year after the signing of a formal treaty between England and Holland, following the marriage of Mary, daughter of Charles II's brother James, Duke of York, who had converted to Roman Catholicism, to William of Orange (1650–1702; reigned 1689–1702), the implacable foe of Catholic France. This was a desperate ploy on Charles's part to bridge the gap between his and his court's preference for Catholic France over his country's and his Parliament's preference for Protestant Holland.

Dryden establishes his credentials as a patriot as well as he positions his own poetic practice by carefully contrasting an excessive concern with form with a practical attention to accuracy: his discussion of *Phèdre* (1677) by the French neoclassical playwright Jean Racine (1639–99) focuses on the 'excess of generosity', as Dryden sees it, shown by Hippolitus in his concern not to accuse his stepmother to his father; he also objects that the character in history has been misrepresented:

> ■ In the meantime we may take notice, that where the poet ought to have preserved the character as it was delivered to us by antiquity, when he should have given us the picture of a rough young man, of the Amazonian strain, a jolly huntsman, and both by his profession and his early rising a mortal enemy to love, he has chosen to give him the turn of gallantry, sent him to travel from Athens to Paris, taught him to make love, and transformed the Hippolytus of Euripides into Monsieur Hippolyte.[23] ☐

This is French contrivance in the interests of an excessive concern with form: against this Dryden places an English concern with practicality and accuracy. It is by implication to set up practice and experience against theory and contrast artificiality with reality.

Having established these credentials, Dryden turns his attention to an attack upon him by John Wilmot, Earl of Rochester (1647–80), made in the latter's *An Allusion to Horace* (*c.* September 1680).[24] In a long and rather rambling discourse, Dryden painstakingly defends the professional writer and distinguishes him from the 'men of pleasant conversation' who are 'ambitious to distinguish themselves from the herd of gentlemen, by their poetry'. Dryden comments:

> ■ And is not this a wretched affectation, not to be contented with what fortune has done for them, and sit down quietly with their estates, but they must call their wits in question, and needlessly expose their nakedness to public view?[25] ☐

There was a particular gibe in this last phrase, as Rochester and his cronies of the 'merry gang' as they were sometimes called, had been accused of doing this literally, especially in October 1677, when rumours of Rochester and others cavorting naked in Woodstock Park provoked Rochester to write to Henry Savile explaining that he and his friends were merely drying themselves off after bathing and complaining that he, Rochester, was 'a Man whom it is the great Mode to hate', a reference to the play *The Man of Mode*, by Rochester's friend Sir George Etherege (*c.* 1635–91), in which Rochester, thinly disguised if at all, had cut such a dash as Dorimant.

Dryden's patient, if long-winded, appeal is on behalf of the professional writer against the corruption of purpose by such divided aims as Rochester clearly displays when considered as a writer. Dryden's famously modest assessment of himself towards the end of his life as having been 'always a poet, and never a good one'[26] is the profes-sional's self-judgement: his quality may be in doubt but his commit-ment never. Rochester was, if anything, occasionally a poet and never a good one.

What Dryden is doing is to establish a basis for his practice in the play he has written. He is carefully negotiating the aesthetic pressures of classical doctrine and the social pressures of the gentleman poet to define an English national poetry that is not ignorant of classical doctrine but not prepared to abandon the sources of its peculiar strengths and is not ashamed of its professional status. The usefulness of Shakespeare as a reference point for such an endeavour is quite clear: himself untroubled by classical doctrine and equally a professional man of the theatre, the quality of his work, acknowledged as widely as it still was, affords Dryden both a source and an authority.

Finally then, Dryden acknowledges his debt to Shakespeare as 'he who began dramatic poetry amongst us' and concludes:

■ The occasion is fair, and the subject would be pleasant to handle the difference of styles betwixt him and Fletcher, and wherein, and how far they are both to be imitated. But since I must not be over-confident of my own performance after him, it will be prudence in me to be silent. Yet, I hope, I may affirm, and without vanity, that, by imitating him, I have excelled myself throughout the play; and particularly, that I prefer the scene betwixt Antony and Ventidius in the first act, to anything which I have written in this kind.[27] □

The closing sentence is particularly striking. The hesitant rhythm with which it begins, so heavily qualified, rises to an impressive declaration: 'by imitating him, I have excelled myself'. This is not vanity: it is the lit-eral truth. Dryden is writing fully in the spirit in which Ben Jonson had written about *imitatio*: he is only saying that he has done better than he has ever done and that it is because of the absorption of the influence of the master spirit of Shakespeare that he has been able to accomplish this. It is not his achievement that he is praising as much as the influ-ence that has enabled him to transcend his abilities, to rise above him-self. It remains to be seen what was made of his attempt by a critic determined to do what he could to right what he believed to be a wrong emphasis of long-standing in English literary history that had led to many misplaced and false judgements, among which was a misjudge-ment of *All For Love* that was itself a consequence of a more serious mis-understanding of the significance of Shakespeare's achievement overall. To put this right, and to put right the misreadings of more than two centuries of cultural practice, especially in literature and criticism, was the mission of the modernists.

Leavis begins by quoting from the Introduction to the *World's Classics* volume *Restoration Tragedies*, written by Bonamy Dobrée:

■ *All for Love* is beyond doubt a proud and lovely masterpiece; it is the fine flower of Dryden's genius. It was at one time, indeed for a very long time, fashionable to decry it in comparison with *Antony and Cleopatra*, but Dryden was not trying to do at all the same kind of thing as Shakespeare. Free opinion will be forced to admit that though Shakespeare's play contains finer poetry than Dryden could ever write – as he would have been the first to admit – Dryden's has a more tragic effect.[28] □

Leavis asserts that, in his view, 'Dryden and Shakespeare seem to be doing things so different in kind as to make a serious and sustained comparison obviously impossible'[29] but recognises that the view 'would not be generally found surprising either in the academic world or in the world of literary fashions (the critic, Professor Bonamy Dobrée, had standing in both)', in which comment he manages to imply that neither world has any authority in matters of critical judgement, a view often expressed by Dr Leavis. Leavis's name is associated with an intense seriousness in matters of critical judgement, a seriousness he claimed not to find in much that passed for literary criticism. In this he may be seen to be following Wordsworth, who comments in the Preface to *Lyrical Ballads* on those 'who talk of poetry as a matter of amusement and idle pleasure; who will converse with us as gravely about a *taste* for Poetry, as they express it, as if it were a thing as indifferent as a taste for rope-dancing, or Frontiniac or Sherry'.[30] For Leavis, the Scylla and Charybdis between which literary criticism had to steer its course were the world of academic study, with its disinterested pursuit of knowledge, and the world of literary fashion, which was buoyed up by opinion. Critical judgement, for Leavis, involves a commitment that may be thought of, in kind and in degree, as existential.[31] It will be necessary to digress slightly to expound more of Leavis's opinions in order to understand the thinking behind the discussion of the two plays more fully.

In his 1972 set of essays entitled *Nor Shall My Sword*, Leavis offers a striking account of the nature of critical judgement:

■ It is in the study of literature, the literature of one's own language in the first place, that one comes to recognize the nature and priority of the third realm (as, unphilosophically, no doubt, I call it, talking with my pupils), the realm of that which is neither merely private and personal nor public in the sense it can be brought into the laboratory or pointed to. You cannot point to the poem; it is 'there' only in the re-creative response of individual minds to the black marks on the page. But – a necessary faith – it is something in which minds can meet.[32] □

This passage situates judgement very precisely between what in another kind of discourse might be called the 'objective' and 'subjective' poles of our experience and places Leavis in a tradition that has resisted this bifurcation of our experience, a tradition that includes William Blake (1757–1827), as the title of this volume itself indicates, and William Wordsworth (1770–1850). Wordsworth's objections to the word 'taste' must be placed alongside his careful discrimination in the same Preface of the work of the 'Poet' from that of the 'Man of science'.[33] For Wordsworth, the Poet is the guardian of a common sense while the Man of science obsessively gathers isolated fragments in a lonely and even selfish pursuit. Blake's figure of Sir Isaac Newton (1642–1727) absorbed by his abstract diagrams and oblivious of the richly variegated rock on which he is sitting will bear comparison with Wordsworth's Newton from *The Prelude* (1850), where his statue's outstretched forefinger seems to the undergraduate Wordsworth

■   the marble index of a mind
Voyaging on strange seas of thought, alone.[34] □

Leavis's views in fact suggest a theory much larger in scope than the words 'literary criticism' might at first sight imply. There is a theory of the development of language and a theory of history, a theory of personal existence and of the significance of the creative writer. A reasonably indicative passage is this from *The Living Principle*:

■ I referred to literature a short way back as the supreme creative art of language. Perhaps I ought now to take notice of two points about English that have some bearing on my argument. The first is that English is spoken in North America by many more people than in this country, and that the American ethos has great prestige and, apparently, irresistible influence. The idea that American English has (in 'zest', 'energy', 'inventiveness' and so on) an obvious vital superiority over British English, and that this superiority calls for mature consideration in its bearing on the cultural future, needn't be discussed as profoundly relevant to the preoccupation of this book: the criteria of 'superiority' that are implied lack interest. And this brings us to the other point: the creative conditions that produced the English language that made Shakespeare possible have vanished on that final triumph of industrialism – even more completely in America than here. Something of those conditions were behind Dickens' work. They have gone utterly – gone for good; and with them the day-to-day creativity of the English-speaking peoples … It is plain that the quasi-living language represented by the talk of the vast majority of the population couldn't have given the assured take-off and the continuous prompting that Dickens [1812–70] still enjoyed in his time, when speech was still a popular art, belonging to a living culture. And Dickens had

Shakespeare behind him, and, of great creative writers, not only Shakespeare.[35] ☐

Leavis quotes Majorie Grene's *The Knower and the Known* (1966) to make his point:

■ My argument makes it necessary to add an insistent explicitness here. 'The child's discovery, and construction, of the world' is possible because the reality he was born into was already the Human World, the world created and renewed in day-by-day human collaboration through the ages.[36] ☐

His grandest statement of this position is perhaps to be found in *Nor Shall My Sword*:

■ In coming to terms with great literature we discover what at bottom we really believe. What for – what ultimately for? What do men live by? – the questions work and tell at what I can only call a religious depth of thought and feeling. Perhaps, with my eye on the adjective, I may just recall for you Tom Brangwen, in *The Rainbow*, watching by the fold in lambing-time under the night-sky: 'He knew he did not belong to himself'.[37] ☐

The echo of the Victorian poet and critic Matthew Arnold (1882–88) from the essay on Wordsworth is clear: 'Poetry is, at bottom, a criticism of life … the question – how to live?'[38]

The foregoing digression is necessary to make full sense of Leavis's opening remarks on Dryden and Shakespeare:

■ The superiority in poetry that makes it seem to me absurd to compare the two plays in tragic effect … is conclusively manifest in the first twenty lines of *Antony and Cleopatra*. It is an immediately felt superiority in the life of the verse – superiority in concreteness, variety and sensitiveness – that leaves us with 'eloquence' instead of 'life' as the right word for Dryden's verse.[39] ☐

He compares the two 'Cydnus' barge scenes, summarising thus:

■ Our general observation is that Shakespeare's verse seems to enact its meaning, to do and to give rather than to talk about, whereas Dryden's is merely descriptive eloquence.[40] ☐

He comments on Enobarbus's 'assonantal sequence' in Shakespeare:

■ The effect is to give the metaphor 'burn'd' a vigour of sensuous realization that it wouldn't otherwise have had; the force of 'burn'd' is reflected back through 'burnish'd' (felt now as 'burning' too) upon 'barge', so that the barge takes fire, as it were, before our eyes: we are much more than merely told that the barge 'burn'd'.[41] □

There follow several paragraphs of close analysis of the verse of the scene, some perhaps powerfully suggestive rather than entirely convincing, culminating in another striking generalisation, this time concerning the major characters. Dryden's are too stiff to have hopped in the public street as Shakespeare's Cleopatra does, or to have sat in the marketplace whistling to himself as Antony is left in Shakespeare's play because the populace has deserted him to go to gaze upon Cleopatra as she arrives in her barge. Leavis comments:

■ Shakespeare's [characters] have a life corresponding to the life of the verse; the life in them is, in fact, the life of the verse.[42] □

On the other hand:

■ Dryden is a highly skilled craftsman working at his job from the outside. The superior structure with which his play is credited as a theatre-piece is a matter of workmanship of the same external order as is represented by his verse. He aims at symmetry, a neat and obvious design, a balanced arrangement of heroic confrontations and 'big scenes'. The satisfaction he offers his audience is that of an operatic exaltation and release from actuality, a ballet-like completeness of pattern, and an elegantly stylized decorum.[43] □

The contrast is with Shakespeare as 'a realizing imagination working from within a deeply and minutely felt theme'. Where in Dryden there is figurative language, 'there is never any complexity, confusion or ambiguity'. Any development 'is simple, lucid and rational'. A further trenchant comment concerns the expression of emotion, which 'doesn't emerge from a given situation realized in its concrete particularity; it is stated, not presented or enacted'. There is a distinction throughout the analysis between 'telling' or 'narration at a distance' and a kind of poetry 'in which the thing described seems present and not merely told of'. This may be compared with a similar distinction made by György Lukács (1885–1971), by Henry James from time to time (1843–1916) and also by Sir Arthur Quiller-Couch (1863–1944), among many others of different critical persuasions. It reflects a conviction that literature is, or should aim to be, 'concrete' and concerned with what Leavis calls 'realization'.

Leavis's final judgement on *Antony and Cleopatra* is that it is not among Shakespeare's greatest tragedies. He even suggests that he would not substantially disagree with Bradley (a remarkable condescension for the critic whose attack on Bradley's *Othello* was so fierce).[44] He does say though that it 'is a very great dramatic poem'. Leavis offers the hint that the play 'might be an introduction to the study of Shakespeare's imagery' and refers the reader to a discussion earlier in the book (pp. 102–3) of the image at 3.2.47–50:

> ■ Her tongue will not inform her heart, nor can
> Her heart inform her tongue – the swan's down feather,
> That stands upon the swell at full of tide,
> And neither way inclines □

Quoting R.H. Case's Arden footnote comment:

> ■ It is not clear whether Octavia's heart is the swan's down feather, swayed neither way on the full tide of emotion … or whether it is merely the inaction of heart and tongue … which is compared to that of the feather.[45] □

Leavis comments:

> ■ Dryden would not have left it not clear. And Dryden could not have evoked the appropriate dramatic feeling with that vividness and particularity. When we try to say in what ways the passage is incomparably superior to anything Dryden could have produced, we have to think of metaphor as something more immediate, complex and organic than neat illustrative correspondence.[46] □

This last distinction is useful and thought-provoking and will take us back to the heart of Leavis's concerns as a critic not only, as he claims, of literature (because he insists that there can properly be no such thing) but also of life.

It is worth tracing the steps of Leavis's account backwards though, to the point at which he introduces his comparison between the two Cydnus speeches. Leavis quotes Shakespeare and then says: 'How does that look in comparison to Dryden's rendering of it?'

The point is at least ambiguous but it is worth pursuing: of what does Leavis conceive the Dryden passage to be a 'rendering'? Is it a rendering of the incident itself, imagined independently by both dramatists? Or is Dryden's a rendering of Shakespeare's, perhaps in the spirit of Dryden's own discussion of 'imitation', the

> ■ endeavour of a later poet to write like one who has written before him on the same subject: that is, not to translate his words, or to be confined to his sense, but only to set him as a pattern, and to write as he supposes that author would have done had he lived in our age. □

This point needs to be taken together with a further question that arises out of Leavis's account. Commenting on the 'swan's down feather' and Case's rather dry observation that its application is not clear, Leavis says:

■ Dryden would not have left it not clear. And Dryden could not have evoked the appropriate dramatic feeling with that vividness and particularity. □

The question is, what is 'the appropriate dramatic feeling'? More precisely, to what should the dramatic feeling be appropriate? Leavis continues with an important comment about metaphor:

■ When we try to say in what ways the passage is incomparably superior to anything Dryden could have produced, we have to think of metaphor as something more immediate, complex and organic than neat illustrative correspondence.[47] □

Elsewhere in *The Living Principle*, Leavis has some useful comments to offer on Dr Johnson's attitude to Shakespeare, including an interesting discussion of Johnson's account of Shakespeare's language:

■ It is incident to him (Johnson says) to be now and again entangled with an unwieldy sentiment, which he cannot well express, and will not reject; he struggles with it a while, and if it continues stubborn, comprises it in words such as occur, and leaves it to be disentangled and evolved by minds that have more leisure to bestow upon it.[48] □

Leavis acknowledges the existence of unsatisfactory passages in Shakespeare but goes on to say that it is not at all clear that Johnson would not reject passages other, perhaps later, critics would praise.[49] Leavis sees behind this tendency the spirit of the age. He quotes Johnson:

■ Shakespeare, whether life or nature be his subject, shows plainly that he has seen with his own eyes; he gives the image which he receives, not weakened or distorted by the intervention of any other mind; the ignorant feel his representations to be just and the learned see that they are compleat.[50] □

And he comments:

■ But the virtue which Johnson praises involves more than he recognizes – much more than his thought, conditioned by Augustan 'correctness', is capable of grasping unequivocally. The sentence is the more significant in that Johnson's assumption regarding our contact with the external world is explicit in it: 'the image which he receives'. This is the Lockean account of perception as a matter of passively received 'impressions' ['Lockean' refers to the ideas of English philosopher John Locke, 1632–1704] – and it entails the whole conception that Blake was to fight against in defence of human creativity, the enemy being the cultural ethos he associated with the names of Locke and Newton.[51] □

Johnson's praise of Shakespeare's powers of expressing 'nature' directly, 'not weakened or distorted by the intervention of any other mind', brings to mind Dryden's of some years earlier:

■ He was the man who, of all modern and perhaps ancient poets, had the largest and most comprehensive soul. All the images of nature were still present to him, and he drew them not laboriously, but luckily. When he describes anything, you more than see it, you feel it too. Those who accuse him to have wanted learning give him the greater commendation. He was naturally learned. He needed not the spectacles of books to read nature. He looked inwards, and found her there. □

This too may be accused of a Lockean prejudice, although it is more to the point perhaps to recognise that both Dryden and Johnson are struggling with an idea that the world can be too much seen through the medium of other people's books and that it might be possible to see it without the benefit of what Dryden contemptuously calls 'the spectacles of books'. This does not necessarily imply that there is world waiting to be so seen (after all Dryden says that Shakespeare 'looked inwards'), only that what we see would look different if we did not see through the spectacles of books. That Dryden wished it suggests that he could not do it and this in turn suggests that he was indeed rendering Shakespeare or at least rendering some version of an incident as it was rendered in a book. It might be possible to go so far as to suggest that the incident no longer exists, if indeed it ever did, outside its being related. The scene itself is, after all, a relation of an incident. The dramatic incident, in fact, is the relating of the incident. It might be regarded as an imitation in both plays, or as a translation.

This makes the discussion of imitation and translation both urgent and difficult. It demands an approach to the question of what is being rendered that will also be an approach to how the appropriateness of dramatic feeling ought be judged, and it will enable us to decide whether what Leavis says about metaphor should be thought of as an absolute or a relative judgement. Under what conditions, in other words, should we be looking for 'something more immediate, complex and organic than neat illustrative correspondence'? Under what conditions might we be looking precisely for 'neat illustrative correspondence'?

It is reasonable to say that comparison between Shakespare and Dryden is not fruitless if we compare them not with one another but with a third thing that we can call 'Antony and Cleopatra'. This third thing may or may not be a historical incident but it is incident in literature, at least from Plutarch. And our access to the historical is through that species of literature, history. Nicholas Rowe has already been quoted from the Preface to his edition of 1709:

■ For those Plays which he has taken from the *English* or the *Roman* History, let any Man compare 'em and he will find the Character as exact in the Poet as the Historian.[52] □

As has Nahum Tate:

■ I confess I cou'd never yet get a true account of his Learning, and am apt to think it more than Common Report allows him. I am sure he never touches on a Roman Story, but the Persons, the Passages, the Manners, the Circumstances, the Ceremonies, all are Roman. And what Relishes yet of a more exact Knowledge, you do not only see a Roman in his Heroe, but the particular Genius of the Man, without the least mistake of his Character, given him by their best Historians.[53] □

That is, the incident is related in the histories.

This is enough to suggest that the true basis of comparison must be what both dramatists made of Antony and Cleopatra as they had received them from history and literature, for from what other source could they have received them? In addition we must be aware that Dryden set himself to the task with Shakespeare's example before him.

Dryden did not set out to translate Shakespeare though; he set out to produce something to set alongside Shakespeare. He did this by imagining Antony and Cleopatra entirely differently, with a clarity of vision in which there is no place for the sort of feeling the expression of which Leavis so admires in Shakespeare and which demands the kind of metaphor he so praises. To condemn Dryden for not doing it is to condemn him for not attempting to do it. We may say that things are different without having to say whether one is superior to the other. There are advantages to the one not offered by the other; that is true the other way round, however. Dryden has strengths, and not merely strengths that earn him a decent second place. The truth is that Leavis is right. The two are very different. They are related in interesting ways and Dryden certainly seems to lament something that Shakespeare has that he has not but it is simplistic to rank them. Leavis is not merely ranking them of course; he found something in Shakespeare that he believed humanity required and was in danger of losing, and he thought that Dryden and Johnson were part of a 'cultural ethos' that threatened that deprivation. He thought it was the duty of criticism to struggle against that cultural ethos. We may think the danger was exaggerated or perhaps that it has passed; we may have a different solution if we do not. If we do not think it exaggerated or passed and we do not have a different solution, then we will probably continue to rank Dryden and Shakespeare. I shall suggest another path.

CHAPTER THREE

Dryden's Revision of *Antony and Cleopatra*

D ryden sets his play in the aftermath of Actium. Antony has withdrawn into the temple of Isis, shunning all company, including Cleopatra's; Octavius is encamped at the gates of Alexandria, yet there is stalemate:

> ■ Maecenas and Agrippa, who can most
> With Caesar, are his foes. His wife Octavia,
> Driven from his house, solicits her revenge;
> And Dolabella, who was once his friend,
> Upon some private grudge now seeks his ruin:
> Yet still war seems on either side to sleep. ☐   (Act 1 lines 52–7)

The characters are few in number and carefully balanced. Egypt is represented by Alexas, Cleopatra's eunuch, and two priests, Serapion, and Myrsis, who has very little to say, and two maids, Charmian and Iras, the latter having little to say. Rome is represented by Octavius and Octavia and Dolabella and Ventidius, the latter a balance to Alexas; this balance itself balancing the greater balance of Antony and Cleopatra or rather Octavius and Cleopatra, with Antony torn between the one whom he loves helplessly and the principle represented by the other. There is none of the rapid and startling shifts of scene from one part of the empire to another and there is none of the breathtaking poetry of the earlier play. Dryden's aim is altogether different. Tightly focused in terms of place and time, two of the three great 'unities',[1] the play equally tightly focuses on action, the third. Dryden concentrates his attention on the conflict between love and duty, as this manifests itself for Antony in the conflict between what Ventidius calls him to and what Cleopatra calls him to.

In Act I, a brief conversation between Serapion and Alexas fills in the background and then Ventidius enters at line 88. The rest of the Act is a fine dramatic contest between Antony and Ventidius, Ventidius first observing the distraught Antony, unobserved himself, then coming forward to risk his anger at being disturbed and to confront him with memories of what he has been. Dryden himself in his Preface said that he preferred this scene to anything he had written 'in this kind'. It is not possible to give any flavour of this scene by quotation. The scene works as a perfectly imagined and crafted piece of dramatic realisation, not through poetry but through verse, by which distinction I mean that Dryden exploits the rhythmical effects available to language organised on a metrical basis but he does not really exploit the figurative resources of language. An example will have to suffice. Antony, in his rage, calls Ventidius an 'envious traitor' and Ventidius is hurt:

■ Oh, that thou wert my equal, great in arms
   As the first Caesar was, that I might kill thee
   Without a stain to honour!
   Ven.   You may kill me;
   You have done more already, called me traitor.
   Ant. Art thou not one?
   Ven.   For showing you yourself,
   Which none else durst have done? But I had been
   That name, which I disdain to speak again,
   I needed not have sought your abject fortunes,
   Come to partake your fate, to die with you;
   What hindered me t'have led my conqu'ring eagles
   To fill Octavius' bands? I could have been
   A traitor then, a glorious happy traitor,
   And not have been so called.
   Ant.   Forgive me, soldier:
   I've been too passionate.
   Ven.   You thought me false;
   Thought my old age betrayed you: kill me, sir;
   Pray, kill me. Yet you need not; your unkindness
   Has left your sword no work.
   Ant.   I did not think so;
   I said it in my rage: prithee forgive me.
   Why didst thou tempt my anger by discovery
   Of what I would not hear?
   Ven.   No prince but you
   Could merit that sincerity I used,
   Nor durst another man have ventured it;
   But you, ere love misled your wand'ring eyes,
   Were sure the chief and best of human race,
   Framed in the very pride and boast of nature,
   So perfect, that the gods who formed you wondered
   At their own skill, and cried, 'A lucky hit
   Has mended our design.' Their envy hindered,
   Else you had been immortal, and a pattern,
   When heaven would work for ostentation' sake,
   To copy out again.[2] □   (383–413)

It is necessary to attend quite closely to what Dryden is doing. In response to Antony's angry and contemptuous outburst which declares that Ventidius is not his equal:

- Oh, that thou wert my equal, great in arms
  As the first Caesar was, that I might kill thee
  Without a stain to honour! ☐

Ventidius responds in short, measured phrases that dismiss Antony's contempt by ignoring it and making it appear as though Ventidius is in a position to permit Antony to kill him:

- *Ven.*   You may kill me;
  You have done more already, called me traitor. ☐

He meets Antony's

- *Ant.* Art thou not one? ☐

with rising anger

- *Ven.*   For showing you yourself,
  Which none else durst have done? But I had been
  That name, which I disdain to speak again,
  I needed not have sought your abject fortunes,
  Come to partake your fate, to die with you;
  What hindered me t'have led my conqu'ring eagles
  To fill Octavius' bands? I could have been
  A traitor then, a glorious happy traitor,
  And not have been so called ☐

Antony recovers his temper and makes an apology

- *Ant.*   Forgive me, soldier:
  I've been too passionate. ☐

which Ventidius rejects in the same tone he first used:

- *Ven.*   You thought me false;
  Thought my old age betrayed you: kill me, sir;
  Pray, kill me. Yet you need not; your unkindness
  Has left your sword no work. ☐

Antony presses his apology:

■ *Ant.*   I did not think so;
I said it in my rage: prithee forgive me.
Why didst thou tempt my anger by discovery
Of what I would not hear?   □

Ventidius's spirits rise again and in rising make one of the play's best extended figures: the notion that the gods surpassed themselves in making Antony:

■ *Ven.*   No prince but you
Could merit that sincerity I used,
Nor durst another man have ventured it;
But you, ere love misled your wand'ring eyes,
Were sure the chief and best of human race,
Framed in the very pride and boast of nature,
So perfect, that the gods who formed you wondered
At their own skill, and cried, 'A lucky hit
Has mended our design.' Their envy hindered,
Else you had been immortal, and a pattern,
When heaven would work for ostentation' sake,
To copy out again.   □

Ventidius is not Enobarbus: it is clear that this man could not speak Enobarbus's Cydnus barge speech: he is a much simpler character. He has Enobarbus's soldierliness but he has none of that character's complexities and Dryden's world has none of the seductive charm of the world that has so impressed Enobarbus. What this verse does have is a thoroughly workmanlike ability to express the characteristics Dryden wants to express.

The same facility is observable in a marvellous moment earlier. Alexas has caught Serapion and Myris discussing the dire omens that Serapion has witnessed and is chastising them. Serapion takes the opportunity to inquire into the state of affairs and Alexas gives vent to some of his anxieties, wishing both Antony and Octavius dead:

■ Had I my wish, these tyrants of all nature
Who lord it o'er mankind should perish, here,
Each by the other's sword; but, since our will
Is lamely followed by our power, we must
Depend on one, with him to rise or fall.
Serap. How stands the Queen affected?
Alex.   Oh, she dotes,

> She dotes, Serapion, on this vanquished man,
> And winds herself about his mighty ruins;
> Whom would she yet forsake, yet yield him up,
> This hunted prey, to his pursuer's hands,
> She might preserve us all; but 'tis in vain –
> This changes my designs, this blasts my counsels,
> And makes me use all means to keep him here,
> Whom I could wish divided from her arms
> Far as the earth's deep centre. Well, you know
> The state of things; no more of your ill omens
> And black prognostics; labour to confirm
> The people's hearts. □   (71–88)

This is very good dramatic verse: it is supple, varied and expressive. When Serapion asks how Cleopatra is taking it all, Alexas's repeated 'She dotes' over the line break perfectly expresses the mixture of wonder and exasperation that characterises his mood. The rest of the line, the pause before and after 'Serapion' perfectly introduces the phrase 'this vanquished man'. There follows an uninterrupted, almost perfect blank verse line:

■ And winds herself about his mighty ruins; □

artfully spoilt by a falling cadence at the end that perfectly catches Alexas's slightly ruminative note at this point. It is verse to be spoken by actors with an ear for inflections of tone. It is not Shakespeare: it will not seize the imagination and take it into undreamed of regions. It is good, subtle, psychologically realistic and emotionally sensitive verse, craftsmanlike and vividly imagined. Such verse does not tell us that Dryden could not do what Shakespeare was doing; only that he did not. We should not forget that it was Dryden who first put into currency the term 'metaphysics', connected with the verse of John Donne (1572–1631), and that T.S Eliot, in his seminal remarks on the 'metaphysical poets', diagnosed the illness of English verse in the late seventeenth century as having something to do with the achievements of Dryden and Milton. Eliot acknowledges that they both did 'certain things magnificently well' but it is precisely this achievement that is to blame in his view. The Shakespeare Dryden appreciated was not that appreciated by Leavis.

These two Shakespeares are not different and irreconcilable, however; we do not have to choose one or the other, we do not have to say that either Dryden or Leavis were misjudging or overemphasising. The case is slightly different when we come to Donne's verse, because once Johnson has taken up Dryden's hint and expanded it, we do have a very different Donne to the one described by Eliot and Leavis. This is important. This difference of opinion extends as far as differing conceptions of the nature of experience and even of the nature of the world. Eliot's remarks that something happened to the English mind and Leavis's later characterisation of the vision of Blake pitched against that of Locke and Newton go further than this disagreement over Shakespeare goes, although no further than its implications will go if they are pursued. What Dryden has to say about nature and looking inward to see it needs to be considered, as does what Leavis says about metaphor and correspondence. Both are highly suggestive. A key notion here is Dr Johnson's phrase 'an unwieldy sentiment'. This uneasily straddles two suggestions: that Shakespeare is not capable of expressing it; or that it cannot be expressed. It may be that we sometimes mistake fantasies for intuitions but Johnson's age was more ready to dismiss intuitions as fantasies. It was a key conviction of Leavis and Eliot that Augustan 'reasonableness', the work of Locke and Newton and many others, had limited the scope of the creative imagination. Eliot would not share Leavis's estimate of Blake and Leavis would acrimoniously part company with Eliot, pouring angry critical energy into a denunciation of Eliot's later poetry (especially *Four Quartets*: see *The Living Principle* for example); but the two did share, with many others, the general notion that English thinking had been constricted during the eighteenth and nineteenth centuries and was badly in need of reinvigoration. English thinking could not, however, be reinvigorated through further flights of romantic fancy (which had, in their view, simply dissipated themselves into the sentimentality of the Victorians) but in a rediscovery and reinterpretation of its past. The task for critical thinking in the half-century or so after the main work of Eliot and Leavis is to re-evaluate their revaluation. To acknowledge with them that Dryden's Antony and Cleopatra is not Shakespeare's is the beginning: the next step is to say how and to weigh up the significance of the difference.

There is none of the waywardness of Shakespeare's Cleopatra in Dryden's; the Queen we meet in Act II is not made of sterner stuff but she is not capricious. There is a tragic nobility about her and we are in no doubt that she loves Antony. Alexas is subtle but not despicable; Iras and Charmian are no more than they need to be: suitable stage presences to support their queen. There is none of Shakespeare's Egypt in Dryden's play.

Antony narrates the main action of Shakespeare's play and its antecedent events with brisk economy in lines 260ff.; he and Ventidius establish a much meaner Octavius than Shakespeare's in their discussion of him in Act II (lines 110ff.); the balance of the scene is between the rival claims of Ventidius and Cleopatra on Antony, the tipping point coming in lines 400–30 during which the queen manages to touch Antony's hand and through that touch his heart, as Alexas knew she should be able to.

Act III tips the other way. Ventidius introduces Dolabella, whom we learn was a bosom friend of Antony:

■ He loved me too;
I was his soul, he lived not but in me.
We were so closed within each other's breasts,
The rivets were not found that joined us first.
That does not reach us yet: we were so mixed
As meeting streams, both to ourselves were lost;
We were one mass; we could not give or take,
But from the same; for he was I, I he. □   (90–7)

This is a fair example of figurative language as it appears in the play. Another is given slightly earlier when Antony is confidently speaking to Ventidius of the defeat he has just inflicted on Octavius:

■ We have dislodged their troops;
They look on us at distance, and like curs
'Scaped from the lion's paws, they bay far off,
And lick their wounds, and faintly threaten war. □   (53–6)

If we are looking for poetry of the kind we have found in Shakespeare's play, we shall not find it. Leavis's remark is helpful:

■ When we try to say in what ways the passage is incomparably super-ior to anything Dryden could have produced, we have to think of metaphor as something more immediate, complex and organic than neat illustrative correspondence.[3] □

'Neat, illustrative correspondence' describes these passages well. We learn nothing new about what Antony is talking about; we merely see what we expect to see expressed. When Dolabella arrives on stage, Antony reminds him of the moment he first set eyes on Cleopatra:

■ Her galley down the silver Cydnos rowed,
The tackling silk, the streamers waved with gold,
The gentle winds were lodged in purple sails:
Her nymphs, like Nereids, round her couch were placed,
Where she, another sea-born Venus, lay.
Dola. No more; I would not hear it.
Ant.   Oh, you must!
She lay, and leant her cheek upon her hand,
And cast a look so languishingly sweet,
As if, secure of all beholders' hearts,
Neglecting she could take 'em. Boys like Cupids

Stood fanning with their painted wings the winds
That played about her face; but if she smiled,
A darting glory seemed to blaze abroad,
That men's desiring eyes were never wearied,
But hung upon the object. To soft flutes
The silver oars kept time; and while they played,
The hearing gave new pleasure to the sight,
And both to thought. 'Twas heaven, or somewhat more;
For she so charmed all hearts that gazing crowds
Stood panting on the shore, and wanted breath
To give their welcome voice. □   (162–83)

This can be compared to Enobarbus's speech in Shakespeare's play
(2.2.190–218): many of the features of the earlier work appear in
Antony's speech in *All for Love*; the Cupids, the Nereids, the purple sails,
for example. However, Dryden is not intending to do what Shakespeare
has achieved. To start with, he puts the description into the mouth of
Antony and we must pay attention to the careful characterisation of
Antony. Dryden's Antony is not merely vacillating; there is no drama in
that, let alone tragedy. Antony's quality may be discussed by thinking
about a speech of Cleopatra's later in this scene when she is confronted
by Octavia. Octavia says:

■   Shame of our sex,
Dost thou not blush to own those black endearments
That make sin pleasing? □   (441–3)

and Cleopatra replies:

■   You may blush, who want 'em.
If bounteous nature, if indulgent heaven
Have given me charms to please the bravest man
Should I not thank 'em? □   (443–6)

This is not straightforward. Octavia's description of Cleopatra's 'black
endearments', that they 'make sin pleasing', is interesting. If sin were not
pleasing, it would not be attractive; it does not have to be made pleasing.
What she means is that sin appears not to be sin under Cleopatra's influence and indeed Cleopatra appeals to quite another authority, although
she seems to use a word from the same vocabulary as Octavia's when
she says that she has got her charms from 'bounteous nature' and adds,
'indulgent heaven'. What kind of 'heaven' is Cleopatra's? When she
thanks nature/heaven for so gifting her, it is so that she may 'please the
bravest man'. In this phrase are her ideals: 'bravery' and 'pleasure'. We may

gloss 'bravery' as something like 'strength'. Antony is a strong man in Cleopatra's eyes and she seeks to give him pleasure. It is a simple economy and it sits beside Octavia's and Ventidius's as a more primitive economy than theirs.

It is worth considering for a moment the sort of interpretative frameworks Dryden could have assumed that his audience would be able to draw on, especially, in the light of this moment in the play, the significance of Christian historiography. Rome, especially for the Catholic imagination but in historiographical terms for the Christian imagination in general, has a special place in the Christian story. Rome is the great empire, the figure of 'the World' for many writers and believers, against which Christ is placed; it is the place of the martyrdom of St Paul and St Peter and the place of St Peter's bishopric and the writing of the first gospel. It is the place from which the Western church spread out and on which it was, in great part, until the Reformation, based. The Reformation, seeing itself as a struggle with Rome, revived the great significance of Rome as the other. In Dryden's play there is an enclosing irony: Rome may defeat Cleopatra, Antony, and Egypt, but it will itself be eclipsed. In its very arrogant assertiveness at the moment of its triumph, its doom is being written out. Octavia and Ventidius may well present an economy more sophisticated, 'higher' in some senses, than Cleopatra's, but that does not mean that the playgoer is meant to take away the conclusion that it represents the best.

Antony is torn between them. At the end of Act II, Ventidius pleads with Antony:

■   And what's this toy
    In balance with your fortune, honour fame? □

Antony claims it 'outweighs 'em all' and later says

■   Give, you gods,
    Give to your boy, your Caesar,
    This rattle of a globe to play withal,
    This gew-gaw world, and put him cheaply off:
    I'll not be pleased with less than Cleopatra. □   (442–6)

Ventidius's 'toy' is Antony's world and vice versa. There is no misunderstanding more complete.

It is perhaps a mistake to view what Cleopatra has to offer as 'sin' and Antony as merely beguiled. Cleopatra's view, which is Egypt's view, is simpler, more basic, earlier even, but it is different; it is not merely opposite. Cleopatra's Egypt rewards strength with pleasure: it is the triumph of the moment of the body. Rome's reward is the more considered, more reflective, triumph of the mind. Dryden shows Antony not as a weak, indecisive man but as a 'brave' man torn between the triumph of the body and the triumph of the mind. A simpler way of putting it is to talk of pleasure and virtue but that is a Roman way of putting it. Alexas's vexation at lines 384–91 is typical:

■ Cast out from nature, disinherited
Of what her meanest children claim by kind,
Yet greatness kept me from contempt: that's gone ...
She dies for love, but she has known its joys:
Gods, is this just, that I, who know no joys,
Must die because she loves? □

He means by 'greatness' prestige, and by 'joys' sexual pleasure. The feeling is that for Alexas at least there is nothing else under the sun. Roman 'virtue' is not so much objectionable to such a view as it is unintelligible.

Physical strength, Cleopatra's 'bravery', stands poised between aspiration upwards towards Roman 'virtue' and mere satisfaction in pleasure. Dryden's moral purpose in the Cydnos barge description is to show the attractive power of pleasure over the mind of a strong man. Shakespeare's purpose is more complicated, just as Shakespeare's Egypt is more complicated than Dryden's Egypt. Shakespeare's Egypt is a matter of pleasure but we feel more strongly the unnaturalness of that devotion to pleasure than we do in Dryden, in which we do not feel it at all.

An example may suffice. Enobarbus describes the barge at one point thus:

■   The poop was beaten gold;
Purple the sails, and so perfumèd that
The winds were love-sick with them. The oars were silver,
Which to the tune of flutes kept stroke, and made
The water which they beat to follow faster,
As amorous of their strokes. □   (2.2.199–204)

Two figures demand comment: in the first the image is of the winds, the force propelling the barge, as 'love-sick' and merely pursuing the barge, which is, presumably, proceeding under its own force; the second is more complex and picks up 'beaten' from line 199. The image is of the water being 'beaten', and so made 'amorous of their strokes' confuses the ideas of affection in 'strokes' with assault or punishment. This, combined with 'love-sickness' and the notion of an inverted natural sequence (the winds do not propel the barge but pursue it), offers an image of the utmost contrivance and contrariety to nature. It is clear that Enobarbus does not judge (or at least that he withholds his judgement) but the impact of this scene not only on him but, more importantly, on Antony, is quite unambiguous:

- *Maecenas.*   Now Antony
   Must leave her utterly.
   Enobarbus.   Never. He will not. □   (2.2.238–40)

This is not a matter of choice: what she has to offer Antony is, in Eno-barbus's opinion, irresistible. Dryden shows us a simple choice, tragic in this case, between pleasure and virtue, and leads us carefully to under-stand that the choice of pleasure is not merely vicious because Antony is not merely vicious and neither is Cleopatra.

As analysis ever more clearly defines the difference between Dryden's play and Shakespeare's play, the question becomes more urgent as to what Dryden meant by saying 'In my style I have professed to imitate the divine Shakespeare'. It is clear in his treatment of the subject that he did not seek to 'imitate the divine Shakespeare' but wrote something quite different. He claims to have abandoned rhyme in order to make his stylistic imitation the closer but there is more to Shakespeare's dra-matic verse than being 'blank', as Leavis's criticism makes clear. It may seem that inviting the comparison was not wise of Dryden, unless he intended the comparison to focus on what was peculiarly his own, and, in so doing, he would, by contrast, bring into focus what was peculiarly Shakespeare's own.

There is enough evidence in earlier plays to see *All for Love* as the natural development of Dryden's work in the heroic vein.[4] The insistent contest between love and honour was a set piece, while in *All for Love* it is a real struggle between a more realistic love and a more realistic honour. The theme is not despicable, although its presentation in the 'love and honour' plays does it little credit. The theme may even be dis-cerned in Dryden's later struggles with his own religious faith. His con-version to Catholicism struck (and strikes) many as opportunistic but if he were merely a turncoat he could have turned his coat again in 1688 when he maintained his position at not inconsiderable risk. If for honour we read duty, then the theme appears as a version of a struggle between public and private, self and soul, even reason and emotion. Even such a broad summary is sufficient to identify how far away is Shakespeare's play.

It is not enough to say that Dryden has simplified Shakespeare's play, or that Shakespeare's key characters are more complicated than Dryden's, although each of these statements is true. We need to specify the com-plications to make a decent judgement that they are advantages or that Dryden's simplifications are disadvantages, if that is the kind of judge-ment we think right. Dryden may equally be said to have refined and streamlined his characters to provide a focus on a central conflict that is clear and thus dramatic. This is not to say that Shakespeare is undramatic: only that he looked elsewhere for his dramatic focus. *All for Love* is a misleading title if we think of exalted meanings for the word 'love': Antony sacrifices family, loyalty and principles for a vision of heroism in which strength and bravery are rewarded with pleasure. This is a vision not only other than Rome's, which he lets go, but older than Rome's, and it may be that a Restoration audience, in serious mood, may be able to reflect that just as one age was replaced with a better one, so too was that replacing age itself replaced.

This is not the vision of *Antony and Cleopatra*, or at least it is not a vision that can easily be sustained by the play, or an interpretation that convinces readily. The contrast between the two shows how much more clearly Shakespeare's play is focused on the process by which Antony is drawn in and not on the conflict that his being drawn in represents: crudely put, the play's interests are psychological rather than moral. This is reflected in the question at issue as far as Leavis is concerned: the importance of poetry. In *Antony and Cleopatra* the dramatic action is realised within characters as much as it is between characters and that action is more complex than it is in *All for Love*. *All for Love* cannot afford to divert attention away from its dramatic focus because of the nature of that focus: the conflict in Antony between the calls of Rome and Egypt. The issue is the moral contrast between the two. For *Antony and Cleopatra* the complex, convoluted, inward world of the sonnets is more appropriate as first Antony and then Cleopatra struggle with themselves, and for that reason the poetry must be both more complex and more foregrounded than it can be in *All for Love*. This is not to say that Dryden simply chose not to do what Shakespeare chose to do, but could have done it if he had so chosen to do: there is no evidence that Dryden could have done so. There is no evidence that he wanted to do so and failed. The question is what kind of poetry is not only appropriate to particular times and circumstances but can be achieved in those times and circumstances. Dryden's time not only could not have achieved *Antony and Cleopatra* but it would not have wanted to and could not have comprehended it and this is why it could not have achieved it. This is why Johnson expresses impatience with what he sees as 'unwieldy sentiments' and this is why, for Leavis, and for others, rightly grasping Shakespeare's achievement was so important to understanding how to act in the early twentieth century as a critic and a creative writer.

Such a discussion raises an important question that has far-reaching implications. If we are to discuss what could or could not be done at a particular time, what do we mean? Do we mean that there were no sufficiently capable individual persons available or do we mean that something other was the cause? If we mean that something else was the cause, what do we mean? For Leavis and Eliot, the cause was to be found in something Eliot called 'the English mind' and in what Leavis called 'the cultural tradition'. This was more than the individual mind, more than individual minds considered altogether: it was what Leavis tried to capture in the compound 'creative-collaborative'. He did not wish to diminish the importance of the individual mind but neither did he wish to grant it sovereignty. The question of language may be used as an illustration. No one invents language: everyone learns to speak as others already speak. However, individual speakers may say things hitherto unsaid. For Leavis, language was the supreme 'creative-collaborative' achievement, definitive of what he called 'the human world'. To discuss the differences between these two plays was for him more than expressing a preference of taste and in this he was in agreement with Wordsworth, Matthew Arnold and Dr Johnson, however differently they may have expressed similar thoughts.

All for Love closes with a piece of plotting more reminiscent of *Othello* than *Antony and Cleopatra*, as both Ventidius and Alexas scheme with increasing desperation against the pair, scheming that results in Act V in Antony's bungled suicide and Ventidius's more successful attempt, in Cleopatra's suicide and, somewhat irrelevantly, that of both Iras and Charmion. It is left to Serapion to speak the epitaph over the two:

■   Sleep, blessed pair,
    Secure from human chance, long ages out,
    While all the storms of fate fly o'er your tomb;
        And Fame to late posterity shall tell,
        No lovers lived so great, or died so well. □

It is important to reflect that this is Dryden's Egypt's judgement on them: Shakespeare ends with his Rome's judgement, in the shape of Octavius's remarks:

■ No grave upon the earth shall clip in it
    A pair so famous. High events as these
    Strike those that make them, and their story is
    No less in pity than his glory which
    Brought them to be lamented. □   (5.2.353–7)

It is perhaps typical of Octavius that he should put himself into the final picture but it is also a just judgement: the play leaves us with his victory and, by implication, Rome's. The lovers are given the courtesy of a rather ambiguous description, 'famous', where Dryden allows Serapion the more partial judgement: they lived 'great' and died 'well'. Octavius compliments their part in the 'high events' and grants them 'pity' and 'glory' but he closes with himself, and their funeral procession will be a prelude to his triumphal parade:

> ■   Our army shall
> In solemn show attend this funeral,
> And then to Rome. □   (5.2.357–9)

Dryden's Shakespearean imitation may focus more closely on the conflict between love and honour than is ever true of *Antony and Cleopatra* and that may be grounds for thinking that he was 'imitating' very much in the manner he describes: 'to write as he supposes that author would have done had he lived in our age'. He has brought to bear on the story a framework of values more in keeping with his own age than with Shakespeare's, although it also true that the play is emotionally more complex than this simple formula suggests. Antony's summary of his ambitions, 'My life has been a golden dream of love and friendship', focuses another theme of the play, the envious comradeship he enjoys with Dolabella and also with Ventidius, although that is of a different sort, and the two friendships are compared and contrasted throughout the play. The conclusion we draw is that Antony cannot have both love and friendship and that the contrast between these two is even greater than the contrasts between love and honour. Act IV is particularly rich in condemnation of the fickleness of both men and women provoked by love. *Antony and Cleopatra* contains many touching scenes of male friendship but nothing as intense as those in *All for Love*.

H.H. Furness commented that 'for full eighty years, from 1678 to 1759, it usurped Shakespeare's tragedy on the stage; and, indeed, in these latter days came perilously and incomprehensibly near to shaking the allegiance of Sir Walter Scott [1771–1832]'.[5] David Garrick revived Shakespeare's play in 1759 at Drury Lane,[6] cutting Shakespeare's forty-three scenes to twenty-seven and reducing shifts of location to a minimum as painted sets were used. Philo, Demetrius, Ventidius and Scarus disappear and their lines are given to Thidias (renamed Thyreus) and Dolabella. Thyreus delivers Enobarbus's Cydnus barge speech in scene 1 (it is in Act 2 in Shakespeare). Gallus, Menecrates and Varrius are dispensed with and entire scenes vanish, including 3.1, 3.4 and 4.1–3: 657 lines are cut in all. Double entendre is bowdlerised. Pompey and Octavia appear but only in one scene each. Cleopatra's role is spectacularly enhanced and the political discussions between Antony, Pompey and Octavius are lost. Her part is substantially unchanged. The love story is emphasised at the expense of the political dimension, becoming essentially ahistorical; Caesar is humanised and Enobarbus softened. All this is to bring Shakespeare closer to Dryden.

Dryden's play survived, however. J.P. Kemble (1757–1823) produced a patchwork of Dryden and Shakespeare for Covent Garden in 1813, which Hazlitt saw;[7] Macready put Shakespeare's play on at Drury Lane in 1833, still with some admixture of Dryden. The first production of Shakespeare without any Dryden was Samuel Phelps's at Sadler's Wells in 1849.[8] What emerges from this stage history (which takes us well into the subject matter of the next chapter, the Romantics and the Victorians) is the persistence of Dryden's central shift of emphasis: the reduction of the political intrigue of empire and the clarification of the dramatic conflict. The complexity of Shakespeare's play, the deliberate (it must be assumed) placing of two complex psychological inward dramas in a dramatic conflict with each other within a wider context of the intricate political manoeuvrings of both great and lesser characters, is quite lost.

CHAPTER FOUR

Romantics to Victorians: 'This enchanting Queen'

The stage practice of the eighteenth century with respect to *Antony and Cleopatra* has its counterpart in the criticism of the nineteenth in that, from the point of view of the modernist critic at least, Shakespeare's distinctive practice is not being recognised, or, worse still, it is being reinterpreted in such a way as to bring it within acceptable bounds. The strong tendency in the nineteenth century is to see the play as very much about Cleopatra, whose charms influence even the most judicious and excite the less judicious into extravagance.

The great German critic Augustus Wilhelm Schlegel praises Shakespeare's 'three Roman pieces' for the restraint Shakespeare shows in excluding 'foreign appendages and arbitrary suppositions' while he 'fully satisfies the wants of the stage'.[1] The suggestion implicit in this is that there is, at least potentially, a conflict between 'the wants of the stage' and the demands of history, that is, history is undramatic. Schlegel takes a different view from Johnson's but shares the terms that Johnson employs: 'under the apparent artlessness of adhering closely to history as he found it, an uncommon degree of art is concealed'.[2] Johnson had dismissed the play's construction, accusing it of following history and relating the events 'without any art of connection or care of disposition'. Schlegel argues that Shakespeare seizes 'the true poetical point' of events and gives 'unity and rounding' to what he describes as 'a series of events detached from the immeasurable extent of history without in any degree changing them'.[3] This is a bold stroke. The suggestion is that, properly chosen, an extract from history may become dramatic when exhibited on the stage; rather as an *objet trouvé* is not art in itself in its usual surroundings but becomes art when detached from them and exhibited on its own.

He admits, however, in his specific treatment of *Antony and Cleopatra*, that perhaps Shakespeare tried to bring under his control too great a variety of events, and he reflects that the great difficulty of creating historical drama is that the play must be 'a crowded extract, and a living development of history'.[4] To take a set of events out of history is to risk them becoming unintelligible. Shakespeare overcomes the problem in *Antony and Cleopatra* by only alluding to a great many things that cannot appear on the stage and the weakness of this approach is that 'a work of art should contain every thing necessary for fully understanding it within itself'.[5]

Schlegel's picture of Antony is a familiar one: in him 'we observe a mixture of great qualities, weaknesses, and vices, violent ambition and ebullitions of magnanimity: we see him sunk in luxurious enjoyments and nobly ashamed of his own aberrations'.[6] An insufficiently resolute figure, he is continually 'manning himself to resolutions not unworthy of himself, which are always shipwrecked against the seductions of an artful woman'. Schlegel makes a connection others will make in this respect: the picture of Antony in the toils of Cleopatra's seductiveness is 'Hercules in the chains of Omphale, drawn from the fabulous heroic ages into history, and invested with the Roman costume' (Ovid tells the story of the subjugation of Hercules by Omphale, the Amazonian Queen of Lydia).

Cleopatra is 'an ambiguous being made up of royal pride, female vanity, luxury, inconstancy, and true attachment' and Schlegel judges the relationship as being 'without moral dignity', yet recognises that it 'still excites our sympathy as an insurmountable fascination' and comments: 'As they die for each other, we forgive them for having lived for each other'. Octavius, by contrast with these two great beings, displays 'heartless littleness' and Schlegel comments that Shakespeare 'seems to have completely seen through [him] without allowing himself to be led astray by the fortune and the fame of Augustus'.

Coleridge rated the play very highly indeed, doubting even 'whether it is not in all exhibitions of a giant power in its strength and vigour of maturity, a formidable rival of the *Macbeth*, *Lear*, *Othello* and *Hamlet*'. He identifies an important paradox:

■ There are scarcely any [plays] in which he has followed history more minutely, and yet few even of his own in which he impresses the notion of giant strength so much, perhaps none in which he impresses it more strongly. This is owing to the manner in which it is sustained throughout – that he *lives* in and through the play – to the numerous momentary flashes of nature counteracting the historic abstraction, in which take as a specimen the death of Cleopatra.[7] □

He declares the 'motto' for the play's style '*feliciter audax*' and claims that this 'happy valiancy of style is but the representative and result of all the material excellencies so expressed'. He makes an interesting suggestion: that the play should be compared with *Romeo and Juliet* 'as the love of passion and appetite opposed to the love of affection and instinct'.[8] His insight into Cleopatra is compelling:

■ The sense of the criminality in her passion is lessened by our insight into its depth and energy, at the very moment that wc cannot but pcrccive that the passion itself springs out of the habitual craving of a licentious nature, and that it is supported and reinforced by voluntary stimulus and sought-for associations, instead of blossoming out of spontaneous emotion.[9] □

It is instructive to compare this with Schlegel's picture. Schlegel's Cleopatra is essentially a weak person; capable of 'true attachment', she is nonetheless so influenced by 'royal pride' and 'female vanity' and a love of luxury that she is incapable of constancy. This is a moral picture rather than a psychological picture: we need no complex psychology to explain the moral dilemma. She knows what she should do and she does not do it; she knows what she should not do and she does it. Coleridge, on the other hand, invites us to sympathise with a psychological morbidity that may be moral in its origins but has passed beyond those origins into a condition of being. She has enjoyed deliberately stimulated luxury for so long that she is almost incapable of a feeling not deliberately induced and supported. She is not so much criminal as so far gone in her abandonment that she earns our pity. This may not be Shakespeare's figure (and it is certainly not Dr Johnson's) but it is a speculation that can be supported from the text and realised in performance. This raises the question that will loom much larger in the twentieth century of the extent to which we can talk of Shakespeare's Cleopatra at all, or indeed of any of his characters, as though we might read his intentions off his text, even if we could be quite certain what that text was.

Hazlitt (1778–1830) describes the play as 'a very noble play' but goes on to say that it is 'not in the first class of Shakespear's productions' although standing next to them. He thinks it the finest of the historical plays:

■ that is, of those in which he made poetry the organ of history, and assumed a certain tone of character and sentiment, in conformity to known facts, instead of trusting to his observations of general nature or to the unlimited indulgence of his own fancy.[10] □

There is a tantalising set of oppositions in this formulation: 'facts' and 'fancy' pre-eminently. It is not impertinent to observe that Dickens will make tremendous rhetorical play with this alliterative opposition in *Hard Times* (1854), by which time, and in whose hands, the opposition has become entrenched. It is not so here, at this time and in these hands, but the distinction is observed. A neutral, intervening term is introduced as well: 'general nature'. We must imagine that there is the specificity of 'known facts', the categorical level of 'general nature' and a third realm of 'fancy'. The interesting question is what is the relationship imagined by Hazlitt between the three? In the answer to that question lies the answer to the further question, what is the 'certain tone of character and sentiment' that belongs properly to 'known facts'?

There is a clue in Hazlitt's praise of Shakespeare's powers of characterisation as they are displayed in this play:

■ He brings living men and women on the scene, who speak and act from real feelings, according to the ebbs and flows of passion, without the least tincture of pedantry of logic or rhetoric.[11] ☐

He gives as an example the passage in which Cleopatra wonders aloud what Antony is doing while he is absent from her, claiming that 'Few things in Shakespear ... have more of that local truth of imagination and character'. He offers as his judgement of the character the view that:

■ Cleopatra's whole character is the triumph of the voluptuous, of the love of pleasure and the power of giving it, over every other consideration.[12] ☐

And he concludes that:

■ She had great and unpardonable faults, but the grandeur of her death almost redeems them. She learns from the depth of despair the strength of her affections. She keeps her queen-like state in the last disgrace, and her sense of the pleasurable in the last moments of her life. She tastes a luxury in death. After applying the asp, she says with fondness –

Dost thou not see my baby at my breast
That sucks the nurse asleep?
As sweet as balm, as soft as air, as gentle.
Oh Antony![13] ☐

Hazlitt's picture of Cleopatra does not have the psychological depth of Coleridge's and there is something quite unsatisfactory about the phrase 'the strength of her affections' in the passage just quoted because, although Antony might be supposed to be their proper object, it is clear that Hazlitt thinks she is more concerned with the manner of her death than with the affections he has stated are so strong. The phrase has a rhetorical mannerism about it that does not convince either: it is too antithetically balanced and unlike Schlegel's comment on the lovers 'As they die for each other, we forgive them for having lived for each other', which shows the same rhetorical structure, it has no moral complexity, her despair and her affections having nothing necessarily to do with each other. It is not even true of the play. Schlegel's somewhat baffled acknowledgement that she is capable of true attachment along with her pride and vanity is much nearer the mark. Hazlitt is trying to turn the play into a rather sentimental tragedy of true attachment learned too late: it is more the tragedy of true attachment too tied up with other considerations ever to have become clear enough to have influenced anything.

Hazlitt commends those moments in which Antony's previous character is recalled and uses the opportunity to attack the doctrine of the unities:

■ The jealous attention which has been paid to the unities both of time and place has taken away the principle of perspective in drama, and all the interest which objects derive from distance, from contrast, from privation, from change of fortune, from long-cherished passion; and contrasts our view of life from a strange and romantic dream, long, obscure, and infinite, into a smartly contested, three hours inaugural disputation on its merits by the different candidates for theatrical applause.[14] □

It is difficult to imagine a theatre audience coping with a play that really did offer 'a strange and romantic dream, long, obscure, and infinite': the novel will do this much better. Hazlitt has, though, thrown a spotlight on the play's main weakness: it really is trying to do what the novel will do much better.[15]

However, it manages to achieve locally what it cannot perhaps fully realise overall. Hazlitt quotes 4.14.1–13 and comments:

■ This is, without doubt, one of the finest pieces of poetry in Shakespear. The splendour of the imagery, the semblance of reality, the lofty range of picturesque objects hanging over the world, their evanescent nature, the total uncertainty of what is left behind, are just like the mouldering scenes of human greatness. It is finer than Cleopatra's passionate lamentation over his fallen grandeur, because it is more dim, unstable, unsubstantial.[16] □

That other scene of cloud imagery, Prospero's speech in *The Tempest* at 4.1.146ff., may be in Hazlitt's mind at this point.

Anna Jameson (1794–1860; *Characteristics of Women*, 1833) regarded the great triumph of the play as being 'to make the extreme of littleness produce an effect like grandeur':[17]

■ To heap up together all that is most unsubstantial, frivolous, vain, contemptible, and variable, till the worthlessness be lost in the magnitude, and a sense of the sublime spring from the very elements of littleness.[18] □

Cleopatra is 'a brilliant antithesis' and 'a glorious riddle' and Mrs Jameson concludes that 'the woman herself would be distracting, if she were not so enchanting'. While other Shakespearean heroines, however complex, offer 'the idea of unity and simplicity of effect … in the midst of variety', Cleopatra's character is marked by its *'consistent inconsistency'* (Mrs Jameson adds, 'if I may use such an expression'), such that the 'the impression is that of perpetual and irreconcilable contrast'. Shakespeare has taken all the various elements 'and fused them into one brilliant impersonation of classical elegance, Oriental voluptuousness, and gipsy sorcery'.[19] Nowhere is she more fully realised than in her death:

■ Coquette to the last, she must make Death proud to take her, and die, 'phoenix-like', as she had lived, with all the pomp of preparation – luxurious in her despair. □

What is so striking is that her distaste of humiliation allows her to overcome her physical cowardice, which led her to desert the battle of Actium, so that:

■ The idea of this frail, timid, wayward woman dying with heroism, from the mere force of passion and will, takes us by surprise.[20] □

The insistent paradoxes of Mrs Jameson's portrait irritated M.R. Ridley[21] and often amount to nothing more than enthusiasm for the character portrayed (just as much criticism of a negative cast often amounts to nothing more than revulsion for the character portrayed: Shaw's is an example), although this last observation is clear-sighted and true. Part of the power of the play lies in our acknowledgement that unworthy people and events can provoke a sense of greatness almost in spite of themselves and indeed even of ourselves as members of audiences.

Charles Bathurst (*Remarks on … Shakespeare's Versification*, 1857) thought the play 'carelessly written' but with 'a great deal of nature, spirit, and knowledge of character' and 'several most beautiful passages'.[22] He singles out Cleopatra's 'dream of Antony' and moments when 'the verse bursts out of its trammels, as in the speech about the cloud'. Bathurst is not exercised by the question of the dramatic potentiality of history, because he regards the play as dealing with the side issues of history. As a result, the play 'is historical; but it is chiefly the anecdote of history, not the dignity of it'. This is at least in part due to Plutarch's influence: Bathurst says that Shakespeare's source is 'in great degree, a collection of anecdotes'.

The business of the play is 'tenderness, even weakness', tenderness of feeling is remarkable throughout but especially in the death of

Enobarbus. Bathurst sees Shakespeare's purpose as being to elevate Antony:

■ He represents him as, what he certainly was not, a man of the most noble and high spirit, capable at times, notwithstanding the luxury he afterwards fell into, of a thoroughly soldier-like life, and full of kind and generous feelings. □

Bathurst comments, perceptively:

■ He [Shakespeare] seems to delight in supposing the melancholy meditations of a great and active character, when losing his power, and drawing to his end. □

As with Hazlitt, the image of Prospero perhaps comes to mind.

Edward Dowden set out in *Shakspere: His Mind and Art* (1875), one of the most popular books of Shakespeare criticism of all time, to show that the creative mind can be inferred into the work by a careful study of the evolution of the work from the beginning to the end. It is a remarkable study. The primary difficulty with any biographical study, however, is that there is always a tendency to justify the work from the life as a picture of the life and although Dowden struggles to avoid this pitfall, he is not always successful. His comments on the Roman plays are among his successes in this respect. He remarks on the difference between *Julius Caesar* and *Antony and Cleopatra*, comparing it as passing from 'a gallery of antique sculpture' into 'a room splendid with the colours of Titian and Paul Veronese'. In the characters of *Julius Caesar* there is 'a severity of outline', whereas those of *Antony and Cleopatra* 'insinuate themselves through the senses, trouble the blood, ensnare the imagination, invade our whole being like colour or music'.[23] The contrast holds good throughout. Whereas *Julius Caesar* is dominated by the idea of duty, the later play is obsessed with pleasure and 'the remorseless Nemesis of eternal law', Brutus the stoic is contrasted against Antony the wayward, inconstant, 'soiled with the stains of passion and decay'. Dowden's contrast between Portia and Cleopatra excites him to say 'Does the one word woman include natures so diverse?' However, 'the spirit of the play, though superficially it appears voluptuous, is essentially severe'.[24] By this Dowden means that Shakespeare is 'faithful to the fact'. Antony and Cleopatra are politically powerful: 'a third of the world is theirs'. Theirs is not the passion of youth 'with its slight, melodious raptures and despairs'. Their passion is 'the deeper intoxication of middle age, when death has become a reality, when the world is limited and positive, when life is urged to yield up quickly its utmost treasures of delight'. Antony is 'daily dropping away from all that is sound, strong, and enduring':[25]

■ The pathos of *Antony and Cleopatra* is like the pathos of *Macbeth*. But Shakspere like Dante allows the soul of the perjurer and murderer to drop into a lower, blacker, and more lonely circle of Hell than the soul of the man who has sinned through voluptuous self-indulgence. □

Dowden makes an interesting distinction: the fascination exerted by each over the other 'is not so much that of the senses as of the sensuous imagination', and he goes on to say:

■ Measure things only by the sensuous imagination, and everything in the world of oriental voluptuousness, in which Antony lies bewitched, is great. □

Dowden is struggling, as other critics have struggled, with the notion of 'greatness' that tragedy is associated with: Cleopatra's beauty, passion and pleasure, Antony's strength and prodigality, 'toil after the infinite'. However, he cannot see Cleopatra's passion for Antony as love:

■ We do not mistake this feeling of Cleopatra towards Antony for love; but he has been for her (who had known Caesar and Pompey), the supreme sensation. She is neither faithful to him nor faithless; in her complex nature, beneath each fold or layer of sincerity, lies one of insincerity, and we cannot tell which is the last or innermost.[26] □

The 'sensuous imagination', as he has already implied, is not a reliable measure of 'greatness':

■ No one felt more profoundly than Shakspere, as his Sonnets abundantly testify, that the glory of strength and of beauty is subject to limit and to time. What he would seem to say to us in this play, not in the manner of a doctrinaire or a moralist, but wholly as an artist, is that this sensuous infinite is but a dream, a deceit, a snare.[27] □

Perhaps sensible that such a critique of the attractions of a life of pleasure may risk a moralising tendency, Dowden insists that the 'ethical truth lives and breathes in every part of his work' and that 'ethical truth' is tragical:

■ At every moment in this play we assist at a catastrophe – the decline of a lordly nature. At every moment we are necessarily aware of the gross, the mean, the disorderly womanhood in Cleopatra, no less than of the witchery and wonder which excite, and charm, and subdue. □

This spirit of Cleopatra is the focus of the difficulty:

■ The presence of a spirit of *life* in Cleopatra, quick, shifting, multitudinous, incalculable, fascinates the eye, and would, if it could, lull the moral sense to sleep, as the sea does with its endless snakelike motions in the sun and shade.[28] □

Nowhere is this more clearly exemplified than in her death, in which 'there is something dazzling and splendid, something sensuous, something theatrical, something magnificently coquettish, nothing stern'.[29]

Dowden contrasts Shakespeare's Cleopatra with Milton's treatment of Dalila in *Samson Agonistes* (1671):

■ Yet Shakspere does not play the rude moralist; he needs no chorus of Israelite captives to utter invective against this Dalila. Let her possess all her grandeur, and her charm. Shakspere can show us more excellent things which will make us proof against the fascination of these.[30] □

The greater though is not Octavius: 'who never gains the power which passion supplies, nor loses the power which passion withdraws and dissipates'.[31]

Swinburne contributes what can only really be described as a fantasia on what he calls 'the thought of Cleopatra', the mere touch of which, he claims, causes the greatest poets (and only the greatest) to rise even higher than they usually can do. He credits the 'marvellous and matchless verses' of *Zim-Zizimi* by the French poet Victor Hugo (1802–85) (in *La Légende des Siècles*, 1859) with the ability to evoke 'all the splendour and fragrance and miracle of her mere bodily presence' and ventures the belief that some

■ may remember that to their own infantine perceptions the first obscure electric revelation of what Blake calls 'the Eternal Female' was given through a blind wondering thrill of childish rapture by a lightning on the baby dawn of their senses and their soul from the sunrise of Shakespeare's Cleopatra. □

Swinburne's approach to the historico-political aspects of the play confidently reflects Antony's 'Let Rome in Tiber melt':

■ Never has he given such proof of his incomparable instinct for abstinence from the wrong thing as well as achievement of the right. He has utterly rejected and disdained all occasion of setting her off by means of any lesser foil than all the glory of the world with all its empires.[32] □

This is odd stuff. It is not criticism; it is praise. It is not praise of Shakespeare but of his creation, and not only of his creation but of the vision of her that she seeks to create and, as a consequence, it is not a critical appraisal of Shakespeare's creation as she is seen by the audience or by the reader. Swinburne's excited and lavish prose is in danger of parodying itself. Anna Jameson appears restrained in comparison.

Arthur Symons wrote of Cleopatra in a similar vein that she is 'the most wonderful of Shakespeare's women, and not of Shakespeare's women only, but perhaps the most wonderful of women'. For good measure, this makes *Antony and Cleopatra* 'the most wonderful ... of Shakespeare's plays'.[33]

Georg Brandes is more judicious. He realises that Shakespeare's aim is, as it was in *King Lear*, 'to evoke the conception of a world-catastrophe'.[34] Brandes points out the need to indicate that 'the action was not taking place in some narrow precinct in a corner of Europe, but upon the stage of the world'. All the comings and goings of messengers and changes of scene serve to 'give the impression of majestic breadth, of an action embracing half of the then known world'. Also the play needs a counterpoise to Antony and Cleopatra themselves, and that is found in the groups surrounding Octavius Caesar and Pompey, and in Octavia. In the contrast between Rome and Egypt, Brandes sees the play siding with Rome: he suggests that unlike *Clavigo* (1774), by the German writer Johann Wolfgang von Goethe (1749–1832), in which love is the virtue and ambition the temptation, in *Antony and Cleopatra* 'it is love that is reprehensible, ambition that is proclaimed to be the great man's vocation and duty'. He accepts that 'the great attraction of this masterpiece lies in the unique figure of Cleopatra', but affirms that 'the greatness of the world-historic drama proceeds from the genius with which [Shakespeare] has entwined the private relations of the two lovers with the course of history and the fate of empires'. For Brandes the meaning of the play lies in the 'sense of *universal annihilation*' that accompanies the 'crumbling to pieces of Roman greatness', fourteen years after the events chronicled in *Julius Caesar*:

■ Just as Antony's ruin results from his connection with Cleopatra, so does the fall of the Roman Republic result from the contact of the simple hardihood of the West with the luxury of the East. Antony is Rome. Cleopatra is the Orient. When he perishes, a prey to the voluptuousness of the East, it seems as though Roman greatness and the Roman Republic expired with him.[35] □

The finality of this picture is what gives the play its resonance:

■ This is no tragedy of a domestic, limited nature like the conclusion of *Othello*; there is no young Fortinbras here, as in *Hamlet*, giving the promise of brighter and better times to come; the victory of Octavius brings glory to no one and promises nothing. No; the final picture is that which Shakespeare was bent on painting from the moment he felt himself attracted by this great theme – the picture of a world-catastrophe. ☐

Mungo MacCallum, whose *Shakespeare's Roman Plays and their Background* will be discussed later, quotes further from Brandes, and these additional phrases give an even deeper sense of the awe with which Brandes contemplated Shakespeare's picture of the declining empire:

■ The might of Rome, stern and austere, shivered at the touch of Eastern voluptuousness. Everything sank, everything fell – character and will, dominions and principalities, men and women. Everything was worm-eaten, serpent-bitten, poisoned by sensuality – everything tottered and collapsed.[36] ☐

MacCallum himself is very much a Victorian but the fuller treatment of his work belongs with a consideration of those critics who have followed his lead and are determined to see *Antony and Cleopatra* as a 'Roman' play.

A.C. Bradley is perhaps second only to Dowden as a popular critic of Shakespeare and, while Dowden stressed the life and Bradley stresses the objectivity of the work, he is as much of a Victorian as Dowden. Victorian criticism is profoundly influenced by the novel, the form at which the age triumphantly succeeded, and is often almost fatally obsessed with biography, either of the author or the characters. Bradley is famously associated with a tendency to mix in to his criticism imagination of the characters as though they were characters in a novel, that is, with much more detail to them than is supplied by or perhaps authorised by the play.

Bradley included his treatment of the play in his *Oxford Lectures on Poetry* (1909); the essay was first published in the *Quarterly Review* of April 1906. Bradley had published his lectures on the four great tragedies in 1904. The separation is crucial: Bradley explicitly rejects any significant connection between the four great tragedies and *Antony and Cleopatra*: 'To regard this tragedy as a rival of the famous four, whether on the stage or in the study, is surely an error.'[37] He continues:

■ One may notice that, in calling *Antony and Cleopatra* wonderful or astonishing, we appear to be thinking first of the artist and his activity, while in the case of the four famous tragedies it is the product of this activity, the thing presented, that first engrosses us. ☐

Believing that, although he is stating the distinction sharply, it is a distinction often felt, he concludes: 'It implies that, although *Antony and*

Cleopatra may be for us as wonderful an achievement as the greatest of Shakespeare's plays, it has not an equal value'. To bracket the famous four with *Antony and Cleopatra* is not merely to make an error in valuation but involves 'a failure to discriminate the peculiar marks of *Antony and Cleopatra* itself'.

In the Introduction to *Shakespearean Tragedy,* Bradley distinguished *Richard III* and *Richard II, Julius Caesar, Antony and Cleopatra* and *Coriolanus* as

■ tragic histories or historical tragedies, in which Shakespeare acknowledged in practice a certain obligation to follow his authority, even when that authority offered him an undramatic material.[38] ☐

These plays cannot be what Bradley calls 'pure tragedy'. In his first lecture in the series, 'The Substance of Tragedy', Bradley makes it clear why especially *Antony and Cleopatra* cannot be considered 'pure tragedy'. In the first place, the definition he advances involves the death of the hero. He points out that in *Antony and Cleopatra*, as in *Romeo and Juliet*, the death of the heroine is involved but he has ruled out *Antony and Cleopatra* as a 'tragic history' and he rules out *Romeo and Juliet* as 'an early work, and in some respects an immature one'. He reaches a preliminary definition of tragedy as 'a story of exceptional calamity leading to the death of a man in high estate'.[39] This man 'should have so much of greatness that in his error and fall we may be vividly conscious of the possibilities of human nature'.[40] His most subtle passages concern the effort to explain the sense of fatalism engendered by the plays in terms of a moral order, which leads to his conclusion:

■ We remain confronted with the inexplicable fact, or the no less inexplicable appearance, of a world travailing for perfection, but bringing to birth, together with glorious good, an evil which it is able to overcome only by self-torture and self-waste.[41] ☐

It is difficult to see, from the very beginning of this account, how *Antony and Cleopatra* might be made to square with it; although whether it is enough to identify the use of North's Plutarch as the disqualifying factor must be doubted: his initial definition rules out a most important feature of the play, that is, Cleopatra's part, and it is important to note that his dismissal of another play that is otherwise 'a pure tragedy' is very unsatisfactory. Having identified the five 'pure' tragedies, he excludes *Romeo and Juliet* as 'an early work, and in some respects an immature one' and thus relieves himself of the difficult task of reconciling a play in which 'the heroine is as much the centre of the action as the hero'[42] with four of which he can justly claim that they set forth stories 'of exceptional calamity leading to the death of a man in high estate'. It would have been interesting to follow what is already a subtle argument through the further coils that complication would have thrown around him: his view is so dependent upon the identification of the inner struggle of a single man that the movement from that to the inner struggle of the heroine would surely have defeated it.

Bradley notes that *Antony and Cleopatra* is rarely acted and identifies a lack of dramatic excitement in the first three acts as a cause of this lack of theatrical popularity:

> ■ People converse, discuss, accuse one another, excuse themselves, mock, describe, drink together, arrange a marriage, meet and part; but they do not kill, do not even tremble or weep … We hear wonderful talk; but it is not talk, like that of Macbeth and Lady Macbeth, or that of Othello and Iago, at which we hold our breath. □

His important point is not that this makes the play inferior to other plays, so much as that it makes it distinct from them: it is not trying to do what they are trying to do and should not be mistaken for trying to do so nor set down because it has failed to do so. Bradley points out that the structure would have allowed Shakespeare to make some very dramatic scenes: a scene, or scenes, of his breaking from Cleopatra to marry Octavia; the counter-stroke of his return would have afforded, if not incident then at least powerful emotions (which, incidentally, Dryden does). Shakespeare does not. The break is not really believed: we are neither encouraged nor really permitted to believe it. The return is only reported; it is not even shown. This is because 'it was essential to its own peculiar character and its most transcendent effects that this attempt should not be made, but that Antony's passion should be represented as a force which he could hardly even desire to resist':[43]

> ■ By the very scheme of the work, therefore, tragic impressions of any great volume or depth were reserved for the last stage of the conflict; while the main interest, down to the battle of Actium, was directed to matters exceedingly interesting and even, in the wider sense, dramatic, but not overtly either terrible or piteous: on the one hand, to the political aspect of the story; on the other, to the personal causes which helped to make the issue inevitable. □

To Shakespeare, Octavius is 'one of those men, like Bolingbroke and Ulysses, who have plenty of "judgement" and not much "blood". Victory in the world, according to the poet, almost always goes to such men; and he makes us respect, fear, and dislike them'.[44] Bradley's dislike is almost personal: as such it is perceptive. He is especially good on

Octavius's dismissal of Antony's challenge and his calling Antony 'the old ruffian':

> ■ There is a horrid aptness in the phrase, but it disgusts us. It is shameful in this boy, as hard and smooth as polished steel, to feel at such a time nothing of the greatness of his victim and the tragedy of his victim's fall.[45] □

   Bradley acknowledges the problem concerning Octavia: Plutarch says that Octavius loved his sister and Octavius says in the play that he does but Shakespeare has let it appear as though Octavius is using her. Bradley says he thinks that Shakespeare was not much interested in settling the question and left it to the actor. This will not do. There is no problem in the play if we ignore Plutarch and, as Bradley notes, Plutarch himself construes Octavius's behaviour towards Octavia in at least one instance as motivated by political expediency. Her travelling to Antony from Rome to Athens was countenanced by Octavius (Plutarch tells us) 'not for his respect at all (as most authors doe report) as for that he might have an honest culler to make warre with Antonius if he did misuse her, and not esteem of her as she ought to be'.[46] Bradley notes this and adds 'The view I take does not, of course, imply that Octavius had no love for his sister'.[47]
   Bradley acknowledges 'the feeling of fate' and admits that there is something of the man of destiny about Octavius, and about the struggle between Antony and Octavius, but obstinately insists that 'there seems to be something half-hearted in Shakespeare's appeal here, something even ironical in his presentation of this conflict'. He adds perceptively: 'The struggle in Lear's little island seems to us to have an infinitely wider scope'.[48] This is indeed ironic, as the geographical scope of *Antony and Cleopatra* is the then known world. Bradley compares 'the cold and disenchanting light' shed on the Trojan War in *Troilus and Cressida* and he comments on *Antony and Cleopatra*:

> ■ We turn for relief from the political game to those who are sure to lose it; to those who love some human being better than a prize, to Eros and Charmian and Iras; to Enobarbus, whom the world corrupts, but who has a heart that can break with shame; to the lovers, who seem to us to find in death something better than their victor's life.[49] □

   Much of Bradley's lecture is given to a discussion of *Antony and Cleopatra* that adds very little to what other critics before or since have said; it is one of the least satisfying of Bradley's discussions, unpunctuated with those brilliant speculative insights into the childhood or whatever part of the characters' lives is wholly untreated by the play under consideration, and stuffed, instead, with bombast. He is struggling throughout against a sense of disappointment: his theory of tragedy has no room for this play. He says:

> ■ In any Shakespearean tragedy we watch some elect spirit colliding, partly through its error and defect, with a superhuman power which bears it down; and yet we feel that this spirit, even in the error and defect, rises by its greatness into ideal union with the power that overwhelms it.[50] □

This feeling, Bradley says, is unusually strong in *Antony and Cleopatra*, yet, in conclusion, he remarks:

> ■ A comparison of Shakespearean tragedies seems to prove that the tragic emotions are stirred in the fullest possible measure only when such beauty or nobility of character is displayed as commands unreserved admiration or love; or when, in default of this, the forces which move the agents, and the conflict which results from these forces, attain a terrifying and overwhelming power. The four most famous tragedies satisfy one or both of these conditions; *Antony and Cleopatra*, though a great tragedy, satisfies neither of them completely.[51] □

He repeats his view that this is not a defect, as the play is not aiming at achieving this kind of success. It brilliantly succeeds in doing what it does, but Bradley remains unspecific about what that is. The clue is in his discussions of Coleridge with which he begins. He picks up 'angelic strength' from Coleridge[52] and expands upon it with a real zest and flourish:

> ■ One is astonished at the apparent ease with which extraordinary effects are produced, the ease, if I may paraphrase Coleridge, of an angel moving with the wave of a hand that heavy matter which men find so intractable.[53] □

Bradley comments perceptively on the way Shakespeare handles Plutarch:

> ■ how the artist, though he could not treat history like legend or fiction, seems to push whole masses aside, and to shift and refashion the remainder, almost with the air of an architect playing (at times rather carelessly) with a child's bricks. □

This sheer artistry is what reduces the play: Bradley believes that *Antony and Cleopatra* is linked with the Sonnets (as Dowden had said) and with *Troilus and Cressida*, as reflections upon Shakespeare's own experience, but, by the time he has come to the later play, 'not only is the poet's vision unclouded, but his whole nature, emotional as well as intellectual, is free. The subject no more embitters or seduces him than the ambition of Macbeth'.[54] However, the artist is not so impersonally absorbed either; although Bradley does not so much as say so, the lecture is suffused with a sense of falling short. His remarks on Antony and Cleopatra are an attempt to breathe life into his response: Antony is even described (ludicrously) as a poet. Antony is an orator: he has a feeling for a fine phrase. Shakespeare is the poet who puts the fine phrases into his mouth and who has a much deeper feeling for them than his character does. Both Antony and Cleopatra say things that are marvellous and yet the feeling persists that they cannot be as fully aware of them as we are or as the writer must have been, and this is part of the feeling of the play and what nags at Bradley, although he does not spell it out (and perhaps is not quite aware of it himself). Antony and Cleopatra are always speaking to an audience, even when they appear to be trying to be sincere, and although they express their feelings, it seems that they are always at least half-aware of the effect they are having. It is this self-conscious artistry that is so much less satisfactory than the kind of artistry that loses sight of itself in its vision of what it is addressing that Bradley has identified in this play.

On the relationship itself, Bradley errs on the side of generosity:

■   Neither the phrase 'a strumpet's fool', nor the assertion 'the nobleness of life is to do thus', answers to the total effect of the play. But the truths they exaggerate are equally essential; and the commoner mistake in criticism is to understate the second.[55]   □

Bradley sees in their love 'the infinity there is in man', much as Dowden had done. The design of the play is to highlight Antony being drawn irresistibly into his passion, while underplaying any possibly distracting element (such as Octavia), and contrasting this movement with the world in which and increasingly against which it is being played out, the political world of Octavius and the others. Its main result is to present positively the passion and the tragic deaths of the central characters. Where Bradley is unconvincing is in his treatment of the central characters. A comment about Cleopatra is not an unfair selection: 'That which makes her wonderful and sovereign laughs at definition'.[56] Of Antony he remarks, among other things, 'The joy of life had always culminated for him in the love of women: he could say "no" to none of them: of Octavia herself he speaks like a poet. When he meets Cleopatra, he finds his Absolute'.[57] This is not really criticism.

Bradley's identification of Cleopatra as Antony's 'Absolute' places him firmly in the camp of Romanticism as that was described and vilified by

George Bernard Shaw in his Preface to *Three Plays for Puritans* (1900). Shaw begins by claiming that his years as a theatre critic had adversely affected his health and claims that this effect is the result of the stultification of the theatre by a doctrine of art that he describes as 'sensuousness'. This doctrine of art is nowhere so pernicious as it is in the representation on stage of love. The problem is that audiences are unwilling to accept anything other than the genteel in the manner of representation, while insisting that love be the implicit motive behind all conduct represented. Shaw contrasts the storytelling of the Arabian Nights:

■ In the Arabian Nights we have a series of stories, some of them very good ones, in which no sort of decorum is observed. The result is that they are infinitely more constructive and enjoyable than our romances, because love is treated in them as naturally as any other passion. There is no cast iron convention as to its effects; no false association of general depravity of character with its corporealities or of general elevation with its sentimentalities; no pretence that a man or woman cannot be courageous and kind and friendly unless infatuatedly in love with somebody … rather, indeed, an insistence on the blinding and narrowing power of lovesickness to make princely heroes unhappy and unfortunate. These tales expose, further, the delusion that the interest of this most capricious, most transient, most easily baffled of all instincts, is inexhaustible, and that the field of the English romancer has been cruelly narrowed by the restrictions under which he is permitted to deal with it. The Arabian storyteller, relieved of all such restrictions, heaps character on character, adventure on adventure, marvel on marvel; while the English novelist, like the starving tramp who can think of nothing but his hunger, seems to be unable to escape from the obsession of sex, and will rewrite the very gospels because the originals are not written in the sensuously ecstatic style.[58] □

Life will come to imitate this form of art, and Shaw gives an increasingly exaggerated and fearsome catalogue of the likely misfortunes to which we shall all be subject:

■ Jealousy, which is either an egotistical meanness or a specific mania, will become obligatory; and ruin, ostracism, breaking up of homes, duelling, murder, suicide and infanticide will be produced (often have been produced, in fact) by incidents which, if left to the operation of natural and right feeling, would produce nothing worse than an hour's soon-forgotten fuss. Men will be slain needlessly on the field of battle because officers conceive it to be their first duty to make romantic exhibitions of conspicuous gallantry. The squire who has never spared an hour from the hunting field to do a little public work on the parish council will be cheered as a patriot because he is willing to kill and get killed for the sake of conferring himself as an institution on other countries. In the court cases will be argued, not on juridical but romantic principles; and vindictive damages and vindictive sentences, and the repudiation or suppression of sensible testimony, will destroy the very sense of law. Kaisers, generals, judges, and prime ministers will set the example of playing to the gallery. Finally the people, now that their compulsory literacy enables every pen-man to play on their romantic illusions, will be led by the nose far more completely than they ever were by playing on their former ignorance and superstition.[59] ☐

Is it a wonder, Shaw asks, 'why I call the Puritans to rescue [the theatre] again as they rescued it before when its foolish pursuit of pleasure sunk it in "profaneness and immorality"?'[60] Art has become the instrument of 'a systematic idolatry of sensuousness' and he feels that:

■ when I see that the nineteenth century has crowned the idolatry of Art with the deification of Love, so that every poet is supposed to have pierced to the holy of holies when he has announced that Love is the Supreme, or the Enough, or the All … that Art was safer in the hands of the most fanatical of Cromwell's major generals than it will be if ever it gets into mine.[61] ☐

   Shaw's irony is extensive: his objections to the 'sensuous' are not so much moral as they are aesthetic: he objects to the sumptuousness of the theatrical style of his time and he contrasts that sumptuousness of presentation with the paucity of what is presented. He concludes: 'The pleasures of the senses I can sympathise with and share; but the substi-tution of sensuous ecstasy for intellectual activity and honesty is the very devil'.[62] So when he comes to dismiss *Antony and Cleopatra* as follows, it is not unclear what is in his sights:

■ Shakespear's *Antony and Cleopatra* must needs be as intolerable to the true Puritan as it is vaguely distressing to the ordinary, healthy citizen, because, after giving a faithful picture of the soldier broken down by debauchery, and the typical wanton in whose arms such men perish, Shakespear finally strains all his huge command of rhetoric and stage pathos to give a theatrical sublimity to the wretched end of the business, and to persuade foolish spectators that the world was well lost by the twain. Such falsehood is not to be borne except by the real Cleopatras and Antonys (they are to be found in every public house) who would no doubt be glad enough to be transfigured by some poet as immortal lovers. ☐

The logic of the position is pessimism, Shaw claims ('The lot of the man who sees life truly and thinks about it Romantically is Despair'), and he calls for an end to the age in which it held such a prominent position:

■ Surely the time is past for patience with writers who, having to choose between giving up life in despair and discarding the trumpery kitchen scales in which they try to weigh the universe, superstitiously stick to the scales and spend the rest of the lives they pretend to despise in breaking men's spirits. □

He admires August Strindberg (1849–1912), and Jonathan Swift (1667–1745), and other 'resolute tragic-comedians', who 'force you to face the fact that you must either accept their conclusions as valid (in which case it is cowardly to continue living) or admit that their way of judging conduct is absurd' but he has no time for 'your Shakespears and Thackerays' (a reference to the Victorian novelist William Makepeace Thackeray, 1811–63), who 'huddle up the matter at the end by killing somebody and covering your eyes with the undertaker's handkerchief, duly onioned with some pathetic phrase'. Shaw's judgement is trenchant: 'I hate to think that Shakespear has lasted 300 years, though he got no further than Koheleth the Preacher [supposed author of the Old Testament book, *Ecclesiastes*], who died many centuries before him'.[63]

In his sense of history, Shaw is very much of his time, although on the progressive wing for that time; there is much of the attitude of Karl Marx (1818–83) and Friedrich Engels (1820–95) in this, and that theme will be picked up later in this book when these ideas re-enter critical thinking in the latter part of the twentieth century. There is also much of the desire to shock respectable opinion for which Shaw had earned much of his reputation. Although the remarks seem dated, the central principle is important: *Antony and Cleopatra* may not enshrine timeless truths so much as opinions widely held at the time of the play's performance and for some time afterwards. In which case, what is its worth after that time has passed into history?

Shaw's withering anti-Romanticism marks the end of an era and the emergence of a new trend in the arts at the turn of the nineteenth and twentieth centuries. In many ways himself very much a Victorian, he has one foot in the new age, that of the modernists.

CHAPTER FIVE

Modernists: 'No more but e'en a woman'

One strong feature of the modern period was a renewed interest in the drama and theatre practice of the Elizabethan and Jacobean eras and one of the great figures in this revival was Harley Granville-Barker. Granville-Barker sits astride the divisions and complications of this period in which the modern is struggling to be born out of the remains of the Victorian. Granville-Barker's own plays show much of the tastes of the time but his talents and interests are shown to best advantage in his contribution to *A Companion to Shakespeare* (which he edited with G.B. Harrison) and in the *Prefaces to Shakespeare* (1927–45). In his discussion of *Antony and Cleopatra,* Harley Granville-Barker writes against Dr Johnson's assertion that the events are narrated 'without any art of connection or care of disposition'. His master trope contrasts music and architecture:

■ We should never, probably, think of Shakespeare as sitting down to construct a play as an architect must design a house, in the three dimensions of its building. His theatre did not call for this, as the more rigorous economics of modern staging may be said to do. He was liker to a musician, master of an instrument, who takes a theme and, by generally recognised rules, improvises on it; or even to an orator, so accomplished that he can carry a complex subject through a two-hour speech, split it up, run it by diverse channels, digress, but never for too long, and at last bring the streams abreast again to blend them in his peroration.[1] □

A later metaphor observes:

■ So Shakespeare weaves his pattern – to find yet another simile – as he goes along, setting colour against colour, coarse thread by fine.[2] □

It is not easy to do justice to Granville-Barker's close commentary through which he shows just what he means: one example may suffice. When he is discussing Ventidius's scene with Silius, he points out that on Shakespeare's stage there would be no perceptible and distracting scene changing and the previous scene, the drunken dinner aboard Pompey's barge, would be a vivid recent memory: 'Enobarbus and Menas would hardly have vanished, their drunken halloos would still be echoing when Ventidius and his procession appeared'.[3] This is important: what Granville-Barker calls Shakespeare's 'stagecraft' may slip beneath the view of a criticism dominated by reading, by close attention to texts. He reminds us that the Act divisions of *Antony and Cleopatra* were invented by Rowe; they do not appear in the Folio. The unimpeded flow of action is a crucial part of the total effect, offering such juxtapositions as he has just described:

> ■ For the fact is that Shakespeare's work never parcels up very well. He was not among those writers who industriously gather material, sort and arrange and re-arrange it before they fit it together. When his mood is operative he creates out of an abundance of vitality, and it is no good service to him to start obstructing the flow of it. He keeps, for all his fervour, a keen sense of form; it is largely in the marriage of impulse and control that his genius as a pure playwright lies. When inspiration flags, he must come to contriving. He is business-like at that, quite callously business-like sometimes. But even to the most work-a-day stuff he gives a certain force. And should carelessness – for he can be wickedly careless – land him in a tight place, there is, to the practised observer, a sort of sporting interest in seeing him so nimbly and recklessly get out of it.[4] □

This is a valuable passage to have at hand during most considerations of Shakespeare's work or criticism of Shakespeare's work. It is a practitioner's insight; alive to theatrical considerations not as abstractions but as immediate practical concerns. It reminds us that Shakespeare wrote for the theatre, whether or not primarily he did so determinedly, and the theatre must always be in our minds when we consider the work.

The experience of the practitioner lends to Granville-Barker's somewhat garrulous commentary on the battle scenes a loose cogency: this collection of fragments that has so irritated and baffled other commentators is shown to be just the sort of fluid, continuous action Granville-Barker has said is Shakespeare's characteristic quality as a dramatist. He is especially good on the rapid emotional shifts of scenes 10–14 of Act 4, showing how the very fragmentariness and frenetic activity of scenes 10–13 issues into the strange calm of scene 14 and 'Eros, thou yet behold'st me?', with its extended, misleadingly playful conceit upon which Granville-Barker comments brilliantly: 'If we were not first thrown off our emotional balance we might find the fantasy that follows – for all its beauty – too much an intellectual conceit, and too long-drawn out.' As it is 'we should feel with Antony the relief this strange sense of dissolution brings from the antics of passion'.[5] Granville-Barker's concluding point should never be forgotten: 'We have been ideal spectators, we know what happened, and why; and just such an impression has been made on us as the reality would leave behind. It is a great technical achievement, and one of great artistry too.'[6] The distinction is an important one and it lies behind Bradley's struggle with himself: Bradley magnificently concedes the artistry, but he cannot admit the art. There is something missing from this great tragedy for him that places it in the second rank behind the famous four. Granville-Barker cannot tell us what it is and this makes him a lesser critic than Bradley. When we have finished Granville-Barker, we are no more sure what the difference between the technical and the artistic might be than when we started. Bradley has told us what it is: it is a matter of what the play is about.

John Middleton Murry takes on this great responsibility, to address what the play is about. His description of Cleopatra at 5.2.93–4 as 'a child, lost in a dark forest, wavering and timorous: caught between her vision of a world made magnificent by Antony, and her knowledge of a world made dead by his death' is brushed by the gust of psychoanalysis and is a subtle response to the great poetry of those lines; his discussion of the later lines (214–21) is inspired.[7] He picks up especially

■   I shall see
  Some squeaking Cleopatra boy my greatness
  I' the posture of a whore □   (219–21)

reminding his readers that that was what was actually happening as the actor spoke the lines. He describes the moment as a 'super-dramatic device'. It is anti-dramatic in the sense that it shatters (or, risks shattering) the dramatic illusion but Murry wants the implication to be that the tactic raises the moment above the ordinary level of the drama rather than depressing it below that level. Murry compares *Julius Caesar* 3.1.112–17:

■ *Cassius.* Stoop, then, and wash.
    They smear their hands with Caesar's blood
                          How many ages hence
    Shall this our lofty scene be acted over
    In states unborn and accents yet unknown!
    Brutus. How many times shall Caesar bleed in sport,
    That now on Pompey's basis lies along
    No worthier than the dust. □

In these two moments, characters envisage their present actions being re-enacted in their future and that envisaged future re-enactment is the audience's present experience. This lends a ceremonial, a ritual element to the moment. Murry's own exposition tends markedly in this direction.

He quarrels with the word 'device', claiming that the method here is 'quite intuitive'. Shakespeare possessed the 'deliberate and conscious technical cunning' suggested by the word 'device' but is here using another faculty:

> ■ He challenges the dramatic illusion, because he can, and because he must. First, because he can: he has created the imaginative reality of his Antony and Cleopatra. For us they *are*. Second, because he must. In the confidence, in the ecstasy, in the 'intensity' of his own creativeness, he must seize the opportunity that has offered itself naturally of directly confronting the order of reality which he has created with the order of actuality which is.[8] □

Murry is very good on the way Shakespeare uses the word 'royal' and the meanings he packs into it. He is particularly good on Charmian's beautiful lines:

> ■ Now boast thee, death, in thy possession lies
> A lass unparallel'd. Downy windows, close;
> And golden Phoebus never be beheld
> Of eyes again so royal! □   (5.2.317–20)

Murry points out that the range from 'Royal Egypt' (4.15.70) to 'the maid that milks' (4.15.74) is captured in the 'lass unparallel'd'. The progress through 'downy windows', 'golden Phoebus' and ending on the word 'royal', Murry rightly says, makes that word mean

> ■ all that has gone before – all that was gathered up, before, into the 'lass unparallel'd' – all this, moreover, bathed in the majesty of 'bright Phoebus in his strength' [which Murry borrows, bizarrely, from *The Winter's Tale*].[9] □

He then takes the word 'royal' towards something he struggles desperately to express. On the way he says some useful things:

> ■ We know the meaning, before we know the word; the various, rich and infinite significance is first given to us, then at last the word which captures and crowns it.[10] □

That is a good way of describing the progress of poetic meaning as it is achieved often in Shakespeare's dramatic work. Murry sees in the scene between Dolabella and Cleopatra, with which he began and to which he returns now and again, 'the incommensurability of her experience and his'.[11] This is again a useful phrase: Dolabella's 'Gentle Madam, no' is sensitive but unbelieving; Cleopatra's 'You lie up to the hearing of the gods' at once distracted, hysterical, triumphant and even chilling. It is for a moment as though she knew something for a certainty that we cannot even hope to believe. However, Shakespeare may also be seen to be playing with different versions of things and not affirming the reality of a spiritual realm at all. Murry stakes his all on the affirmation of the spiritual and it leads him into some strange comparisons. He sees Antony's banquet of Act 4 scene 2 as a sort of Last Supper, quite explicitly: 'It is, if I may dare to put it thus, the Last Supper of Antony – sacramental, simple and strange.'[12] He approaches balance at one point only to swerve away from it:

> ■ A pathetic illusion, some may call it. But it is something rather different from this. Royalty – it is the great burden of this play – is no external thing; it is a kingdom and a conquest of the human spirit, an achieved greatness. □

True, but Shakespeare's treatment of these two in his play is far more equivocal than Murry is allowing.

This is still more true of his treatment of the loyalty of Enobarbus and finally of Cleopatra herself. Murry himself mentions the key to unlocking his misunderstanding: 'Shakespeare, who has written the tragedies, knows more about it [royalty]'.[13] True again: to understand loyalty as well as royalty, one must look to *King Lear* and then back to *Antony and Cleopatra* and contrast Enobarbus and Kent and see what a different world there is in his later play. When Murry gets round to it, he makes the important point that it is the poetry of the play that convinces us of such things as he has been asserting, such as the royalty of Antony. He then falls into the trap, as so many do:

> ■ We say to ourselves: 'the man *is* noble!' If then he does monstrous things, as Macbeth and Othello do, we can but ascribe it to his falling into the clutches of some superhuman power.[14] □

Or we can recognise, with a sinking feeling, the power of poetry and the uncertainty of our judgements. The striving for the superhuman, the effort to exceed oneself and one's condition that Murry so keenly wants that he sees it in the play are not unintelligible emotions, and they are not unintelligible to Shakespeare or undiscoverable in his works, but they are not simply affirmed. They may not be affirmed at all, let alone simply. They may be presented as possibilities, as dreams, as illusions. The illusion may be a trap; it may be a glory. The plays rarely allow a reader or audience member to carry away a certainty unchallenged.

Part of the problem is the rather exalted theory of poetry that Murry seems to have:

■ We have watched Antony ennoble the sacrifice of his friends, and be the more ennobled by that sacrifice [this is Murry's summary of what he calls Antony's 'Last Supper']; and we have watched him die royally. Then we have watched the mysterious transfusion of his royal spirit into the mind and heart of his fickle queen. And all this we have watched, not merely with the bodily, but with the spiritual, eye; we have heard it, not merely with the bodily, but with the spiritual, ear.[15] □

He develops this, musing:

■ The poetic utterance passes, without jolt or jar, into the dramatic deed, as though utterance and act were but a single kind of expression. □

And further:

■ Indeed, one might say that the inward life and creative process of such a drama as this is the gradual invasion and pervasion of the characters by the poetry of their own utterance. Their acts gradually, and reluctantly, move into harmony with their utterance; and, as the acts slowly change their nature, so the quality of the utterance becomes more rich and rare. To this process of attachment of deed to poetry, there is, it seems, but one inevitable end. The total suffusion of the character by poetry is death.[16] □

This becomes 'the total self-sacrifice of one human being for another in death, is the only true symbol we have and can recognise for Love', which then leads towards the Crucifixion by which 'Time is suffused and made incandescent by Eternity'. The problem with this is that it has taken the reader a long way from *Antony and Cleopatra*. It is doubtful whether the account Murry gives of the Crucifixion is at all applicable to that play. Neither Antony's nor Cleopatra's deaths can be described convincingly in such terms. Yet the point about poetry shaping their deeds is fascinating. The keyword is 'reluctantly'. This picture will very well answer Bradley's unhappiness as well, because it suggests that tragedy is not inevitable, in one sense, but a result of their overheated imaginings of themselves. The word that Bradley was avoiding, 'factitious', is, indeed, not the right word but there is an elusive quality of contrivance about it all, as though they were depicted as having to own up to their exaggerated sense of themselves, as though they were the victims of their self-publicisation. Murry comments later: '[Shakespeare's] task was to load the particular act of death with all the significance it could contain'. This is a concrete comment on a concrete dramatic situation.

Cleopatra is a reflex of Antony: 'But when he dies, her poetic function is to maintain and prolong, to reflect and reverberate, that achieved royalty of Antony's'.[17] Murry interprets the theme of death in the last Act as 'this note, as of a musing dream'[18] and suggests that 'it seems to us as though Cleopatra henceforward moves in a trance, governed by some secret music of the kind that marked the passing of God from Antony'. This sort of critical activity may best be described as free fantasia, or perhaps a rhapsody, dipping down every now and again for fresh sustenance from the text, but making free play with it and expanding its own inventions considerably beyond what, to many, the text may seem to warrant. Murry returns to Cleopatra's words to Dolabella and his treatment of them is a good example of the licence assumed by his approach. He describes them as 'visionary words' and then says that 'some would call them rhetorical'. There is an argument to be had here, but not for Murry: 'But to me the epithet seems quite meaningless'. He admits that the words are marked by hyperbole, 'but hyperbole is an empty grammatical label'. Well, in fact, 'rhetorical' is not in itself meaningless, although its application to Cleopatra's words may be held to be inappropriate, and 'hyperbole' is not an empty grammatical label but is a term that, when applied to Cleopatra's words, is not only intelligible but, it may be argued, perfectly appropriate. Murry's own hyperbole is a smokescreen. He continues: 'The point, and the only relevant point about them, is that they do body forth, against a mighty background, the nature and meaning of Antony.' It is quite possible to assert that this is just not true. This is the problem with such impressionistic criticism: it may be true, and equally it may not be true.

John Russell Brown, in his Introduction to the Casebook from which these selections are taken for discussion, says that he thinks Bradley's essay on *Antony and Cleopatra* is 'one of his ... finest achievements as a critic', claiming as evidence that

■ no one had said before, for example, that Cleopatra's 'ecstasy' at the end of the play appears 'not factitious, but an effort strained and prodigious as well as glorious, not, like Othello's last speech, the final expression of character, of thoughts and emotions which have dominated a whole life'.[19] □

Bradley, however, does not quite say this. He says:

■ Why is it that, although we close the book in a triumph which is more than reconciliation, this is mingled, as we look back on the story, with a sadness so peculiar, almost the sadness of disenchantment? Is it that, when the glow has faded, Cleopatra's ecstasy comes to appear, I would not say factitious, but an effort strained and prodigious as well as glorious, not, like Othello's last speech, the final expression of character, of thoughts and emotions which have dominated a whole life?[20] □

The very delicacy, the tentative, infinite tact of this makes the important phrase 'comes to appear' a matter of subjectivity. The 'we' who 'close the book in triumph' (we are back in the study again – are these things true for the member of the audience in the theatre?) and who 'look back on the story' are being appealed to only as individual sensitivities and not as minds. It was this tendency in Bradley, and in nineteenth-century criticism at large, that provoked the contributors to *Scrutiny*, the journal founded by F.R. Leavis, and one such, H.A. Mason, demonstrates the method and the manner of that periodical in a piece as far removed from Murry and Bradley's impressionistic improvisations as could, at the time, have been imagined. Characteristically entitled '*Antony and Cleopatra*: telling versus showing', Mason's essay pointedly notes: 'We are *told* I don't know how many times that he [Antony] was a supreme specimen of humanity', however, 'the Antony who is presented dramatically never makes us believe in these reports'.[21] Mason further argues:

■ I cannot believe that Shakespeare tried very hard to make us feel, feel intimately, what he so often talks about. He has not made us know what it is for a man to be like Mars, nor has he brought us near knowing what it would be like for a man to be like Bacchus. We do not get near enough to the root and springs of action that could make a life of love-making and drinking and general jollity seem the expression of a force of nature. And for those who do not require the values of Love and War to seem god-like before they can be deeply roused by them, I would say that on the human level we do not get the effective answer to the common-sense moral judgment on Antony's behaviour. □

Mason observes shrewdly of the last Act:

■ So much of the play is now a matter of suggestion, of response to an almost magical play with words, to activities of what I must be content to style the imagination without providing a working definition of the word, that one man's say-so becomes unusually impertinent.[22] □

He might have said that by the same token almost any one's say-so becomes unusually authoritative. Mason's complaint is against Shakespeare. He claims that Shakespeare 'was seduced by "angelic strength" into organic weakness'.[23] His version of Bradley's judgement that the play must not be set down as second-rate against the great tragedies because it was not trying to be like them is the more severe: 'When I call this play a failure, I do not mean that Shakespeare tried for tragedy and failed: it seems to me he just did not try.'[24] Mason is firm on Wilson Knight's extravagance[25] (which is also Murry's incidentally). Knight says of Cleopatra's final words: 'We find an imaginative parallel in the Crucifixion'. Mason comments:

■ We may wonder whether 'parallel' is the right word for

Now no more
The juice of Egypt's grape shall moist this lip

and

I will not drink the fruit of the vine, until the kingdom of God shall come

when we think of the manner of the two deaths.[26] □

Mason's point is that Cleopatra's words are richly imbued with her characteristic sensuality:

■ Her power is to be able to keep it up to the last and to show her sensual nature dominant, to end with velvety jokes drawn from memories of love passages involving the complexities of bodily touch.[27] □

Mason comments, perhaps dryly, that he is not tempted 'to create a "mystique" or a "philosophy" of the extremes of love', which is most certainly what Murry (to whose invocation of the Last Supper Mason's strictures may well be applied) and Wilson Knight do, but from which Bradley restrains himself, bothered by a consciousness of what he will not quite bring himself to call 'factitious'. Even L.C. Knights, a seasoned writer for *Scrutiny*, is apparently seduced by the play. He claims that Shakespeare

■ Infused into the love story as he found it in Plutarch ... an immense energy, a sense of life so heightened that it can claim to represent an absolute value:

Eternity was in our lips, and eyes,
Bliss in our brows' bent; none our parts so poor,
But was a race of heaven. (I.iii.35–7)[28] □

His evidence is, of course, the poetry: 'It is the richness and energy of the poetry in which all of this is conveyed that, more than any explicit comment, defines for us the vitality of the theme.' He quotes Wilson Knight with approval, insisting on 'the impregnating atmosphere of wealth, power, military strength and martial magnificence' and the cosmic imagery and imagery of natural fruitfulness. This is all very well but Wilson Knight does what Knights is in danger of doing and that is detaching the poetry from the specific dramatic context. Bradley has already called Antony a poet, as he called Othello a poet in his lecture on that play.[29] Leavis stingingly rebuked Bradley for the latter, observing that in a poetic drama all the characters spoke poetry and this did not make them poets. It is not wrong to draw attention to thematic imagery; however, it is wrong to forget the dramatic context in which each element occurs that contributes to the theme. It is Cleopatra who is claiming that 'Eternity was in our lips': it is up to us to judge whether we believe it.

Knights' apparent submission turns out to be tactical, however: he is fully aware that the power of the poetry does not create reality, only illusion:

■ The figure that Cleopatra evokes may not be fancy – the poetry invests it with a substantial reality; but it is not the Antony that the play has given us; it is something disengaged from, or glimpsed through, that Antony. Nor should the power and beauty of Cleopatra's last great speech obscure the continued presence of something self-deceiving and unreal. She may speak of the baby at her breast that sucks the nurse asleep; but it is not, after all, a baby – new life; it is simply death.[30] □

Franklin Dickey comments wryly that 'the tradition which makes Antony and Cleopatra "famous patterns of unlawful love" and modern criticism are so much at odds'.[31] He reminds us that Dryden could appeal to a traditional view within which Shakespeare was himself writing, although of course neither poet was bound to submit to it. As Dickey summarises the tradition with admirable brevity and some wit, there is not much to be said for Cleopatra or Antony. He points out that Shakespeare's lovers are simply 'so much more complex and appealing' than those of his predecessors and he describes the tendency to see the lovers as ennobled by their passion as 'somewhat Nietzschean'.[32] He points out too, as do Knights and Mason, that this view of the play can only be maintained by overlooking a good deal of it. His summary is blunt:

■ Traditionally Antony and Cleopatra threw away a kingdom for lust, and this is how, despite the pity and terror that Shakespeare makes us feel, they appear in the play.[33] □

Dickey is more sympathetic to Octavius than many other commentators are: 'Certainly his comments on Antony's defeat are not empty rhetoric'.[34] This is not an argument in itself but it is a useful hypothesis to try out.

How convincing a picture can be constructed of Octavius, the man of feeling? Such a figure is certainly an essential component of a more complex picture and Dickey is right to say:

■ Shakespeare is always shifting his viewpoint so that each magnificent wayward gesture is countered either by a glimpse of its futility or by a sober estimate of its cost both to the lovers and to the universe.[35] □

As a result, Shakespeare succeeds where the others had only moralised:

■ The *contemptus mundi* [contempt for the world] which other playwrights preach in vain follows upon our awe at the sight of the most glittering world conceivable lying in ruins. □

Dickey's measured and thoughtful analysis lies between Bradley and Murry's essentially Romantic convictions and Mason's and Knights' sternly anti-Romantic, or anti-Victorian convictions. Bradley is a great critic; he is disturbed by a sense of inadequacy, although he does not want to embrace the conclusion that seems to be offered, which Mason eagerly embraces, that the play is a failure. Dickey offers a way out of the dilemma. The play is a triumphant success: it succeeds where the earlier moralists had failed; it fully dramatises where they had merely preached. Bradley and Murry want to believe in the grand passion (Bradley says that the 'passion that ruins Antony also exalts him, he touches the infinite in it');[36] Mason and Knights moralise. It is an irony of literary critical history that, if Dickey is right, history has come full circle and reunited the tradition from which the story of the lovers originally emerged with a later version of it. The Romantic, or Nietzschean, if Dickey is right, excursion has come to an end in the campaign of the contributors to *Scrutiny* against the survivors of the adventure. Cleopatra, 'the enchanting queen' is, in her own phrase, 'no more but e'en a woman'.

CHAPTER SIX

The Editions: 'The varying shore o' the world'

So far the narrative of this Guide has been a mixture of simple chronology and a suggestion that modernism, in the shape of F.R. Leavis, has a pivotal role in turning simple chronology into a history. This chapter marks out briefly a third option: the dispassionate scholarly survey of various attempts to turn simple chronology into history. The various editions of single plays considered here each take upon themselves the responsibility for a survey, however brief that may be, of opinion, of 'the varying shore o' the world' of views of this play.

The number of editions in which Shakespeare's plays have appeared during the course of the twentieth century is an indication of the 'Industrial Revolution of Shakespeare studies' as Muriel Bradbrook (1909–93) has called it.[1] After the great labours of the eighteenth-century editors, perhaps only the upsurge in publication of editions that began shortly before the twentieth century began can be compared. This chapter will take the reader from the beginning of the twentieth century, with Case's Arden edition of 1906 as revised by Ridley, through to the end of the century, with John Wilders' Arden edition of 1995, by way of Barbara Everett's Signet, Emrys Jones's Penguin and David Bevington's New Cambridge. While not being exhaustive, this survey aims to be representative.

The first to be considered here will be Case's 1906 Arden edition of which Bradley said, 'Nothing recently written on Shakespeare, I venture to say, shows more thorough scholarship or better judgement than Mr Case's edition in the Arden series'.[2] Case's 1906 Arden edition was reprinted seven times, and revised and reset in 1954 by M.R. Ridley, which Arden designated the ninth edition. Thus even one imprint has seen the play through many editions.

Case dates the play between 1606 and 1607, citing the changes Samuel Daniel made to his *Cleopatra* for the 1607 edition of *Certaine Small Works*.[3] The critical introduction is argued very closely, with a strong sense of the discriminations that need, in his view, to be made. These concern both er and the manner of the work. He begins by citing Coleridge, pressed the doubt:

■ Whether the *Antony and Cleopatra* is not, in all exhibitions of a giant power in its strength and vigour of maturity, a formidable rival of the *Macbeth*, *King Lear*, *Hamlet*, and *Othello*.[4] □

However, according to Case, *Antony and Cleopatra* is not equal to these works: first because it is unlike them in its essential structure as it 'belongs to a type of play defective in construction and absorbing centre of interest'. It is a chronicle play. Such plays have their qualities. There is a 'vivid presentation' of the elements of the story 'but historical fact is lopped and telescoped only so far as is indispensable to a stage-plot'.[5]

The theme of the play has, Case notes, been compared with that of *Macbeth* and *Coriolanus*, but once again the treatment accorded this theme, a consequence of the type of play dictating a structure proper to that type of play, is defective. The character of Antony, as it is revealed in the chronicled version to which Shakespeare has committed himself, does not lend itself to tragedy as, at the end:

■ all that is great in him, his heart-winning magnanimity in its various manifestations, is conspicuous as ever, and to this is now added the capacity for devotion and self-forgetfulness which he pitifully lacked before.[6] □

Furthermore, the characters are presented as motivated by more than one pressure: 'In this play, as in life, things extraneous to passion strengthen its hold for good or evil'.[7] Antony would certainly have returned to Cleopatra in any case, but the play suggests that the 'holy cold and still conversation' of Octavia and his having to take an inferior position to Caesar's are factors in his decision. In the same way, in Cleopatra's case, her aversion to the prospect of being put on show as one of Caesar's triumphs seems at least as strong a motive in her deciding to take her own life as is her love for Antony. The result is that *Antony and Cleopatra* is not to be compared with the great tragedies because the 'appalling situations' of the heroes of *Macbeth* or *Othello*, 'set between retrospect and prospect of horror',[8] are utterly unlike that of either Antony or Cleopatra.

The depiction of Cleopatra, so often the central question in critical discussion, allows Case to take up and develop the theme he has broached in his discussion of Antony, namely that a complex of passions is operating in the central characters. Shakespeare departs from his source once again, in that his picture of Cleopatra is 'of coarser fibre' than that depicted in Plutarch, and here 'coarser' does not only indicate a quality in the drawing but in the nature of what is drawn. What Case calls 'the arts of irritating perverseness' employed in the first act, which are Shakespeare's invention and are not described in Plutarch, are more marked than the 'flickering amusements' with which Plutarch shows Cleopatra trying, later, to attract Antony away from Octavia.[9] Case invokes Johnson, who remarks 'the feminine arts, some of which are too low, which distinguish Cleopatra'.[10]

Case is preparing an argument and it has to do with something else concerning which Shakespeare has departed from his source. Case is in no doubt that Shakespeare allows us to believe that Cleopatra's motive for death is complex, and a carefully argued discussion of her motives leads to the cautious conclusion that although we cannot ignore her desire not to be paraded as part of Caesar's triumph, we must consider carefully 'how far we are justified in regarding this, and this only, as what enabled her to "be noble" to herself'.[11]

This is a subtle argument and one which depends upon his disarming the reader's prejudices, as it is quite possible to react quite differently to Cleopatra's motives as they are presented by the play and thus to react quite differently to her death. A different reaction diminishes the play, as Eliot's famous undermining of Othello's last words attempts to do. By claiming that Othello is 'cheering himself up',[12] Eliot makes us think that Othello is thinking only of himself. If Cleopatra is thinking only of herself, then why should an audience feel anything but contempt for her?

Case's comments on the verse of the play are important, revealing as they do an attitude to the poetry that is at first sight at variance with his identification of the play as a chronicle. The work displays the changes in Shakespeare's handling of verse evident (Case says) since *Hamlet*, which Case believes makes the verse less musical 'in its effort to become a more spacious continent of his multiplying thought'. The verse depends upon the actor speaking it to render it 'musical'; accent is more freely distributed, 'which gives grip and strength at the cost of some ruggedness'. It is to no avail, however: 'ellipse and ambiguous phrase show that no relaxation of metrical constraints could accommodate the ideas and images demanding utterance'.[13] It is not easy to see what a welter of 'ideas and images demanding utterance' might be doing in a chronicle play and Case does not attempt an explanation, noting only that this development in Shakespeare's verse assists in confirming the date of the play, but it is a matter that asks for explanation and his successor goes some way to giving one, as shall be seen.

Case's view presented as a general view is of divided hearts, of compromised motives. In Antony it is the 'grave defect in a nature generously endowed with noble traits'; his treatment of Octavia is 'cold-blooded and heartless', not to mention his disabling infatuation with Cleopatra. In Cleopatra herself it is the confusion of motives surrounding her death: her love for Antony conflicts with and is compromised by her dislike of ignominy. Case's argument is subtle but his picture allows us to conclude that the case is not proven. Enobarbus's death is itself compromised: 'we must add to remorse the small favour shown to master-leavers by Caesar'. In each case there is 'something extraneous that helps to determine [their] fate'.[14] This is part of the truth to life demanded by the chronicle. A similar structure may be observed in Caesar; his resolve and clear judgement is softened by such notes as his generous and sad valediction at 5.1.35. No one is clear-cut. If some are selflessly attracted by the noble and selfishly affected by the base, others are confused in different ways: Enobarbus's remorse is not relieved by any consolation for his desertion; Caesar's purity of motive is confused by his pity for the man he knew and once respected. But these are not the wholesale destructions of goodness of character one has come to look for in tragedy; this is just life in its formlessness as chronicle records it. Case reminds us of the context within which Shakespeare's play appears; the context of plays about the story. The point gained in mentioning the other plays on the same theme is to emphasise Shakespeare's originality and define it to some extent. Shakespeare took a subject already treated by at least two distinguished if not popular writers (Case asserts that he knew the Daniel and also Brandon)[15] and subjected it to a radical revision. Case does not think the revision wholly successful; his successor disagreed.

Ridley's central contention is that the play should not be seen in the context of the great tragedies, first because it is a love tragedy and secondly because 'we are left at the end of *Antony and Cleopatra* with less sense of waste than at the end of any of the others'. This is because of the central characters themselves: 'Their passion ennobles them as nothing else ever has or ever could, but also, if they themselves were nobler, it would not.' We are not to conclude that the play is a failure because Shakespeare did not set out to write a tragedy in the mould of the big four: 'he tried to write a drama of a different order, and royally succeeded'.[16]

Ridley recognises the limitations of the source material only too clearly: 'the story is itself undramatic'.[17] Shakespeare overcomes the great difficulty that the spectacle of such a man wasting what talents he has on an infatuation is hardly likely to edify or even entertain by showing us that he really is 'the triple pillar of the world' and rushing us from one part of the world to another so that 'we feel the surge of great events'.[18] This has a consequence for our sense of Cleopatra, as the one influence who can win him away from this great position of power and responsibility.

Ridley's continuation of Case's Introduction starts by acknowledging the significance of three accounts of the play those of A.C. Bradley, Lord David Cecil (1902–86), and John Dover Wilson, in his Introduction to the Cambridge edition of the play. Ridley does not comment on Bradley, merely describing his essay as 'probably the finest piece of concentrated criticism which even this great critic achieved' but Lord David Cecil's essay strikes Ridley as odd. Cecil concentrates on the political aspects of the play and argues that the central theme is not love but success. Ridley dismisses this view, saying only that Cecil 'must find the play much duller than most of us do'.[19] Lord David Cecil's opinion is not all that eccentric, however, and it is a response to the difficulty of classifying the play and thus identifying with confidence just where it is aimed.

Dover Wilson, introducing the *New Shakespeare*, has the merit, according to Ridley, of drawing attention to a reading of the Seleucus scene, which A. Stahr had pointed out in Plutarch (who had in turn been cited by Furness).[20] The passage is certainly instructive and makes clear that the Seleucus scene was set up by Cleopatra in order to deceive Caesar into thinking that she wanted to live. North's marginal comment reads: 'Cleopatra finely deceiveth Octavius Caesar, as though she desired to live.'[21] This of course proves nothing about what Shakespeare did with the scene and Ridley comments that Wilson 'overplays his hand',[22] exhibiting 'a generous error to which he is liable',[23] that is, the desire to see characters of whom he approves as wholly laudable. Ridley asks what happens between Act 4 scene 15 and Act 5 scene 2: 'Under the immediate shock of Antony's death she rises to a mood of exaltation'[24] but that does not last. She would make terms if she could dictate terms and it is only her realisation that Caesar will not treat with her that determines her to kill herself. This is a rebuttal in effect of Case's argument. Ridley's own judgement is more astringent. The last Act allows us to appreciate 'the cutting and balanced precision of Shakespeare's delineation of Cleopatra'. In that Act she is 'the great queen, and is indeed fire and air', but the first four Acts give us a different picture: 'it would be hard to find anywhere in literature a more unsparing picture of the professional courtesan'.[25] He makes an important distinction between complexity and variety, declaring that Cleopatra is not complex in her motives but varied in her manner. Some critics, he claims, have been baffled by her because they were unable to make this distinction. She is 'the past-mistress in her ancient art',[26] that is, the art of the courtesan, which she has practised upon Pompey and Caesar, but her aim now is love and it is also Antony's. However, Ridley is unconvincing here, as he is driven to qualify, step by step, his initial assertions to the point at which they become confused and unclear:

■ It is the merest fatuity of moralizing to deny the name of 'love' to their passion, and write it off as 'mere lust'. No doubt it is not of the highest kind of love; it is completely an *égoisme á deux* [meaning that they are both equally self-regarding rather than concerned more with the other person in the relationship], and has no power to inspire to anything outside itself; but it has in it something that should be an element in the highest kind of love; and at least it is the passion of human beings and not of animals, of the spirit as well as of the body. It was not by her beauty (of which by all accounts the gods had not been lavish) but by her superb vitality that Cleopatra took Antony captive and held him.[27] □

Ridley's task is to prove what he asserts, that the love of this pair 'is of the spirit as well as of the body', and he does not do that; perhaps he cannot. It is not an edifying spectacle to see a cautious critic back-pedalling as he is doing here from an assertion he should not have made. Having conceded that it is not 'the highest kind of love', he offers to identify an element that kind of love should have, which theirs undoubtedly possesses, and then leaves us to guess what that is (although it cannot be 'mere lust', it will not be so easy to distinguish from it); having realised that the pass has now been lost, he sticks up for them by reminding us of what we already know, that Antony and Cleopatra are not animals, but his argument that a love not based on conventional attractions is therefore of the spirit is full of holes. The final sentence is almost a shamefaced confession of defeat; at least, it is a defiant refusal to admit that defeat.

Ridley is as baffled as the critics he condemns, having come so much further than they did. He is surely right that 'Shakespeare's portrayal of Cleopatra at the end of the play is far more subtly penetrating, and more unsparing, than some of his critics would like it to be',[28] but it seems that he does not have the courage of his initial convictions when it comes to facing Cleopatra at the end. This is interesting, and suggestive, as making judgements about Cleopatra seems to be altogether harder than making judgements about Antony. Ridley is clear about Antony:

■ Antony has a magnificent vitality about him, to which both men and women react; but he is a creature of impulse, he has no eye for the stars, and cannot steer a course; he wants what he wants strongly, and he wants it immediately; he is generous, and even his faults are on a grand scale; he can descend to folly, but never to meanness.[29] □

What Ridley is saying is that he will be no statesman and that is true. It is not true of his rival: we must never forget that Octavius will become Augustus. Secondly, we must beware of words like 'vitality' (compare Cleopatra's 'superb vitality') and especially of adjectives such as 'magnificent' and 'grand'. We must be sure that we know what they mean before we use them and it is not at all clear that Ridley is sure what he means by them or, if he is, he does not make that meaning clear to those who may not instinctively fall in line with the implicit judgement. 'Vitality', like 'vigour', is like 'strength'. It is easy to see that a man physically strong may act badly or well, it is only slightly less easy to see that a man gifted with strength of will may act well or badly; equally a man gifted with vigour or vitality may act badly or well: the point is being able to tell the difference. Ridley has already said of Shakespeare's treatment of Cleopatra that he at least could tell the difference and there is no reason to think that Shakespeare's treatment of Antony is any less clear-sighted or that Ridley's confusion over Cleopatra does not proceed from similar causes to those responsible for his confusion over Antony. Antony's treatment of Octavia may not easily be described as 'mean' but it is not all that easily described as anything else.

Ridley's conclusions about the play are instructive. After all our critical intelligence has exhausted itself:

> ■ We know in our hearts that what in this play Shakespeare has to offer us is a thrill, a quickening of the pulses, a brief experience in a region where there is an unimagined vividness of life.[30] □

Here then is the explanation of Antony's 'magnificent vitality' and Cleopatra's 'superb vitality': the 'unimagined vividness of life' offered by the play. Ridley does not dismiss our 'intellectual exercises and their results' but he does set them against this experience quite clearly. The results of our cerebration 'drift down the wind like the idle thistledown that for this play they are'.[31] It is not an unattractive vision but it is one that can be placed at the tail end of late Victorian Romanticism, just as clearly as Case's distaste for the 'ruggedness' and the lack of 'music' of Shakespeare's later dramatic verse puts him so clearly before Grierson's Donne and Eliot's and Leavis's championing of that accent in English verse. This is not of course to say that the attitude is wrong, it is just to identify its place in a developing literary critical history.

On the other hand, Ridley is very perceptive about Octavius. 'The relentless power of Rome' is something of which we never lose sight and at the end of the play Octavius 'is Rome, looking down ... on the "pair so famous" over whom her chariot wheels have rolled'.[32] The counterpart to the 'aesthetic' is history, meaning politics, power, economics and ultimately science and technology; the material world against the spiritual world, the body against the soul. This is why it is not true to say that our intellectual exercises are wasted: the view that they are 'idle thistledown' may be the view of the world into which Antony would step and into which Cleopatra appears to be inviting him to step, but it is certainly not merely by that token the view of the play. The experience of the play is surely the experience of the equal balance of Rome and Egypt and not of the dominance of one over the other.

Ridley's final comments conclude that 'the peculiar glory of this play is not in its dramatic quality at all. It is in its poetry.'[33] Here he parts company again with Case, although it may be said that though they disagree in the detail, they share an overarching view, which is visible in their shared commitment in the end to the vision of the world we associate in the play with Cleopatra.[34] Ridley singles out the use of echoes in the play (such as those in 5.2.192 recalling 4.15.66 and those in 4.14.99 being recalled by 5.2.294); he identifies the use of unexpected words or juxtapositions (he cites 'the odds is gone', 4.15.66); he reserves special commendation for the quality of a poetry absolutely matched to its occasion so that if it is quoted apart from its context it loses its significance. Ridley cites 5.2.308 and comments that if it is put in a less unexpected context, 'the description, let us say, of a happy and carefree mother', then it is unremarkable. However:

> ■ Put those same words in the mouth of the great queen, standing in her full and final majesty, robed and crowned for the stroke of her last fatal lover, with the asp at the breast that had suckled her children, and the world catches its breath.[35] □

It is difficult at this point to forget, for example, Leavis's description of Othello's last moments as a *coup de théâtre* (a sensational theatrical moment), staged by Othello himself,[36] and make the comparison with a more obviously staged *coup de théâtre* and recognise that we shall be denied the satisfaction and the pleasure of the moment if we are in any doubt about Cleopatra's right to stage it. Ridley is surely right about the poetry and what it is meant to do but it may still be asked whether he has plumbed the depths of the play as far as his own expressed determination might have led us to expect him to do. There is another, subtler, dramatic satisfaction to be had in watching someone who has no right to stage such a *coup de théâtre* but is determined to so anyway. The experience is not tragic, but then Ridley is among many who will say that the play is not tragic anyway.

One who agrees with that view is Barbara Everett in her Introduction to the Signet edition of the play, published in 1963 under the general editorship of Sylvan Barnet of Tufts University. The Signet features generous selections from Bradley's essay on *Antony and Cleopatra*, John Danby's *Poets on Fortune's Hill* and North's Plutarch. Its notes are helpful to the reader rather than scholarly (not that the scholarship is lacking, merely that it is unobtrusive); the General Introduction is a good summary of the state of knowledge regarding Shakespeare and the Elizabethan and Jacobean theatre of his days, and the Introduction, by Barbara Everett, is an engaging essay on the play.

Everett agrees that *Antony and Cleopatra* is not a tragedy. She summarises the fate of the protagonists and comments that:

> ■ There can be a large difference between a play's 'subject', summarized in detachment, and the full effect of the play itself. Antony and Cleopatra's

fates and fortunes are not presented with the kind of tragic or dramatic intensity that such an outline might suggest. Rather they and their world are presented in a series of leisurely – at first sight, almost casual – insights, that include in their range the great and the small, the significant and the insignificant: a fortunetelling and a great battle, a political conference and a wild party, a memory of the lovers' first meeting and a death in a monument, a woman slapping a messenger and a countryman giving a lecture on the nature of asps.[37] ☐

She points out that

■ The whole play is constructed ... out of a pattern of juxtapositions and contrasts, with the point of view continually shifting and changing.[38] ☐

This is reflected in the characterisation as well: unlike the earlier tragedies in which characters change as a process of development through which potentialities for good or evil are realised, *Antony and Cleopatra* is peopled by characters dominated by fluctuations of mood:

■ Quick fluidity and changeableness of character becomes the norm, almost the rule: and in such a world, tragic motivation becomes impossible and tragic responsibility is largely absent. Men seem to be moved by impulse and instinct, chance and expediency; and the guilts and terrors, shames and miseries of the early tragedies are very largely absent.[39] ☐

The key to the play is time: 'In politics as in love, the procession of time moves in a continual destruction'. As a result, the play is 'natural' rather than 'supernatural', 'physical' rather than 'metaphysical':

■ Caesar's ambition is to 'possess the time' by possessing the world for a while; Antony and Cleopatra live only in the present instant, and lose the world for good.[40] ☐

Everett suggests that the basic attitude of the play belongs to the world of comedy rather than tragedy:

■ Cleopatra's world is essentially a world of 'play': a world, that is, that studies to find fit expression for the exuberance of natural energies and needs no justification for what it does.[41] ☐

It is inevitable that this attitude will not prevail against a single-minded will like Caesar's, bent to the vision of 'universal power and universal peace', to which he is committed. It is equally inevitable, it may be added, that that vision will appear unattractive by way of contrast and not necessarily any more substantial either. As Everett has already suggested though, Caesar's possession of the world, in the vision of the play, is only 'for a while'.[42]

Everett concludes:

> ■ One phrase of Cleopatra's – her 'Here's sport indeed', as she draws the dying Antony to her – bears all the profound comic pathos and tragic irony that fills and characterizes the play. Yet this mingled experience is as strong as it is complex; it has a power and vitality that is Antony's when, in defeat, he 'mocks the midnight bell':
>
> > Let's have one more gaudy night: call to me
> > All my sad captains; fill our bowls once more;
> > Let's mock the midnight bell. (3.13.183–5)   □

It is this final effect that she has in mind at the beginning of her Introduction, when she says of the play, that

> ■ It is, in final poetic and dramatic effect, one of the most triumphantly harmonious, coherent, and 'finished' plays that Shakespeare ever wrote, from first to last line bearing the impress of a unified purpose powerfully carried out.[43]   □

She points out that such significant critics as Bradley and Wilson Knight thought the play not a tragedy at all, although the Folio editors had done, calling it *The Tragedie of Antony and Cleopatra* and placing it in the last section (*Tragedies*) of the First Folio. For Ernest Schanzer, it was a 'problem' play, like *Julius Caesar* and *Measure for Measure*, presenting a radical moral dilemma left unresolved at the play's close.[44] However, Everett, while agreeing that *Measure for Measure* or *Troilus and Cressida* are difficult to classify, believes that this is because they are incomplete as works of art and it is therefore 'easy to see in them (or to imagine one sees) the marks of changing purpose, or of discordances within the given materials',[45] which make it difficult to classify them. She sees in *Antony and Cleopatra* both tragic and comic potential. It is tragic in that it contains 'the expression of irremediable loss, incurred consciously and borne responsibly', but it is comic in that it contains 'the expression of an ineffaceable light-heartedness'. In case this mode of expression is difficult to accept, she offers another word, 'highheartedness', as a gloss.[46]

She sums up the power struggle in the play and comments, 'to describe the play in these terms is to give it something of the discipline, and something of the limitations, of any game of power'[47] and she argues that the play transforms the action and event of Plutarch's narrative into 'a process of tragic and individual experience'.[48] Even relatively minor characters such as Pompey have their moments of dignity and solemnity, as has Enobarbus, and none of these moments has any political or historical importance, 'their significance and their weight lie in a different sphere of value'.[49] The voice of Rome is the voice of the game of power: it is 'the voice of common judgement and social wisdom'[50] and not only does Caesar speak it but Antony can too. He can also speak Cleopatra's language: 'a language of immediate individual experience, sensory in its apprehension, exalted or intense in its tone, and arrogant in its claims'. In such a language 'the intense experience of an exceptional individual becomes its own rationale'.

There is a simpler way of putting this:

■ Antony and Cleopatra are ... proud: proud of being themselves, and proud of being greater than anyone else in the world. Nor are they monstrous in this, for the whole world of the play is governed by the ideal of pride, and in it 'honor' and 'nobility', 'greatness' and 'reputation' are the very fabric of existence.[51] □

This is precisely their undoing as

■ All that makes them admirable is inextricably confused with its own corruptions: their energy, vitality and power are self-defeating ... All Antony's courage reveals itself as inextricable from blind and irrational violence, and his generosity from sensual obsession; all Cleopatra's vitality and self-possession reveals itself as wayward, demanding, and treacherous.[52] □

The end towards which all this moves is that 'in defeat – a defeat which is the loss of an ideal, as well as the loss of the world – both grow, paradoxically, more gentle, more human, and more wholly sympathetic'.[53]

It is worth recalling Dr Johnson's remark that 'the events, of which the principal are described according to history, are produced without any art of connection or care of disposition'.[54] Johnson saw no difficulty in the classification of the play: he only saw that the editors of the First Folio, who 'divided our author's works into comedies, histories and tragedies, seem not to have distinguished the three kinds by any exact or definite ideas'.[55] This was, he thought, only an effect of the development of literary culture from rude beginnings touched by natural genius to the more consciously directed work of his own day. For the editors of the First Folio:

■ History was a series of actions, with no other than chronological succession, independent of each other, and without any tendency to introduce or regulate the conclusion. It is not always very nicely distinguished from tragedy. There is not much nearer approach to unity of action in the tragedy of *Antony and Cleopatra* than in the history of *Richard II*.[56] □

Barbara Everett's essay shows the ability to discover formal completion in a work in which Johnson could find none because he was looking for kinds with which he was familiar and which meant something to him. It is highly unlikely that Everett's essay would have enlightened him: it belongs to a further age, an age that responded more feelingly to the dilemma between the worlds presented by the play and saw more in it than an exercise in a familiar iconography, to illustrate which she quotes John Danby: 'Shakespeare's study in Mars and Venus – the presiding deities of Baroque society, painted for us again and again on the canvases of his time'.[57]

The *New Penguin Shakespeare*, edited by Emrys Jones, was published in 1977 and comes with an additional authority, 'Used and Recommended by The Royal Shakespeare Company'. The edition is even more workmanlike than the Signet. There is no General Introduction and no footnotes: these being supplanted by a Commentary at the end of the play into which all the material for footnotes at least as full as those of the Signet and, in many cases, fuller has been gathered, the purpose of this arrangement being perhaps to encumber the reader as little as possible, although footnotes are generally more convenient than endnotes in practice.

Emrys Jones concentrates his attention on the form of the play, making the same point that Ridley and Case had made that the story itself is undramatic as it appears in the source material, and quoting Bradley's judgement that the play was defective in its construction. However, he has a very different conclusion:

■ Though it runs the risk of looking structurally incompetent, it is in fact a marvel of formed dramatic writing.[58] □

Jones starts by pointing to the fact that the play is made up of short scenes and by further noting that these scenes are themselves often 'atomistically constructed'.[59] He draws a parallel with Plutarch's narrative method, which consists in an accumulation of detail and is itself almost without plot. In this respect the play runs the risk of seeming to return to the early Elizabethan popular drama that was often no more than a series of pageants.[60] Jones considers whether its stage history cannot be accounted for by this feature, among others: the more obviously shapely *All for Love* replaced it on the stage for nearly two hundred years; and although it was performed in the last century, it was not of frequent appearance (Jones notes that one of the practical difficulties is that the play requires a first-class male actor who is prepared to be upstaged by a first-class female actor to the extent of having to disappear entirely before the climactic final scenes). Jones describes the play as essentially composed for a small theatre and speculates that it may have been written for the Blackfriars, with all the possibilities of intimacy that venue would have offered.

Although the play gives the impression of spaciousness, covering vast distances and without a clear time scheme (a function of its lacking a clear plot), it works through often highly delicate verbal effects as well as quite intimate stage groupings. Alone among the Roman plays, it has no crowd scenes. Furthermore, it is a play about talk. The talk is 'endlessly opinionative' and the people who do the talking are the 'top people in the world': the play presents us with a 'world awash with the tide of merely human opinion'.[61] There are no frames of reference that offer stable judgement, only the conflicting opinions of opinionated and powerful people. Jones points out that the play is set in a pre-Christian era but written for an audience in a Christian country. Such an audience could be expected to note the contrast between the world in which it stood and the world evoked by the play. It might be worth reflecting, although Jones does not, that the English Reformation had complicated the picture, in that the final court of appeal may be the Church but there was no settled agreement on what that Church was. In that respect, there is a parallel to be drawn with the play and not just a contrast, that is, there is a conflict between rival authorities and an empire breaking asunder. Whether Shakespeare saw this or not there is, as Jones points out, in the continual presence of the sea in the play, an ever-present signifier of this moving tide of opinion that offers a reflection that things and people are both ever-changing and ever the same.

Jones sees this as a form of historical realism. This is what life is like for people known to us as historical figures: they do not know how things are going to turn out, they are 'making themselves up' (in Jones's striking phrase), while for an audience they are fixed. He compares *Antony and Cleopatra* with the other two plays from Plutarch of this period, *Coriolanus* and *Timon of Athens,* and remarks that in both we see a hero presented to us in a mass of detail and under continual observation and subject to continual comment. The function of the soothsayer in *Antony and Cleopatra* is, according to Jones, to draw the contrast between the existence of the future from which the audience is looking back on these people and the people themselves who have no idea what the future will be and, in that scene at least, very little real interest in it.

He analyses the galley scene briefly and effectively to show Shakespeare's technical grasp in detail. Six characters interacting are sharply distinguished by their contributions to a movement that points to the final movement of the play: as the feast moves to its climax, attention is focused on Antony and Lepidus; as Lepidus becomes increasingly helpless, the contrast shifts to Caesar and Antony, leaving Caesar at the end of the scene in control. In the background, briefly moving into focus, is Menas's offer to give Pompey the whole world if he will only say the word. Jones comments:

■ The entire scene – world-sharers in a drunken party, floating on the sea – creates a wonderfully suggestive image of the paradoxes of political power.[62] □

The shapelessness of the sea is called out by one of his most suggestive comments, on Antony's wonderful speech at 4.14.2, that, in this speech, we see Antony

■ decomposing into that sea of matter out of which all life comes – and which in the play is imaged in the formless but fecund mud of the Nile.[63] □

There lies behind some of the play's key images an image of the primal chaos out of which all order is brought and to which it may return. Something of this is glimpsed by Jones when he notes that Plutarch describes the pair of lovers as having made 'an order between them which they called *Amimetobion* (as much to say, "no life comparable and matchable with it")',[64] and cites 'Let Rome in Tiber melt' (1.1.33). He suggests that the *contemptus mundi* (contempt for the world) shown in this speech might have called forth some spark of recognition in the religiously minded in his audience, as Antony's reply to Cleopatra's 'I'll set a bourn how far to be beloved (1.1.16)', 'Then must thou needs find out new heaven, new earth', Jones suggests, recalls Revelation, 21.1: 'And I saw a new heaven, and a new earth'. These links are tenuous: they may occur to some readers and not to others; they may be picked up in the theatre or they may not. It would be unconvincing to argue that Shakespeare had intended them to be picked up. This is one of the dangers of impressionistic criticism, although Jones demonstrates the strength of the approach over and over in this Preface.

The line of thought he is pursuing suggests that the play offers a meditation on the different kinds of order that may be drawn out of chaos, a meditation in which the political ambitions of Caesar form only one possibility of order and the lovers' aspirations another. If this is so, then what Jones is saying suggests that all forms of order are seen as equally unstable by the play.

Returning to the question of form, Jones proposes a view in which the play breaks into two parts at 3.6, with the rejection of Octavia and the return to Egypt. Jones draws attention to the long sequence from 3.7 to 4.15, claiming that this has often been 'uncomprehendingly maligned', whereas it is, properly conceived, 'a great imaginative achievement, made possible only by formidable technical resourcefulness'.[65] The contrast between the two parts, Jones proposes, allows us to see in the second part a much greater concentration, even an impression at least of the unity of place, or its focus perhaps, and of a concentration of time, which now seems to be running out rather than standing still. The final breach with Caesar that is Antony's rejection of Octavia precipitates war and the rapid movement with which Caesar closes on the pair and destroys them.

This two-part structure echoes Plutarch, who divides the two parts with a long account of Antony's Parthian campaign with which Shakespeare does not concern himself, and it overcomes the sense of arbitrariness induced by the five-Act structure introduced by eighteenth-century editors. Attempts to make the play fit that shape may be doomed to failure, while Jones's bipartite structure, although radical, does fit the work. This is especially true if the nature of the first part is considered more carefully still, as Jones does. He argues that Antony, 'by committing himself to a life of sensations rather than thoughts ... is choosing to live his life precisely as a succession of moments'.[66] The response to the play that characterises Case and Ridley is not out of place; it merely overemphasises parts of the play at the expense of others. The first part shows us the dreamlike, irresponsible world that draws Antony and imitates, so Jones insists, the formlessness of life itself: 'the untidy-looking arrangement serves to bring out the untidiness of life',[67] and 'he [Shakespeare] also wished to imitate the immense capaciousness of the world'.[68]

This is a dangerous argument, although Jones insists that this appearance is produced not only deliberately, but with 'unlifelike, wholly artistic, economy and rhythm'.[69] Deliberately to compose something shapeless is, deliberation notwithstanding, to compose something shapeless. Economically composed shapelessness is still shapelessness. 'Rhythm' offers hope but it must be considered further than Jones is able to do here: 'A consideration of the play's form will inevitably end in paradox.'[70] It need not however, and paradox is only sometimes true: it is frequently only annoying.

However, Jones has offered the makings of a significant view of the play in this essay: the bipartite structure and the insight into what lies behind the play as a whole will, if put together, provide a powerful perspective. The shape envisaged by Jones's essay is perhaps best imagined as a spiral, something like a whirlpool. At its outer edge, as the play starts, odds and ends are drawn into a sluggish but gathering stream: at the break point identified by Jones, it is now too late to turn back; the energy of the stream has become clear and the play is concentrated towards a final drawing down into its depths of all those who have succumbed to it. Those depths are the chaos out of which the various orders evoked for us by the play have been drawn. A meta-theatrical image is feasible: the theatre as both chaos and order. In the convincingness and insubstantiality of its representations, the stage is pre-eminently placed to present such a vision.

Jones believes that the age would probably judge the lovers depraved; he seems to be assuming that that is the direction in which 'cultural pressures' would tend and that Shakespeare may have made the same assumption and further assumed that his audience was likely to take the same view. It is also possible that he himself shared this view, at least to some extent. However, 'since he was writing a tragedy, he deliberately and perhaps instinctively went on to modify this view, to show to what extent sympathy and even admiration could be aroused for the doomed pair'.[71] It is not impossible to imagine such a project being attractive, simply from the point of view of Shakespeare the commercial artist, both as a challenge to his skill and as an attraction to the audience, as what Ridley calls 'a thrill'. Jones presents the lovers judiciously. No one speaks up for their love other than they themselves but when they do so they speak of 'spiritual enlargement': Jones cites 'Let Rome in Tiber melt' (1.1.33). Their desire for and expectation of reunion after death 'cannot be dismissed as contemptible'.[72] Apart from other considerations, Antony's generosity and the love he shows for and inspires in his followers is not a negligible factor and is indeed one of the key elements of Cleopatra's 'dream' of him: 'For his bounty,/There was no winter in't; an autumn it was/That grew the more by reaping' (5.2.85). Cleopatra bestows a bounty of a different kind: her last scene provides what this play, with its peculiar form, has so far withheld – an ending.

The final impression left by the play, Jones believes, is one of beauty. He stresses how polished is the surface of the play and goes further than Ridley (who had insisted that the success of the play was in its poetry rather than its dramatic qualities) and defines the quality of the play's poetry as 'lyric'. Jones asks whether Shakespeare was imitating Horace, as in *Romeo and Juliet* he had imitated the Italian poet Petrarch (Francesco Petrarca, 1304–74).[73] If he were, it would be appropriate had James I (1566–1625; King of England, 1603–25) seen the play, as then the poet of the original Augustan age – the reign of the Roman Emperor Augustus (27 BC–AD 14) – would have provided the inspiration for a play witnessed by the 'Augustus' of his own age, who had brought a universal peace to his realm. As we have no way of knowing whether King James did and no way of proving this fancied influence of Horace, such speculation remains only attractive.

The *New Cambridge Shakespeare*, edited by David Bevington, appeared in 1990. It features an extensive and comprehensive Introduction so thoroughly supported by footnotes that it is clear that the general reader has been overtaken by the undergraduate student as the consumer envisaged by the product. The Introduction presents an interesting critical problem in itself: it is so admirably comprehensive and at the same time so carefully inclusive that it forcefully reminds us that, without some discrimination, we are in danger of surrendering to a view of the play as a hopeless muddle. Indeed, Bevington himself asks at one point:

■ Is this all the play has to offer – a sense of a tragic disparity which has a very pointed appeal for the modern sensibility?[74] □

Although the essay is comprehensive, there is a theme to be detected and it is fairly given in the following remark:

■ The history of critical reaction suggests that the play is a kind of Rorschach test for us and for those who have written about the play, most of them males.[75] □

The essay opens with a discussion of 'Date and sources' and closes with a long and useful section on '*Antony and Cleopatra* in performance'; between these are sections on 'The contrarieties of critical response'; 'The ironic gap between word and deed'; 'Transcending limits'; 'Genre and structure'; 'Style' and 'Stagecraft'. The overriding organising principle is dilemma: opening with a survey of the conflicting opinions to be found in the critical history concerning Antony and Cleopatra and their relationship, Bevington moves on to a structural principle of the play, the contrast between what characters do and what they say and between what they say about themselves and what others say about them, particularly Antony, Cleopatra and Octavius. 'Transcending limits' deals with the disparity between the lovers' aspirations and their fate. Do the lovers transcend the limits imposed by the world? Sexual politics and psycho-mythologising about the feminine principle lead into a discussion of Antony's 'bounty' contrasted with Caesar's meanness. Some interesting points about the relationship between sex and drama are made and about the role of art and acting in both. The section 'Genre and structure' features discussion of several attempts to pin the play down, some even discovering elements of Aristotelian structure;[76] Maynard Mack's emphasis on contrasts and mirroring episodes and themes is treated sympathetically.[77]
   On sources and parallels, Bevington says:

■ [Pembroke and Daniel] portray the lovers as heroic victims of their own passionate excesses and remorseless destiny, regretfully aware of their failures but ready to face death with resolution and the expectation of an afterlife together in the world of the dead.[78] □

He sees Shakespeare's vision of the lovers as 'complex and ennobling',[79] emphasising the use of sources in mythology and in other arts to enhance this vision. He points to the parallels with Hercules and Omphale as well as with Venus and Mars and he quotes the remarks of Northrop Frye concerning Cleopatra at least semi-approvingly:

■ She has affinities with a kind of goddess figure that both Hebraic and Classical religions keep trying to subdue by abuse: she is a whore and her children are all bastards; she is a snare to men and destroys their masculinity, making them degenerate slaves like Circe; she is an Omphale dressing her Hercules in women's clothes; she has many characteristics of her sister whore of Babylon. ☐

Her world is 'the night side of nature, passionate, cruel, superstitious, barbaric, dissolute, what you will' and can 'bring a superhuman vitality out of Antony that Rome cannot equal, not in spite of the fact that it destroys him, but because it destroys him'.[80] Bevington comments that in such a view 'Cleopatra's mythic ancestry helps illuminate her dangerous fascination'.[81]

Summarising some scholarly attempts to place the play in its ancient context, Bevington remarks that

■ Shakespeare wrote about the ancient Roman world pretty much as he found it in Plutarch and his other classical sources, but he also wrote for his own generation.[82] ☐

He says earlier that

■ *Antony and Cleopatra* could not have been written as it stands in Roman times. The vision of a tragic and ennobling love is indebted to Ovid and Virgil, but it also owes much to the kind of exalted vision of love we find in later Western culture in the *liebestod* [love-death] of Tristan and Isolde.[83] ☐

Bevington tends to read the play in terms of gender politics, for example seeing Octavius as

■ The voice inside the play for those male readers who cannot entertain the wholeness of Cleopatra and are threatened by the challenge she represents to a male desire for control. ☐

and

■ Caesar's recollection of the Antony of former days ... expresses the Spartan ideal of soldiership in such overstated terms we sense in his words the need to fend off in himself any urge to the contrary. ☐

and

■ In his cynical remark that 'want will perjure/The ne'er-touched vestal' (3.12.30–1) we see a glimpse of a personal need to demean women and control them because they are, in his mind, both inferior and dangerous. ☐

He sums up this line of thought:

■ In the end he possesses everything – except, that is, what he most
envies and yet hates, the life and spirit of Antony and Cleopatra.[84] □

This is ingenious speculation, and not untrue to the play, but every piece
of it could be countered with an alternative view. The 'wholeness' of
Cleopatra can just as easily be seen as her petulant desire to have her
cake and eat it and the challenge she represents as being to orderliness
rather than to control (a desire not necessarily exclusively male – Octavia
shares it); there is no evidence to suggest that Octavius is doing anything in his overstatement of his Spartan case other than expressing his
disgust for the contrary state into which he believes Antony has sunk;
it is true that he does say that 'Women are not/In their best fortunes
strong', but it is to stretch the point to say that this implies that he sees
them as 'both inferior and dangerous' or that there is any evidence at all
of 'a personal need to demean them'. In the same way, there is no evidence that he expresses anything other than respect for a fallen enemy
at the end of the play and none that he hates and envies 'the life and
spirit of Antony and Cleopatra'. There is much evidence that he is contemptuous of their selfish pleasure seeking and this is not so unusual a
view as to prompt the reader or the watcher to psychoanalytical subtleties.
More precisely, one may pursue this line of interpretation, but one is
not compelled to do so any more than one is compelled to accept it once
it has been offered. It is a mark of the richness of Shakespeare's poetry
that it will bear such teasing out without breaking.

Bevington pursues this line of argument further:

■ What is different from Shakespeare's other tragic portrayals of sexual
conflict is that Antony finally holds to a vision of wholeness in which he
can be sustained by, and participate in, the feminine principle embodied
in the Egyptian world and most of all in Cleopatra – the principle of life,
the generative, exotic, fertile power of nature itself that encompasses
both the slime and the sun, both life and death.[85] □

It is 'better to be Antony and lose than Caesar and win'.[86]

Having reviewed critical opinion on the questions of genre and
structure, Bevington comments:

■ Shakespeare's style in this play is finally perceived, then, as one of
wholeness fashioned out of antithetical elements.[87] □

Bevington's summary of the performance history of the play is admirably
thorough. He notes that there is no record of the play's performance in
its day and that the earliest record of any performance is not exactly a

record: it is the entry in the Lord Chamberlain's records for 1669, which states that the play was 'formerly acted at the Blackfriars'. Sir Thomas Killigrew's 'King's Men' were 'allowed' the performance rights in 1669 for *Antony and Cleopatra* and twenty other plays. Killigrew's company acted at the Theatre Royal in Bridge Street but there is no evidence that they made use of the performance rights they had been allowed. Sir Charles Sedley adapted the play for the Duke's Theatre in 1667 and Dryden's *All For Love* appeared in 1678. Bevington observes that these strictly neo-classical accounts of the story may seem to be departures suited to the fashions of the times, but it is important to remember that the treatments of the story contemporary with Shakespeare are similarly 'classical' or, more precisely, Senecan, reflecting the importance of the work of Seneca to Elizabethan and Jacobean theatre. The Countess of Pembroke's *Antonius* (1592) was never publicly acted: it was a translation of Robert Garnier's strictly Senecan *Marc Antoine* (1578), which owed much to the *Cléopatre captive* (1552) of Étienne Jodelle (*c.* 1532–73); Samuel Daniel's *The Tragedy of Cleopatra* (1594) was another closet drama (that is, a drama not written for stage performance), and Samuel Brandon's *The Virtuous Octavia* (1598) is, as Bevington notes, 'no less Senecan in its hostility to the popular stage'. Bevington brings the theatre history up to Peter Hall's 1987 production at the National Theatre and his survey is thorough.[88]

John Wilders' Arden edition pays tribute to David Bevington's edition as a 'model of thoroughness and good sense'.[89] Wilders makes the comparison between Rome and Alexandria in familiar terms:

■ For the Romans the ideal is measured in masculine, political, pragmatic, military terms, the subservience of the individual to the common good of the state, of personal pleasure to public duty, of private, domestic loyalties to the demands of empire. Alexandria, on the other hand, is a predominantly female society for which the ideal is measured in terms of the intensity of emotion, of physical sensation, the subservience of social responsibility to the demands of feeling.[90] □

He quotes Peter Erickson who suggests that these worlds meet in Antony:

■ Octavius finds in Antony a heightened image of his own abstemiousness, Cleopatra's celebration of the bountiful Antony projects a model in which she discovers her own bounty.[91] □

And he quotes Janet Adelman:

■ The contest between Caesar and Cleopatra, Rome and Egypt, is in part a contest between male scarcity and female bounty as the defining site of Antony's heroic masculinity.[92] □

Wilders suggests that such contrasts can be seen not only throughout the play but also as the shaping force in individual scenes. Thus the fanfares of the opening scene suggest the entrance of 'some distinguished leader' but is followed by the appearance of Antony and Cleopatra with her maids and 'with eunuchs fanning her': the reconciliation of Antony with Caesar is immediately followed by a conversation between Maecenas and Enobarbus about the excesses of Alexandria.

Wilders sees 'instability' as the key to the play, taking a familiar leap at one point:

■ Both [Francis] Bacon [1561–1626] and Montaigne express the renewed influence of philosophical scepticism which appeared in Europe towards the end of the seventeenth century, but transformation is also the central theme of Ovid's *Metamorphoses*, perhaps the most lasting influence on all Shakespeare's work and which he must have read as a schoolboy. The Roman poet's prolonged meditation in the last book of the *Metamorphoses* on the ceaseless flux of creation probably lies behind this distinctive element of the play.[93] □

There is no evidence that Shakespeare had read Ovid's *Metamorphoses* as a schoolboy or at any other time that cannot be otherwise explained;[94] the eagerness that wishes so to see Ovid behind *Antony and Cleopatra* is held sufficiently in check by sound scholarly instincts that press for 'probably' in the last sentence to avoid a blatant imposition on the reader's intellect, but the sheer tenacity of the ideology of the classically trained Shakespeare is startling.

Wilders notes that Plutarch condemned Antony while acknowledging his virtues and quotes Dryden:

■ The chief persons represented were famous patterns of unlawful love; and their end accordingly was unfortunate. □

Wilders quotes Dowden's view that the play seems to say that 'this sensuous infinite is but a dream, a deceit, a snare', and Franklin Dickey for whom the play shows 'the terrible end of excessive passion'.[95] A.P. Riemer sees such views as a corrective to 'the elevation of those critics who insisted on seeing Cleopatra as a seventeenth-century precursor of Isolde [in the opera *Tristan und Isolde* (1865) by Richard Wagner, 1813–83],'[96] as Swinburne or Wilson Knight had done.

Wilders comments:

■ Shakespeare's critics, like his characters, tend to interpret his play in accordance with the predispositions they bring to it.[97] □

He quotes Hazlitt's description of Shakespeare's chameleon-like ability to take on his colouring from his surroundings:

■ He was the least of an egotist that it was possible to be. He was nothing in himself; but he was all that others were, or that they could become. He not only had in himself the germs of every faculty and feeling, but he could follow them by anticipation, intuitively, into all their conceivable ramifications, through every change of fortune or conflict of passion, or turn of thought ... He had only to think of any thing in order to become that thing, with all the circumstances belonging to it. □

He adds himself that Shakespeare could also express sympathetically almost any ideal, 'especially the Roman, with which he must have become familiar from his schooldays onwards', allowing himself to insert a further confirmation of Shakespeare's classical education, once again argued on the excellent basis that it must be so.[98] He goes on to say that the question which of the ideals he expresses in the play was truly believed in by him is a question that 'should not be asked'. Why not, it must be supposed, is because it is not susceptible to an answer and not because it would be improper to ask, but it is worth making these things clear or one may be taken to be elevating the dignity of the playwright excessively.

Wilders refers with approval, in summary, to Ernest Schanzer's essay, which, he says, 'does justice to the irreconcilable'[99] and he quotes Janet Adelman who says that 'the extreme of skepticism must be balanced by the extreme of assent'. Complexity, or hybridity, of form is partly to blame. Like *Richard II*, *Julius Caesar* and *Coriolanus*, 'it is both a tragedy and history play'; like *Romeo and Juliet*, 'it is a double tragedy', although the deaths, much separated, produce different effects. Antony is shown to be 'limited intellectually and even imaginatively':

■ He is most miserably degraded, of course, in his failure to perform the decorous suicide which he attempts and which, in retrospect, he likes to think he has accomplished. One has only to recall the death of Brutus to see the difference.[100] □

Wilders notes that the complexities of Cleopatra's last hours have been especially fruitfully explored by twentieth-century criticism:

■ Such uncertainties have been perceived only in the twentieth century, when criticism has concentrated on tensions, ambiguities, counter-cultures and self-contradiction.[101] □

He points out that Bradley, for example, saw 'something half-hearted in Shakespeare's appeal here, something even ironical in his presentation of this conflict'.[102] Wilders notes that G.K. Hunter has claimed that Bradley saw himself as a philosopher-critic who was looking to poetry, as Matthew Arnold had famously suggested that we should, 'to interpret life for us, to sustain us, to console us', and this is something that cannot be found in *Antony and Cleopatra*, as Wilders suggests:

■ Nothing purely good or evil can be found in the play and what seems admirable in one context is shown as ridiculous in another – or, rather, appears as both admirable and ridiculous at one and the same time. A tragedy founded on such assumptions could not satisfy Victorian readers who looked to it to console and sustain them. In the sceptical twentieth century it has been better appreciated.[103] □

On the style and language of the play, Wilders turns first to Plutarch in North's translation. Plutarch describes how Antony, as a young man, had studied oratory in Greece, as a result of which he 'used a manner of phrase in his speeche, called Asiatick, which carried the best grace and estimation of that time, and was much like to his manners and life: for it was full of ostentation, foolish braverie, and vain ambition'. Wilders quotes Rosalie Colie:

■ The Greeks had, naturally enough, characterized Persians and others to the East of Athens as 'Asiatic', meaning sensuous, sybaritic, self-indulgent, rich, materialist, decorated, soft. According to the paradigm, Asiatics lived a life of ease, delicacy, even of sloth, surrounded by ornate works of art and elaborate amusements for body and spirit. Gradually the moral disapproval levelled at their eastern neighbours came to be applied to a style of oratory conceived as 'like' Persian life, a style formally complex, ornate, decorated and elaborate.[104] □

Wilders comments that the language Shakespeare forged for the pair is used nowhere else by him and is the most effective means of making the contrast between Rome and Egypt.

On sources and influences, Wilders ranges widely. He speculates that it was a need to build into the play Plutarch's own voice that led Shakespeare to create the character of Enobarbus, and he quotes Mungo MacCallum who reminds us that Dryden subtitled *All For Love* 'The World Well Lost' and comments that 'we have something of the same feeling in reading Shakespeare and we do not have it in reading Plutarch'. Enobarbus helps to balance this sense of transcendence without being part of the merely 'Roman' criticism of Antony. However, although it is true that Plutarch is a dispassionate commentator, that role can hardly be taken up by a minor character, even one so memorable as Enobarbus, and anyway he has left the play before the point at which that role is really needed, the point at which, if they reach it at all, the lovers reach their moment of transcendence. That surely is where dispassionate commentary is needed if we are to have it at all. Plutarch does not have much to say about Octavius, and Wilders suggests that Shakespeare may have found hints in Simon Goulart's *Life of Augustus*, which North had translated for the 1603 edition of his translation of Plutarch's *Lives*. Mungo MacCallum suggested that Shakespeare consulted the 1578 translation of Appian's *Civil Wars* for details of Pompey's campaign and the rebellions of Lucius and Fulvia.[105]

On other sources, Wilders notes that there are echoes of the Countess of Pembroke's *Antonius*,[106] although he points out that Schanzer remarks that Shakespeare did not get the Cleopatra of the first four Acts from *Antonius*, but he may have been influenced by it when he came to the final scene.[107] Daniel's *The Tragedy of Cleopatra*, dedicated to the Countess of Pembroke, 'was designed as a companion piece to *Antonius*',[108] and his Cleopatra, as Riemer says, 'has none of the vulgarity of Shakespeare's heroine'.[109]

Perhaps more significant are the sources in mythology as they are part of the play's own texture. Wilders points out that Root notes that:

■ In the series of great tragedies, classical mythology plays quite an insignificant part; but in *Antony and Cleopatra* and *Coriolanus* it suddenly reasserts itself with surprising vigour ... A chief characteristic is the frequent allusion to the greater divinities. □

Venus and Mars may come from the *Odyssey* (8.266–328) of Homer or more likely from *De Rerum Natura* (*On the Nature of the Universe* by the ancient Roman philosopher and poet Lucretius, *c.* 95–55 BC), lines 29–40.[110] Wilders comments that the story was a popular subject for Renaissance writers, showing either love overcoming strife or the subjugation of valour by lust: 'In other words, it is capable of both an 'Egyptian' and a 'Roman' reading'.[111]

Hercules's subjugation by Omphale, the Amazonian queen of Lydia, as that story is told by Ovid (*Heroides*, 2.305–58), is also echoed, especially in the aspect of the exchange of garments,[112] and Plutarch compares Antony explicitly with Hercules. Raymond Waddington points to *Gerusalemme Liberata* (*Jerusalem Delivered*, 1575) (16.3–7) by the Italian poet Torquato Tasso (1544–95) and *The Faerie Queene* (1590–6) (5.8.2) by Edmund Spenser (1522–99).[113] Others have pointed to the story of Hercules at the crossroads (*Hercules in Bivio*, recorded in *Memorabilia* by the ancient greek historian Xenophon (*c.* 428–354 BC) (2.1.21–34)).[114] Another comparison is with Aeneas in the fourth book of the *Aeneid*[115] and from this to *Dido, Queen of Carthage* by Christopher Marlowe (1564–93).[116] Adelman points out that Virgil's Dido turns away from Aeneas in the

Underworld and Aeneas grieves briefly before going on to the Elysian fields (Dido is left with the other disconsolate souls on the plains of mourning) to see the spirits of the future heroes of Rome, and Wilders notes that Antony is being partial in his memory of the story, recalling the lover and not the hero.

There is also a connection with Egyptian mythology. Isis is the body of Egypt, flooded by her brother Osiris, the Nile; Isis also looks forward to joining her dead husband in the afterlife.[117] Cleopatra makes this association herself. The habit that both of them have of identifying themselves with great archetypes certainly contributes to the sense of greatness to which they aspire, but as Wilders comments:

> ■ The association of Antony and Cleopatra with these classical archetypes creates a number of contradictory effects. The idea that Antony is another Hercules, another Aeneas, and that Cleopatra is a greater Venus, a second Dido, clearly adds to that sense of their own magnitude which they themselves deliberately create, both in Shakespeare's account of them and in Plutarch's, and it cannot help but make its impression on an audience. At the same time, if we reflect on these allusions, we realize that, by Roman standards, they discredit the protagonists, particularly Antony, who, like Mars with Venus and Hercules with Omphale, abandons heroic virtue for the blandishments of a woman but, unlike Hercules at the crossroads, turns away from the path of Roman virtue and, unlike Aeneas, gives up his obligations to his country for the sake of his love for a foreign queen. The paradoxical, ambivalent nature of the lovers which is central to Shakespeare's play is deepened by their association with their mythological archetypes.[118] □

The connection with Isis, however, although it is given by Octavius as further evidence, if it were needed, of the decadence of Egyptian life (3.6.1–19), offers a further complication to the pattern of contrasts offered by the play: as Wilders points out, it is from the Roman point of view that the classical archetypes show the lovers at a disadvantage; the identification of Cleopatra with Isis may be seen to authorise with divine sanction and place within a divine scheme the very form of life Octavius despises and perhaps fails to understand.

There is a clear contrast between the last two editions surveyed here and the first three, which is not just a matter of the temperament of the editor. The first three editors survey prevailing critical opinion fairly briskly and set out their own views quite clearly. Thus it is not difficult to summarise the views of the play of Case, Ridley, Everett and Jones. Bevington and Wilders spend much more of their time discussing other critical reactions and setting before the reader not so much their own position as a judicious comment on the current state of a game very much as yet undecided. This is partly a reflection of the considerable expansion of work in the area and partly a reflection of the increasingly self-conscious and theoretically sophisticated nature of criticism since the 1960s and 1970s. The next two chapters survey the development of criticism in the twentieth century by considering a specific theme: the 'Romanness' of the Roman plays. Starting with Mungo MacCallum, who first defined the category as more than a loose grouping, and moving on to Robert Miola's comprehensive *Shakespeare's Rome* (1983), the discussion takes in Coppélia Kahn's ground-breaking *Roman Shakespeare* (1997) and an important essay by Ania Loomba, *Gender, Race, Renaissance Drama* (1992). The stage is thus set for a close consideration of some of the main theoretical positions of the late twentieth century.

CHAPTER SEVEN

The Romanness of the Roman Plays (1)

Mungo MacCallum was the first to propose the specific category, 'Roman play'. Dr Johnson had expressed a widely held although not always openly expressed view that the plays were histories, and that this was not to their advantage. MacCallum regarded the common source as significant.

John Velz's 'Retrospect'[1] is a useful point of departure for the essays considered in this chapter. He begins by sketching the main outlines of the debate as lying (broadly) between Nahum Tate and Edward Dowden. Tate remarked in his prefatory address to *The Loyal General: A Tragedy* that in Shakespeare's Roman works 'the Persons, the Passages, the Manners, the Circumstances, the Ceremonies, all are Roman'. Tate insisted that 'Nature will not do [a poet's] Business', he must also have a learned acquaintance with the object he hopes to dramatise, including 'the Customs and Constitutions of Nations' and 'the Histories of all Ages'.

We may gather from Tate's comments that he thought that Shakespeare had such an acquaintance with the objects of his study as Tate claimed was necessary. Velz reminds us that Ben Jonson thought contemptuously of Shakespeare's attempts to reproduce the Roman world. Edward Dowden, rather later, tried to find a middle ground, insisting that:

■ While Shakspere is profoundly faithful to Roman life and character, it is an ideal truth, truth spiritual rather than truth material, which he seeks to discover ... Shakspere was aware that his personages must be men before they were Romans ... He knew that the buttressing up of art with erudition will not give stability to that which must stand by no aid of material props and stays, but if at all, by virtue of the one living soul of which it is the body.[2] □

Velz contrasts the approaches of Tate and Dowden, describing Dowden's as 'Platonism' and Tate's as an 'Aristotelian insistence on the poet's acquaintance with "the Customs and Constitutions of Nations" ',[3] suggesting that we may find Dowden 'rather more lofty than logical', feeling that he has avoided the difficult questions. Velz tells us that Dowden 'transmits in his assertions the consensus of the German aesthetic critics he so greatly admired, and he acknowledges his debt to the English Romantic tradition ... as well'.[4] This is not quite fair: leaving apart the language of body and soul, it is true, as Dowden observes, 'that the buttressing up of art with erudition will not give stability to that which must stand by no aid of material props and stays'. However we wish to speak of what makes a work stand up, we shall agree that erudition is not it. It is probably not unfair to speak of Dowden's criticism as 'Platonism' either; he wished to assimilate his work to the critics he admired, as Velz observes, and they, in their turn, wished to assimilate art to other discourses. We only need to observe in passing that if you do not share their aims, you do not have to take on the idealist apparatus to appreciate the accounts they offer of the works they discuss, and this is as true of Dowden as it is of his mentors. An interesting question with any critic under discussion is whether the theory is necessary. The insight may not have been available to the critic without the theory, but it may be available to the reader without the theory.[5]

Velz observes that MacCallum took a distinctive approach, finding that Shakespeare was, compared with others who had dramatised Roman stories, quite a purist in his treatment of source documents and no other had been able so well 'to reconcile the claims of the ideal and the real'.[6] MacCallum argues that there is no attempt in the Roman works to reconstruct the past but Shakespeare chooses those elements in Roman life that had correspondences in Renaissance England. Velz cites Madeleine Doran's work as a continuation of this line of thought.[7] Doran argues that the perception of analogues between classical and contemporary life was in fact regarded as an aesthetic positive and the appropriate critical response, one 'that takes art on its own terms',[8] should approve and not condemn such fusing of past and present.

Velz argues that the trend of critical scholarship in the twentieth century has been away from the question of whether Shakespeare's Romans are authentic and towards whether his contemporaries thought them authentic. T.J.B. Spencer argued persuasively that they did.[9] But if they thought the Roman world only a reflection of their own, is there any justification for singling out a group of Roman plays at all? Velz thinks there is. He points to J.L. Simmons' attempt[10] and also that of Paul A. Cantor,[11] contrasting them with Reuben A. Brower and Milton Boone Kennedy,[12] who take the ancient world to be a source for a much wider group of Shakespeare's plays than those ordinarily thought of as 'classical'. Cantor and Simmons treat the ancient world as a specific and separate object of attention for Shakespeare.

Simmons' thesis is that Rome is essentially pre-Christian; Rome is the earthly city contrasted with the *civitas dei* (city of God) of St Augustine of Hippo (AD 354–430); it is a world in which an unenlightened humanity seeks certainties it cannot possess. Cantor sees the idea of the republic in Shakespeare contrasted with the idea of empire: the first centred upon a commitment to mutual support and the second a decadent and self-indulgent decline from the republican ideal.

Velz spends some time discussing the rhetorical characteristics of the plays, especially those of *Julius Caesar*, noting that since Dr Johnson's observation of a Roman manner in that play, critics have searched for stylistic formulae to identify the plays. Velz reminds the reader that there are distinctive styles to be observed between the three main Plutarchan plays alone. Velz refers to Bethell and Markels especially.[13]

Finally he discusses the importance of institutions to Shakespeare, both political and social, as these have been discussed by others, and ends with a meditation on the significance of the wall both to Virgil and, he believes, to Shakespeare. The wall is what keeps barbarism out and preserves civilisation within: its vulnerability is most poignantly displayed when the threat comes from within. Tarquin's lust in *Lucrece*; Coriolanus's betrayal; the actions of Titus Andronicus; all these are the consequences, not of invasion from without but of collapse within. Velz concludes:

■ Virgil's mythic vision of Rome as driven (or called) by Fate towards the *Pax Augusta* [peace of Augustus (Caesar)] was 'true' in his generation in just the same way the equally vulnerable Tudor myth was in Shakespeare's generation – that is, it was more true in its piety of invention than literalists are likely to understand. Who is to say that in basing his conception of Rome in five plays and a long poem upon Virgil's view of history Shakespeare was not portraying *Romanitas* [Romanness] authentically?[14] □

Mungo MacCallum begins his essay by stating that the Roman plays belong together not so much because they draw from a common source but more because 'they follow the same method of treatment and that method is to a great extent peculiar to themselves'.[15] He passes then to a summary of some of the surviving classical plays before Shakespeare turned his hand to the subject. *A new Tragical Comedie of Appius and Viginia*, by 'R.B.',[16] which was printed in 1575, is his first example. He notes that there is throughout 'a lavish display of cheap boyish erudition'[17] and, in passing to a translation of Seneca's *Octavia*, makes some useful remarks on the kind of art here represented.

He notes that Latin literature was more accessible to a wider readership than Greek, simply because Latin was more widely read than

Greek. He also notes that some of the characteristics of Senecan litera-
ture made it appealing: 'its tendency to heightened yet abstract portrait-
ure, its declamation, its sententiousness, its violence, its unrestfulness'.
MacCallum traces some of these features in the work of the French
Senecans to whom he next turns his attention. Beginning with Marc
Antoine Muret (also known as Muretus, 1526–85), the author of *Julius
Caesar* (1544), and one of the tutors most affectionately remembered by
Michel, duc de Montaigne, through Étienne Jodelle's *Cléopatre captive*
(1552), *César* (1558) by Jacques Grévin (1538–70) and Robert Garnier's
Cornélie (1573) and *Marc Antoine* (1578). Crossing the channel once
more, MacCallum's trail leads through *Gorboduc* (1562) by Thomas
Norton (1532–84) and Thomas Sackville (1536–1608) and the
Misfortunes of Arthur (1587) by Thomas Hughes, before lighting upon the
Countess of Pembroke's translation of Garnier's *Marc Antoine* as *Antonius*
(later *The Tragedie of Antonius*), first published in 1592 but completed in
1590. In 1594 Samuel Daniel's *The Tragedy of Cleopatra* appeared, dedicated to the Countess of Pembroke. MacCallum comments, almost in
passing, 'its claims, of course, are almost exclusively literary and hardly
at all theatrical'[18] and this is a point to which we shall return, although
he also claims that it is 'among the best original Senecan tragedies that
Elizabethan England produced'. Thomas Kyd (1558–94) translated
Garnier's *Cornélie* as *Cornelia* in 1594.

MacCallum assembles some circumstantial evidence to show what is
not really in doubt, that Shakespeare knew of Daniel's and Kyd's work,
but he is respectably tentative in advancing much of a claim, acknowledging that circumstantial evidence is not proof. He makes a most
important observation concerning parallels with Garnier: that they 'are
neither numerous nor striking'.[19] He sees more coincidences with
Daniel but still judiciously concludes that they 'are interesting, but they
are not conclusive'.[20] He accepts (and the judiciousness of his proce-
dures inclines the reader to accept in turn) that there is a case for considering an influence from Garnier's *Cornélie* or indirectly from Garnier
via Kyd. MacCallum's conclusion is a model of restraint:

■ In all three instances the evidence brought forward rather suggests
the obligation as possible than establishes it as certain.[21] □

McCallum spends more time on *Marius and Scilla* by Thomas Lodge
(1558–1625) than he himself holds that it deserves, pointing out that
there are many other plays, the names only of which have descended
to our own day, and there may be others even whose names have not
done; he mentions Fulke Greville, Lord Brooke (1554–1628), who
claimed to have destroyed a tragedy on the theme of Antony and

Cleopatra in 1601, and Brandon's *Vertuous Octavia* of 1598, which has survived, and concludes:

> ■ It is pretty safe to suppose that they did not contain much instruc-
> tion for Shakespeare, and that none of them would bridge the gap
> between Lodge's medley and Shakespeare's masterpiece.[22] □

He summarises by saying that the progress since the mid-century had been significant. *Appius and Virginia*, for example, introduced Roman stories to the popular audience and the Senecans had tried to dramatise 'the old Roman greatness' and Lodge 'is realistic enough in his way'. However:

> ■ No dramatist had been able at once to rise to the grandeur of the
> theme and keep a foothold on solid earth, to reconcile the claims of the
> ideal and the real, the past and the present. That was left for
> Shakespeare to do.[23] □

MacCallum's approach to Shakespeare's Roman plays is prefaced by a brief discussion of Shakespeare's work as a whole that illustrates some of the difficulties of genre criticism. MacCallum observes that the turn of the fifteenth and sixteenth centuries approximately bisects Shakespeare's career, as before 1600 he had written mostly comedies while after that date he was to write 'many tragedies with a few plays which, on account of the happy ending and other traits may be assigned to the opposite class'.[24] What is absent in the seventeenth century, though, is the history play. More specifically, what is absent is 'the play on native history'.[25] MacCallum argues that the Roman play is a species of the historical play, of which 'the play on native history' is another species. MacCallum shares Dr Johnson's opinion of the history play, saying that it is 'little else than a narrative presented in scenes'. The chronicle history is inherently undramatic, for example in *Henry V*, 'there is no dramatic collision of ideas, no conflict in the soul of the hero'.[26] In summary, 'the distinctively narrative wins the day against the distinctively dramatic'. However, the Roman material is pregnant with dramatic possibilities. Further, it is pregnant with tragic possibilities and these possibilities are realised in Shakespeare's treatment of the material, 'So they are always ranked with the Tragedies'.[27] Nevertheless, they are histories, because Shakespeare was not free to adjust the stories to suit his purposes. In *Lear* or *Othello*, there was no given set of facts:

> ■ But in the Roman plays the main facts were accredited and known,
> and of infinite significance for the history of the world. They could not
> be overlooked, they had to be taken into account.[28] □

MacCallum argues his point at length: Shakespeare was scrupulously faithful to the facts. Yet this does not allow us to imagine that Shakespeare was
attempting to reconstruct the past. MacCallum makes an important
observation at this point:

> ■ It may even be doubted whether such an attempt would have been
> intelligible to him or to any save one or two of his contemporaries. To
> the average Elizabethan ... the past differed from the present chiefly by
> its distance and dimness; and distinctive contrasts in manners and cus-
> toms were but scantily recognised.[29] □

For example, although Shakespeare, in composing *Julius Caesar*, could
draw on national memories of civil war and eventually triumphant strong
government and the experiences of nobles, who out of self-interest or
more principled concerns took sides, 'of zeal for the republican theory
as such he knows nothing, and therefore his Brutus is only in part the
Brutus of Plutarch'.[30] In this way, he 'does not give the notes that mark
off Roman from every other civilisation, but rather those that it possessed in common with the rest, and especially with his own'.[31]

MacCallum adds that Shakespeare even introduces material not
Roman but Elizabethan but concludes that the result is not, as one might
have expected, simply anachronistic: he describes the process as a
'quickening', itself the result of 'the thorough realisation of the subject
in Shakespeare's own mind from his own point of view, with all the
powers not only of his reason, but of his imagination, emotion, passion,
and experience'.[32] Paradoxically, the result is more authentic than the
efforts of more 'scholarly' writers, because while they are more correct
in detail, they are deficient in 'the living energy and principle of it all'.
MacCallum quotes 'the erudite Leonard Digges' (1588–1635), who
expressed his opinion in commendatory verses prefaced to the 1640
edition of Shakespeare's *Poems*:

> ■ So have I seen, when Caesar would appear,
> And on the stage at half-sword parley were
> Brutus and Cassius; O, how the audience
> Were ravished, with what wonder they went thence,
> When some new day they would not brook a line
> Of tedious though well-laboured *Catiline* [Ben Jonson's *Catilina His
> Conspiracy* (1611) was a tragedy set in ancient Rome].[33] □

Digges' verses begin: 'Poets are born, not made'. He believes that
'nature only helped him [Shakespeare]'. He goes so far as to say that

> ■   Look thorough
> This whole book, thou shalt find he doth not borrow

> One phrase from Greeks, nor Latin imitate,
> Nor once from vulgar languages translate □

Digges, MacCallum records, took a Bachelor's degree at Oxford and then studied abroad for many years, being promoted to the honorary degree of Master upon his return: 'a man who, with his academic training and academic status, would not be apt to undervalue literal accuracy'. Digges does overstate his case, however:

> ■   All that he doth write
> Is pure his own – plot, language exquisite – □

As we now know, as surely much of his audience would also have known – indeed he may well have depended upon this and MacCallum is himself arguing that this is one reason why Shakespeare had to stick so closely to his sources – his plots were not his own, although he adapted them to his uses.

The point is the same as Dryden's:

> ■ Those who accuse him to have wanted learning give him the greater commendation. He was naturally learned. He needed not the spectacles of books to read nature. He looked inwards, and found her there.[34] □

Velz used the words 'Platonism' and 'idealism' to describe Dowden's attempt to get hold of a similar idea; in Dowden's case that was perhaps fair, as he acknowledged a debt to German Romantic theorists who were themselves indebted to forms of idealist philosophy, but MacCallum presents himself as a thoroughgoing Aristotelian, painstakingly assembling the facts before making his case inductively. The point is that what they are both trying to get hold of eludes both traditions of thought. MacCallum partially recognises this. He identifies two principles in Shakespeare's approach, contrasting but complementary: the first is that Shakespeare does not allow himself to be dictated to by the past; the second is that he does not allow himself complete freedom with respect to it.

MacCallum contrasts the historian's method and the poet's in an interesting simile: 'the painful mosaic of [the historian] is almost directly opposed to the complete vision, the creation in one jet, which may be rightly expected of [the poet]'.[35] It may be observed, as MacCallum does not, that the nineteenth century is the century of the novel and that the perception of the age was that the province of the novel was the real. Whether set in the past or the present, attention to realistic detail is expected. From the prefaces to Scott's *Waverley* novels (1814–29) to *Middlemarch* (1871–3) by George Eliot (1819–80), the dominant strain is realism. *Middlemarch* offers us a clue to the cultural temper: its interest in the sciences and its kinship with their methods shows one of the great minds of its time struggling to reconcile what Wordsworth in his Preface to *Lyrical Ballads* (1800) had strongly implied were irreconcilable, poetry and science. In this opinion, minds as divergent as Matthew Arnold and Thomas Carlyle (1795–1881) had concurred but the dominance of realism strongly suggests that the real and the practices perceived to be effective in dealing with it were an overwhelmingly superior force. MacCallum is somewhat cloistered within a literary view and loses the advantage of a wider range of vision.

Shakespeare escapes both extremes. On the one hand, 'No unhistorical person has historical work to do, and no unhistorical episode affects the historical action', while on the other hand, in his treatment of the known characters of history, 'starting with a conventional type, [he] leaves us with an individual man'.[36] He does this by not resting content with the necessarily vague impression of a character that history leaves us but by using his imagination:

■ Shakespeare probes and defines it; he tests it in relation to the assumed facts on which it is based; he discovers the latent difficulties, faces them, and solves them, and, starting with a conventional type, leaves us with an individual man. □

This is not very clear. It is particularly not very clear about not inventing anything, because it suggests that history has left things to be invented or at least further clarified by hypothesis as the facts are insufficiently precise. In fact, MacCallum's entire analysis at this point is beginning to break down, although the principles are clear enough, because the extremes may be defined, but the closer we approach a centre common to the extremes, the more difficult we find it to distinguish between fact and opinion and fiction. History is not natural science.

The next stage in MacCallum's argument is concerned with the source material. Having identified, to his satisfaction, Shakespeare's approach to source material, MacCallum then identifies the peculiar character of the material he made use of in his Roman works. Plutarch, MacCallum holds, is not just another source:

■ To put it shortly, in Plutarch's *Lives* Shakespeare for the first and almost the only time was rehandling the masterpieces of a genius who stood at the summit of his art.[37] □

MacCallum comments that 'a book like the *Parallel Lives* was bound to achieve a great popularity in the Renaissance. That it was full of instruction and served for warning and example commended it to a generation that was but too inclined to prize the didactic in literature'[38] and then spends some time setting out the life and literary practice of Jacques

Amyot, who translated Plutarch into French in 1559. Amyot's significance is that he not only translates Plutarch but also modernises the world of the narratives.

MacCallum's discussion of North's translation from Amyot is painstakingly thorough, and makes the equally important point that North completed the process of familiarisation of the Graeco-Roman world and thus 'meets Shakespeare half way'.[39] MacCallum does not assume that Shakespeare had any classical education of any significance: North 'supplied Shakespeare with the only Plutarch that Shakespeare could understand'. North's Plutarch 'furnished Shakespeare with his whole conception of antique history'. In *Coriolanus*, MacCallum notes a freedom with the incidents Plutarch relates but a close dependence upon North's language in connection with those incidents that are retained, and, by contrast, in *Antony and Cleopatra* a closer dependence upon the narrative material and a greater freedom in their presentation.

It is to be questioned what purposes are served by MacCallum's digressions as there is no serious suggestion that Shakespeare drew from either Amyot or Plutarch: scholarship concurs that North is his source. To observe that first Amyot and then North adjusted Plutarch, whether intentionally or not, to their time is of interest to another discussion, but as we know that Shakespeare did not have any other access to Plutarch, we may be permitted to ask whether access to Plutarch is even what he was after. It may be safely assumed that just as he did not trouble himself to check his historical sources for the English histories, he was not concerned about the authenticity of his sources for the Roman histories. Authenticity was not his object. We cannot even know whether it could have been. However, the important point is made that Shakespeare was not drawing on Plutarch, and that his adaptation to his time was not his but also that of the translators: first Amyot and, after Amyot, North.

Several pages are devoted to a thorough inventory of Shakespeare's indebtedness to North's Plutarch, in both details and general fidelity to the narrative structure. MacCallum concludes that the impression given is of 'an anxious desire to avoid tampering with the facts and their relations even when history does not furnish ready-made the material that best fits the drama'.[40] Shakespeare's most significant departure, he argues, is the suppression of some of Antony's worst traits as recorded by Plutarch. He maintains that Plutarch and Shakespeare are like portrait painters: the biographer has assembled 'vivid traits which in their general effect are ignoble and repulsive',[41] while the dramatist 'has idealised his model … by reading the soul of greatness through the sordid details'. The contradictoriness of such an account is brought out more fully:

■ He is still, though fallen, the Antony who at Caesar's death could alter the course of history; a dissolute intriguer no doubt, but a man of genius, a man of enthusiasms, one who is equal or all but equal to the highest occasion the world can present, and who, if he fails owing to the lack of steadfast principle and virile will that results from voluptuous indulgence and unscrupulous practisings, yet remains fascinating and magnificent even in his ruin. □

This is a subtle and honest description of a recognisable reaction. MacCallum is here responding to the romance of debauchery. We have to think carefully about what kind of genius and magnificence are represented by such a picture and we have to be scrupulously honest about their attractiveness or we may have missed the entire point of the play.

Comparison of Plutarch and Shakespeare brings out the point that Shakespeare focuses exclusively on the lovers and MacCallum's summary remark is striking: 'Plutarch has no eyes for the glory of Antony's madness.'[42] Plutarch 'regards the whole affair as a pitiable dotage, or, at best, as a calamitous visitation'. The play is a love tragedy, to be grouped in this respect with *Romeo and Juliet* and *Troilus and Cressida*, the only other plays, as MacCallum points out, named after two persons. He contrasts the three: *Romeo and Juliet* 'idealises youthful love'; *Troilus and Cressida* 'shows the inward dissolution of such love when it is unworthily bestowed'; in *Antony and Cleopatra* 'love is not a revelation as in the first, nor an illusion, as in the second, but an infatuation ... It is the love that seizes the elderly man of the world, the trained mistress of arts, and does this, as it would seem, to cajole and destroy them both'. Thus the play is an amalgam of 'chronicle history ... personal tragedy and ... love poem'.[43]

MacCallum situates the play historically in the period after the struggle between old and new orders dramatised in *Julius Caesar*, when the new order has established itself and the losses are beginning to be felt. The old ideal of the state has gone; the common people are dismissed with contempt; the principle of freedom has been replaced by the exercise of power and the contest to wield it. 'The sense of the majesty of Rome, which inspired both the conspirators and their opponents, seems extinct'.[44] MacCallum discusses the subsidiary characters carefully if briskly, pointing out that the whole pack, on any side, contains no one, save Dolabella, who makes a good impression: 'For there is no moral cement to hold together this ruinous world'.[45] Every one is out for him or herself and the chief object is the pursuit of power or pleasure or both: 'Everywhere the cult of material good prevails'.[46] He takes the story of Enobarbus as a particularly instructive illustration of 'the corroding influence of the *Zeitgeist* [spirit of the time]'. MacCallum discusses Enobarbus carefully, showing how Enobarbus admires not only Cleopatra's 'witchery' but also Antony's magnificence. His summary of Enobarbus bears reflection:

■ The tragedy of Enobarbus' position lies in this: that in that evil time his reason can furnish him with no motive for his loyalty except self-interest

and confidence in his leader's capacity; or, failing these, the unsubstantial recompense of fame.[47] □

He supports Antony because he is Antony, but 'fidelity at all costs to a
person is a forgotten phrase among the cosmopolitan materialists who
are competing for the spoils of the Roman world'. We should, at this
point, consider Kent in *King Lear*, who demonstrates precisely, and in
vivid contrast, what MacCallum rightly calls 'fidelity at all costs to a person'. He points out the difference between Enobarbus's contrition and 'the
miraculous conversions of some wrong-doers in fiction, who in an instant
are awakened to grace for no conceivable cause and by no intelligible
means'.[48] Enobarbus realises that the other deserters have achieved no
security in Octavius's service; the return to him by Antony of his treas-
ure reawakens his sense of Antony's magnificence and 'With that returns
his old enthusiasm';[49] in the light of this consciousness, his behaviour
appears despicable and profitless.

MacCallum asks a chilling question: 'Amongst the struggling and
contentious throng of worldlings and egoists who to succeed must tread
their nobler instincts underfoot, and even so do not always succeed, are
there any honest and sterling characters at all?' MacCallum picks out
Scarus, the valiant soldier; Octavia, whose presence is so telling but so
brief; and Eros, the freed slave who kills himself rather than kill his master. His descriptions of these three, over several pages, are well worth
attending to. By contrast, his treatment of the political leaders, as he calls
them, is, insipid. Lepidus is weak, Pompey half-hearted and Octavius shallow. The weakness of MacCallum's method is the weakness of Bradley's
combined with the weakness of Dowden's: close, careful reading is
allowed to expand almost imperceptibly towards speculation (as
Bradley's does) in pursuit of a moral vision (as Dowden's does). The
strength of the method is shown in strong judgements, such as the clear
vision MacCallum conveys of the world of the play as it is revealed
through the secondary characters; its weakness is that it has nothing
much more to say of these three who, in such a vision, are not really
distinguishable from the secondary characters. At such times, the
expansion seems merely expansive and what is close and careful in
other parts becomes leisurely.

MacCallum's treatment of Antony is not very remarkable, although he
makes a useful comparison with the Mark Antony of *Julius Caesar* and
points to the oratorical skill so very marked in the earlier play. MacCallum
sees this oratorical skill in the later play and interprets it as springing from
a deep-seated opportunism. 'Be a child o' the time' Antony bids Octavius
at 2.7.106, to which Caesar replies ominously, 'Possess it, I'll make answer'.
Antony is, in MacCallum's view, very much 'a child o' the time', not only
the time in general, which MacCallum regards as degenerate as the play

presents it, but a child of the moment, having no fixed purpose other than the infatuation. Thus his impulsive generosity, his moving speeches, even his marriage to Octavia seem to meet with that 'convincing air of sincerity that can only be explained by his really liking it for the moment', as MacCallum says of the marriage proposal.[50] Both these aspects, 'for the moment' and 'really liking it', are true of a way of seeing Antony in this play, as a child, in more than the one metaphorical sense, of the moment.

Of Cleopatra, MacCallum says: 'It is almost impossible to look at her steadily, or keep one's head to estimate her aright. She is the incarnate poetry of life without duty, glorified by beauty and grace; of impulse without principle, ennobled by culture and intellect'.[51] Shakespeare, though, does not lose his head, apparently because (and here MacCallum is at his most Dowdenesque) 'the artist is a man, experienced and critical, yet with the fires of his imagination still ready to leap and glow'. This may be a picture of the artist implied by the work but it does read like a picture from a biography. MacCallum struggles to keep his distance: 'It is her deliberate programme to keep satiety afar by the swiftness and diversity of the changes she assumes; but it is a programme easy to carry out, for it corresponds to her own nature. She is a creature of moods'.[52] His Dowden/Bradley tendencies well to the fore, MacCallum ingeniously rationalises Cleopatra's behaviours in terms of this picture of the 'creature of moods', introducing an aspect of cowardice that leads her not only to flee from Actium but also to temporise with Thidias (or Thyreus as MacCallum styles him). The descriptions are not unconvincing but they are necessarily constructions based upon the evidence provided by the play rather than deductions from it, just as are Dowden's constructions of the artist and Bradley's of the characters.

Indeed, speculation is a necessary ingredient of enjoyment of drama, but it is always important to remember that speculation is directed by predispositions and MacCallum's are towards a version of rationality: the logic of Cleopatra's character as he has defined it. This leads him to a strange view of Cleopatra's sending news of her death to Antony:

■ It is not the most candid nor dignified expedient, but probably it is the most effective one; for violent ills need violent cures; and perhaps there was nothing that could allay Antony's storm of distrust but as fierce a storm of regret.[53] □

This last figure betrays the thinking here: the metaphor is weak and the link between the two states contingent at best. If MacCallum is trying to suggest that Cleopatra is attempting a sort of 'tough love' therapy, then his desire to make her actions seem consistent has overtaken his critical tact. The business of defending Cleopatra by explaining her inconsistencies as consistent with some version of her character is far from exhausted and it must be confronted at its source. This action of hers is no more consistent with any other action of hers than any action of Antony's is consistent with any of his.

MacCallum is perceptive about Antony: has Cleopatra bewitched him as he has said she has bewitched so many others? He has already stated at the beginning of this chapter, 'Such avatars as the Egyptian Queen have often been described by other poets, but generally from the point of view either of the servile devotee or of the unsympathetic censor';[54] he has tried to pursue the same path as he says Shakespeare has pursued as (in MacCallum's words) 'a man, experienced and critical, yet with the fires of his imagination still ready to leap and glow'. What he has also done, however, is to try to find in Shakespeare's Cleopatra the kind of consistency we associate with characters in novels, especially the psychologically realist novels of the nineteenth century. In a novel, Shakespeare's Cleopatra would appear intolerably self-centred and shallow; in his play she appears riveting.

MacCallum does sense the discrepancy. He comments on the scenes following Antony's death (scenes that he says reveals of Cleopatra 'the greatness of her nature'):[55]

■ It is a strange riddle that Shakespeare has here offered to the student, and perhaps no certain solution of it is to be found. In this play, even more than in most, he resorts to what has been called his shorthand, to the briefest and most hurried notation of his meaning, and often it is next to impossible to explain or extend his symbols. □

This is similar to Dr Johnson's view:

■ It is incident to him (Johnson says) to be now and again entangled with an unwieldy sentiment, which he cannot well express, and will not reject; he struggles with it a while, and if it continues stubborn, comprises it in words such as occur, and leaves it to be disentangled and evolved by minds that have more leisure to bestow upon it. □

It may be useful to refer to Leavis's discussion of this and related passages, noted in Chapter 2 of this Guide. Leavis's belief is that this kind of response to Shakespeare does not take Shakespeare at face value but imposes requirements he almost certainly did not feel he had to meet.[56]

MacCallum summarises clearly the most common accounts of the Seleucus scene, commenting on them at length. He points out that Shakespeare departs from Plutarch at a number of points, the effect of which is to focus her demeanour more tightly. She is less distraught: North's Plutarch has her in an 'ougly and pitiefull state' and describes her as 'marvelously disfigured: both for that she had plucked her heare from her head, as also for that she had martired her face with her nailes, and besides, her voyce was small and trembling, her eyes sonke into her head with continuall blubbering'.[57] In Plutarch, at this point, Cleopatra blames her fear of Antony for her actions, but Shakespeare puts that suggestion back to the scene with Thidias; even her violence towards Seleucus is less unconstrained in Shakespeare's play than in Plutarch's account. Further, and more puzzlingly, in Plutarch, Seleucus is just standing by and intervenes 'to seeme a good servant', that is, to ingratiate himself with Octavius; while in Shakespeare's play, Cleopatra invites him to make the disclosure and, moreover, there is no mention of his punishment afterwards. Finally, the scene in Shakespeare suggests a more serious deception than is suggested in Plutarch. Taken together, these changes may suggest that Cleopatra has staged the scene with Seleucus's aid.

Against this interpretation, it may be argued that it is far from obvious that the scene is staged. Subtle is one thing, ambiguous is another. On the other hand, it is at least a bold stroke dramatically to present a Cleopatra who has, among other things, made a very good speech to the effect that death is her only future (5.2.1–8), but who seems to have protected herself just in case by sequestering some of her wealth from the attention of Caesar's accountants. North's translation, and a marginal note he adds to underline it, makes it clear that Cleopatra intends to deceive Caesar into believing that she wishes to live and that she succeeds in her aim.

Summing up, MacCallum is just:

> ■ If we credit our feelings, it is quite true that Cleopatra is taken by surprise and put out of countenance, that she seeks to excuse herself and passionately resents the disloyalty of Seleucus. And again, if we credit our feelings, it is quite true that from the time the mortally wounded Antony is brought before her, she has made up her mind to kill herself, and that she is nobler and more queenly for her decision than she was before or than Plutarch makes her.
>
> Of course, buoyant and versatile, feeling her life in every limb, and quick to catch each passing chance, she may even now without really knowing it, without really believing it, have hoped against hope that she might still obtain terms she could accept undisgraced. And the hope of life would bring with it the frailties of life, for clearly it is only the resolve to die that lifts her above herself. So here we should only have another instance of the complexity of her strange nature that can consciously elect the higher path, and yet all the while in its secret councils provide, if it may be, for following the lower.[58] □

This is very clear, and it is exact. The only puzzle is why MacCallum should regard as 'strange' a nature that accords so well with what he has said of both Antony and the play as a whole, in its lesser characters and in the character of its political leaders. It is a world, as he himself has said, in which there is no 'moral cement'; why should we be surprised that Cleopatra acts exactly as both Antony and Enobarbus before her have acted, at last wresting a little nobility out of a career of scepticism, expediency and self-indulgence?

MacCallum's treatment of the love between the two main characters is the keystone of his discussion of the play. First he states a position he has earlier reached:

> ■ We have noted how in that generation all ties of customary morality are loosed, how the individual is a law to himself, and how selfishness runs riot in its quest of gratification, acquisition, material ambition. Among the children of that day those make the most sympathetic impression who import into the somewhat casual and indefinite personal relations that remain – the relation of the legionary to his commander, of the freedman to his patron, of the waiting-woman to her mistress – something of universal validity and worth.[59] □

He then contrasts sexual love with these relationships that have, after all, arisen out of custom, however withered those customary relationships have become by and large. Sexual love is paradoxical: it appears both to arise from a mutual inclination to which assent is given and to have the character of an overriding force. As MacCallum says, when it becomes an overwhelming passion, 'it will supply the grand effective bond when other social bonds fail … it will enable a man and woman to overleap a few at least of the barriers of their selfishness, and in some measure to merge their egoism in sympathy'.[60]

This is a great statement, but unfortunately perhaps, MacCallum goes on to blur the strong impression it makes by references to the concept developed by Johann Wolfgang von Goethe (1749–832) of *Wahlverwandschaft* (elective affinity: the idea is a convergence of choice and attraction operating at a level below free will) and the *Symposium* of Plato. Such grand company is beside the point and is indeed misleading. MacCallum has got the world of the play quite right: it is degenerate. He has also got a key point right: neither Antony nor Cleopatra is capable of finally transcending their ingrained habit of selfishness for very long, or indeed of doing or feeling anything for very long. His portrait of Enobarbus is revelatory of the whole world of the play: a man motivated by feelings of which he is almost ashamed, or which, at least, he cannot find mirrored anywhere else in his world, and without the strength of conscience that would allow him to rest satisfied with his feelings for a guide, who is finally brought to mortal grief by those feelings. The best part of him is a sort of encumbrance to him. So it is with Antony and Cleopatra in MacCallum's view, although it is a view MacCallum retreats from: the best part of them is a sort of encumbrance to them.

MacCallum is insufficiently alive to an important aspect of the study of Shakespeare: he tends to take the words at their face value. That is, he tends to use the words as though it could be proved from them what the characters feel; as though the characters were being, at least sometimes, sincere. However, convincing though the words may often seem to be, it is not always safe to assume that the characters are capable of being sincere. It is true that they seem to mean what they are saying, sometimes; it is also true that we have reason to believe that they do not understand themselves very well at all. Not only the light thrown on to *King Lear* by Regan's remark concerning her father that 'he hath ever but slenderly known himself' (1.2.293), but the extended analysis of blindness and insight conducted in other plays and in the Sonnets will give plenty of evidence that Shakespeare's work is concerned with self-ignorance and its consequences over and over again. Antony is a great orator and to look at any of his speeches for anything other than oratory is to take a great risk in speculation. Cleopatra is, as Bernhard Ten Brink (*Five Lectures on Shakespeare*, 1895) describes her, 'a courtesan of genius',[61] who boasts of having angled for and caught Antony (2.5.10) and whose words and actions are frequently at variance with one another. Why should we believe anything she says?

It is far from impossible though to see that, in this complex and degraded moral world, the feeling from which neither seems to be able to escape for long, the feeling for one another, whatever its nature, is a light of sorts where there is precious little other light. MacCallum implies this more than once but his retreating from it is an indication that, in 1909, at the University of Sydney, he could not sustain the implications of such a view. If, he says, we do not believe that they are really in love, 'the whole interest and dignity of the theme would be gone'.[62] Further: 'If the love were not mutual, Antony would be merely the toy of the courtesan, Cleopatra merely the toy of the sensualist.' There is another way of looking at it, though: they are both, and at once, the toys of one another, the courtesan and the sensualist, and they know it and give in to it. This is not dignified but it is interesting and there is a sort of goodness in it; that people who have spent their lives indulging themselves in a world that only encourages them should right at the end of their careers find themselves fascinated by something other than themselves and be drawn to their deaths because of it may make us think of the 'something missing' of which Mrs Gradgrind complains in a world similarly deprived as described by Dickens in *Hard Times* (1854). It is, above all, consistent with the description of the play that MacCallum has offered, scrupulously obedient to his responses except where he feels the need to rescue Shakespeare's world from itself.[63]

MacCallum has to take the world he is afraid he is revealing by the hand and lead it through Plutarch back to Plato. Plutarch refers to Plato's famous 'horse of the mind' from the *Phaedrus*, and blames it (that is, 'the unreyned lust of concupiscence' – North) for Antony's downfall. MacCallum suggests Plutarch should have consulted the *Symposium*, particularly Aristophanes's contention that people were once four-legged and four-armed and were split into two because they were too happy and now seek ever to find their lost other halves. This MacCallum relates to Goethe and *Wahlverwandschaft* and the love of Antony and Cleopatra is revealed, fully suited in the panoply of Romantic idealism. Finally, MacCallum is able to reconcile Diotima's counterargument to Aristophanes, which is that people only love the good, with Aristophanes's argument:

■ Truly their love, which at first seemed to justify Aristophanes against Diotima, just because it is true love, turns out to answer Diotima's description after all. Or perhaps it rather suggests the conclusion in the *Phaedrus*: 'I have shown this of all inspirations to be the noblest and the highest, and the offspring of the highest; and that he who loves the beautiful, is called a lover, because he partakes of it'. Antony and Cleopatra, with all their errors, are lovers and partake of beauty, which we cannot say of the arid respectability of Octavius. It is well and right that they should perish as they do: but so perishing they have made their full atonement; and we can rejoice that they have at once triumphed over their victor, and left our admiration for them free.[64] □

This rhetorical triumph (for it is not a logical demonstration) is a measure of how hard MacCallum has had to work to lift the love of these two above his own convictions about it, and his difficulties are real difficulties. Primarily they have to do with the convincingness of some of the key passages, for if we have trouble discerning sincerity in some of Shakespeare's characters, we have no trouble wanting to believe that some of what they say is sincere and great trouble reconciling ourselves to the fact that it may not be, and in working out the implications of that uncomfortable fact.

MacCallum, we have seen, included in this discussion only the three plays based upon Plutarch: *Julius Caesar*, *Antony and Cleopatra* and *Coriolanus*. Charney also excludes *Titus Andronicus* on the basis that the Romanness of the Roman plays comprises their use of Roman costume on the Elizabethan stage and praise of suicide, as well as Plutarchan origins.[65] Traversi follows MacCallum and Charney.[66] Brower's perspective is if not all-encompassing then at least much encompassing, seeing the plays in the light of the epic tradition that shapes, in his view, the tragedies as well.[67] Knight also groups the Roman plays with the tragedies.[68]

Cantor discusses only *Antony and Cleopatra* and *Coriolanus*, contrasting empire and republic,[69] and Phillips, pursuing a political model as well, contrasts the three Plutarchan plays with the idea of the *polis* (city state) that he finds in *Troilus and Cressida* and *Timon of Athens*.[70] Paster sees the plays as being interested in the idea of the city, particularly in moments of change from one kind of city to another.[71] Siegel contrasts and compares the English history plays with the Roman. Leggatt sees both sets of plays as interested in political structures and manoeuvring.[72] Platt follows the sequence from the founding of the republic in *The Rape of Lucrece* to the foundation of empire he locates in *Antony and Cleopatra*. He omits *Titus Andronicus* as playing no part in this sequence.[73] Siegel is interested, as Platt is, in the sequence of Rome's own history.[74] Thomas includes *Titus* with the Plutarchan plays and concentrates on a sense of 'social universe' given by the plays' different visions of Rome, a sense of values rather than of exclusively political ideas.[75]

Simmons emphasises an external interpretative framework, claiming that the three 'Plutarchan' plays see the pagan world of their setting 'in the light of Christian historiography', that world having no 'reference beyond the Earthly City'.[76] This is an interesting view as there is no internal evidence to suggest this perspective, although it is at least reasonable to assume that Shakespeare's audiences would have some familiarity with the broad outlines of Christian historiography and especially of the place of Rome in that historiography, all the more so perhaps as the religious conflicts of the time centred upon papal claims for the pre-eminence of Rome over Protestant objections to those claims.

Robert Miola groups all the Roman works together. He cites Roy Walker, who said: 'Shakespeare's idea of Rome was not built in a day, or built at all. Like other living things it was subject to growth and decay, and to trace the course of that organic development is not to impute to the poet a neat plan of construction, conscious from the outset.'[77] Miola comments: 'The inductive approach he outlined and attempted rests on the notion that the Roman works bear a family resemblance to each other and show signs of internal coherence; it allows, however, for the possibility of change, of "growth and decay".'[78] Miola calls the method 'organic'.[79] He claims that 'The poem and the plays are connected by an intricate, yet largely unnoticed and unexplored, network of images, ideas, gestures and scenes',[80] and of the elements of that network, he goes on to assert that 'Viewed in their entirety, they testify compellingly to the coherence of Shakespeare's Roman vision'. Miola claims that Shakespeare's imaginative concern is with the city itself 'as central protagonist',[81] invoked 'by combining various sources, by reworking the political motifs of invasion and rebellion, and by exploring the thematic implications of three Roman ideals: constancy, honor, and *pietas* [the loving respect owed to family, country, and gods]'.

His discussion of *Antony and Cleopatra* has, however, to acknowledge that the *urbs* (city) itself has at best a marginal presence. It appears as the place through which triumphal processions pass, showing off captured foes to 'the common body' for which the emperor himself has nothing but contempt:

■   This common body,
　　Like to a vagabond flag upon the stream,
　　Goes to and back, lackeying the varying tide,
　　To rot itself with motion. □   (1.4.44–7)

This is a vision revisited in *Coriolanus* and prefigured in *Julius Caesar*. However, although the city itself may not appear, its deepest principles are present. Miola suggests that the entrance of the Romans into Cleopatra's monument at the end of the play draws on an important Roman archetype, originating, he argues, in Virgil's account of Pyrrhus breaking into Priam's *penetralia* (the innermost parts of his palace) and, in Shakespeare's Roman works, figured in Tarquin's rape of Lucrece, the rape of Lavinia and even the assassination of Caesar, on which Antony remarks, concerning Caesar's mantle:

■   Look, in this place ran Cassius's dagger through.
　　See what a rent the envious Casca made.
　　Through this the well-belovèd Brutus stabbed;
　　And as he plucked his cursèd steel away,
　　Mark how the blood of Caesar followed it,
　　As rushing out of doors to be resolv'd
　　If Brutus so unkindly knock'd or no. □   (3.2.172–8)

The domestic metaphor invokes the spirit of the *penetralia*, the private space invaded and even desecrated by outsiders. This archetype reappears in the later play with its terms inverted: the Egyptian other, the threatening outsider, is now figured as the mother with the baby at her breast: Caesar himself now appearing as the destructive invader, threatening the pious family.

Much of Miola's essay is dedicated to identifying parallels in classical literature and his method is commentary. He takes the reader through the play effectively, commenting scene by scene. He points out what he claims is 'a pattern of ironic resemblance' to *Julius Caesar*. Antony and Cleopatra's entrance in 1.1 he sees as a parody of Julius Caesar's triumphal entrance in *Julius Caesar* 1.2; the soothsayer provides a further parallel; the news of Fulvia's death affects Antony as that of Portia's death affects Brutus. In each case there is a more self-gratifying motive to be discerned in the later play. The procession is quite literally a parody: fanned by eunuchs, the couple stroll in quite brazen self-satisfaction and self-celebration, where Julius Caesar was at least able to pretend that he thought he was the saviour of Rome; the soothsayer's dreadful doom in the earlier play is replaced by an opportunity for self-indulgent and ribald chatter among Cleopatra's waiting-women in the later; Antony is clearly more interested in Cleopatra than he is in Fulvia and his being recalled to more public matters has an almost comic element to it, as of course it has nothing of the kind in the earlier play.

Miola turns then to a close discussion of the leave-taking, exploring the parallel with the parting of Dido and Aeneas from Virgil's *Aeneid*. Miola acknowledges the extensive discussion of this moment and this parallel, especially the work scholars have put in to show that sources other than Virgil may have been drawn upon.[82] Miola is indebted to Baldwin for the assumption that, as Virgil was an Elizabethan grammar school staple, Shakespeare was drawing on his school days. Miola makes the point that scholars of Virgil are aware that the Roman poet meant to draw a comparison between Dido and Cleopatra (in the course of the description of Cleopatra's death in *Aeneid* VIII, he makes use of a phrase closely resembling a phrase used during his description of the approach of Dido's death in *Aeneid* IV). Certainly the tension between love and duty is associated with both characters. Miola's detailed analysis and comparison is instructive although dependent at one crucial point on a path through Marlowe and that allows one to suspect an indirect rather than a direct influence, if it mattered greatly. To get the parallel to work, Miola has to transpose key moments and, in a manoeuvre characteristic of such arguments, he then claims that the final, considerable, difference between the two scenes follows 'accordingly'. Miola concedes that there is no 'series of fully worked out correspondences' but asserts that 'remembrance of the earlier scene shapes the present one'. I should only quibble with 'remembrance' as involving an unnecessary importation: let us be content with noting the resemblance and refrain from advancing too much further. Miola is honest about the differences between the two scenes and admits that they are 'fundamental and important'. And they are. Miola acknowledges that there is nothing in Dido's speeches comparable to the scorn for honour and Roman ideals in general shown by Cleopatra, and while Dido is tragic in her passion, Cleopatra is still mistress of her wit, whatever her misgivings. Miola regards this differentiation as a mark of Shakespeare's 'continuing absorption with Virgil',[83] describing Virgil as a 'deep source' and claiming that Shakespeare, being able to 'imitate, refashion, and then ignore' this source in the space of a single scene, displays a freedom with regard to the source that merely demonstrates his indebtedness to it.[84]

Miola's discussion of Pompey's place in things is interesting: he argues that the vision offered by the play is that Roman history is cyclical, and that in *Antony and Cleopatra* features of the history dramatised in *Julius*

Caesar are replayed, but in a degenerate form, by the next generation. This time there is no battle; instead a rather sordid compromise is reached. As Miola pithily summarises Pompey's conduct: 'he sells his birthright for Sicily and Sardinia'.[85] In a similar vein, while Ventidius's victory over the son of the man responsible for the death of Marcus Crassus, a member, along with Pompey's father, of the first triumvirate, seems to have exacted an appropriate revenge, the scene is the occasion for his cynical reflections on the potential disadvantages of success for officers in subordinate positions (3.1.1–27). The presentation of Antony and Octavius as rivals in a slightly shoddy set of contests is a significant departure from Virgil, who presents Octavius as the chosen agent of destiny in a clearly unfolding and preordained plan culminating in a decisive victory (at Actium) over the forces of disorder. Shakespeare not only humanises, he personalises, so that the rhetoric of destiny seems only rhetoric, cynically deployed in a power struggle between selfish men who it is difficult to choose between, as the vices of the one make him more sympathetic than the virtues of the other. It has to be said, however, that the same is true of the rhetoric of love.

Miola devotes some time to attempting to establish a connection between Virgil's *Georgics* III and *Antony and Cleopatra* through a careful discussion of Scarus's 'ribaudred nag' remark (3.10.10) and Enobarbus's aside at 3.7.6–9 about the inadvisability of men and women serving together in armies. At times the discussion is strained, and the links far from obvious and not altogether convincing. Miola's conclusion reveals the weakness of the form of analysis:

> ■ Shakespeare's use of images from the *Georgics* deflates the grandeur of Antony and Cleopatra by bringing them down to the level of beasts; such borrowing, however, simultaneously exalts the human lovers by suggesting that their love partakes in the natural and universal power of *eros*:
>
> > Omne adeo genus in terries hominumque ferarumque,
> > et genus aequoreum, pecudes pictaeque volucres,
> > in furias ignemque runt: amor omnibus idem. (242–4)
>
> > Yea, every single race on earth, man and beast, the tribes of the sea, cattle and birds brilliant of hue, rush into fires of passion: all feel the same Love. □

Enobarbus's remark does all that Miola says here: Virgil is not needed.

Miola's description of Antony's attempt to revive his honour is compelling. He is especially sharp on the ambiguous nature of the enterprise in the eyes of the audience:

> ■ We wonder if Antony is striking a noble pose instead of choosing a noble action, playing a heroic part instead of actually becoming a hero.[86] □

Miola takes a generally sympathetic view of Antony's death, picking
out the way in which the circumstances build up to it: Enobarbus's
repentance and death, which, incidentally, Hazlitt found 'the most
affecting part of the play';[87] Antony's reflections on clouds (4.14.3ff.),
which Markels describes, accurately, as expressing 'a profoundly tragic
view of mutability';[88] and the betrayal of Decretas. His actions seem to
be 'the last honourable option of a Roman soldier in a base world'.[89]
Miola compares the actions of Antony to the deaths of Cassius and
Brutus and notes significant parallels: Cassius commits suicide (and is
assisted) to avoid humiliation as does Brutus; both Brutus and Antony
are seen as having been conquered only by themselves.

However, in Miola's view, Antony repudiates Rome: his divesting
himself of his armour is a symbolic act.[90] Miola sees the suicide as an
attempt at least to rejoin Cleopatra, pointing to Antony's vision of a
reunion between Dido and Aeneas, which, as Miola says, is Antony's
own. Miola comments: 'He decides the archetypal conflict between
duty and love in favour of love'.[91] Further, he argues that the death in
the monument 'unites him with Cleopatra, spiritually and sexually, and
marks a new beginning'.[92]

Antony's death marks, for Miola, the beginning of a final stage in
the movement of the play in which Cleopatra becomes the bride to
Antony's bridegroom. He claims that the ending of the play is a 'transcendent reunion' and says that, for both characters, the change involves
'a repudiation of mythological fancy and a recognition of human real-
ities'. Having said this, Miola's description of Cleopatra's last moments
is heavily mythologised and emblematised, drawing on the work of a
range of scholars who have seen a great variety of references in this
scene, or who have convinced themselves that these things can be seen.
Janet Adelman is quoted, for example, as seeing the serpent as 'a
strange divinity', a contradictory figure who 'kills and gives life, is old
and young, moves and is motionless', further suggesting that the trans-
ferring of the serpent's bite from her arm (in Plutarch) to her breast
makes use of 'the force of an ancient image for Terra, the generative
mother earth, who was frequently portrayed nourishing serpents'.[93]
Miola wants to bring in Cesare Ripa (?1560–1625), whose *Iconologia*
(1611) was used by Ben Jonson for his masques. Ripa's serpents are
symbols of guilt, bad conscience, and 'may lie behind Shakespeare's
portrayal of Cleopatra',[94] or, we may say, they may not. Miola continues the theme, asking whether there are masque elements in *Antony
and Cleopatra*, drawing in Stephen Orgel, who writes interestingly of the
masques that they inhabit an uncertain territory between revels and
antimasque, between order and riot, admitting both but identifying themselves with neither.[95] However, costume and scenery do not make a
masque: it would be more pertinent to discuss Jonson's works as bearing

some relationship to *Antony and Cleopatra*, as they clearly do in the uneasy compromises they offer between the world of duty and the world of licence.

Miola recognises finally that Rome, which at first appears to be 'a place of *gravitas* [dignity and solemnity] in conflict with Egyptian *voluptas* [pleasure]', is more complicated, as criticism has shown;[96] he also recognises that *Antony and Cleopatra* is, in some important respects, a departure from the previous Roman works and, hence, from the Virgilian tradition he has been emphasising throughout. The importance of the family, clear enough in *Titus Andronicus* or *The Rape of Lucrece*, is almost absent from the later play, Fulvia and Octavia being hardly dramatised by Shakespeare at all (in which respect, as in others, he is unlike Robert Garnier or Samuel Daniel, Miola notes, who are more thoroughly in touch with Virgilian *pietas* – sense of duty, loyalty); the character of Cleopatra is given a prominence and a personality quite unfitted to her Virgilian role, that of 'Dido, Circe, Amata, and Juno – the exotic and powerful female who threatens the march of Roman history'.[97] Cleopatra is all that of course, but the play has no sense of Roman history of the kind Virgil is promoting. What Miola has said about Antony is to the point: Rome is seen quite as much as a place of power struggles as a site of virtue and the presentation of Octavius's victory is quite un-Virgilian.

Miola comments on the complexities of the presentation, often overlooked, he suggests, by approaches that take a moral or even a political approach.[98] These approaches often merge into one another and bring out the significance of the reign of Augustus for subsequent history as well as for Roman history, especially for Christian interpretations of history. As Miola points out, 'the Caesar who comes to power in Shakespeare's play, however, little resembles the hallowed Augustus of such legend'.[99] History in this play 'seems undular [wave-like] and cyclical rather than teleological [moving towards a goal]' when it is compared with *Julius Caesar*. Complexity and ambivalence deprive the play of any apparent conviction. The various alternatives seem to be part of a 'vacillating rhythm' that, as Miola observes, 'may be part of some greater harmony' but equally well may be 'merely the movement of the varying tide that rots all things with incessant motion'. This is an important observation and is well put: attempts to find our views reflected in this play are always confounded, ruthless as it is in the exposition of what happens when the contrasting visions of people so radically self-absorbed as to be unaware of any other way of seeing things come into conflict.

Although separated by some years, MacCallum and Miola share many critical assumptions. The critics to be considered in the next chapter have made a break with almost all those assumptions.

CHAPTER EIGHT

The Romanness of the Roman Plays (2)

Coppélia Kahn's focus is on *virtus* (Latin for courage, manhood, military skill, goodness, moral perfection) as a defining characteristic; for her analysis, *virtus* is the essence of the works based upon Roman subject matter. She describes her claim succinctly:

> ■ That Shakespeare's Roman works articulate a critique of the ideology of gender on which the Renaissance understanding of Rome was based.[1] □

She shows that the Renaissance understanding of Rome was in fact based upon an ideology of gender. To do this, she argues first that, in any society, 'the discursive practices of culture make bodily and other differences between human beings into a gender system that makes men as well as women'.[2] Her argument, she acknowledges, owes much to Louis Althusser (1918–90), especially to his theory of 'interpellation'. In French, *interpellation* commonly means being taken in for questioning by the police. Althusser imagines a person being hailed by a policeman who wishes to take him in for questioning and recognising that he is the person addressed by the call. Interpellation, then, involves a call and a recognition: one comes to recognise oneself in being called. We may say that 'society' or 'culture' does the calling: prior to being called we are unaware that we are anything at all; once we are called we recognise ourselves as the one who is called in the manner in which we are addressed. As Judith Butler (1956–) has argued, as soon as a baby is born and someone calls out 'It's a girl!', then a series of such 'interpellations' (as Althusser would say) begin, as a result of which the person comes to recognise themselves as the one called in the way in which they are called; as what they are being called as.[3]

Kahn argues that masculinity in Shakespeare's works is 'an ideology discursively maintained through the appropriation of the Latin heritage for the early modern stage'.[4] This 'appropriation' is further defined as 'the intertextuality of Shakespeare and the Latin authors he read'. 'Intertextuality' is a notion associated with Julia Kristeva (1941–) and means that any text may be considered as a mosaic of references to other texts and cannot thus be regarded as autonomous or bounded but can only be understood as an incident in a continuing process of textual production, a continuous weaving of text (in Latin, *textus* means woven).[5] The connection with a notion of discourse can easily be made: all conversation, thought, spoken or written, can be conceived of as an incident in continuing 'intertextuality'. Kahn's concern is to show the 'degree to which Romanness is virtually identical with an ideology of masculinity' in these plays, which, she claims, has hitherto gone unnoticed.

Kahn briskly summarises largely twentieth-century discussion of Shakespeare and Rome, quoting Hunter's remark that for the English Renaissance 'the Roman past was … not simply *a* past but *the* past',[6] and making the link with the chronicle tradition of Geoffrey of Monmouth (?1100–55) and others that Britain was founded by Brutus, grandson of Aeneas, the founder of Rome.[7] Kahn then surveys Renaissance education with the aid of Anthony Grafton and Lisa Jardine and T.W. Baldwin,[8] even employing some of Baldwin's argumentative strategies, as indeed she has earlier in remarking 'the intertextuality of Shakespeare *and the Latin authors he read* (my emphasis)'. Discussing William Page's grammar lesson from *The Merry Wives of Windsor*, Kahn comments that Page is learning the fundamentals of Latin grammar 'probably much as young William Shakespeare had'[9] and describes the grammar book as 'probably one written by William Lilly [1602–81] and John Colet [?1467–1519] and commanded by Edward VI [1537–53] to be used in all schools'. For 'probably' read 'possibly' or 'perhaps not at all'. Furthermore, an analogy between education and the commonplace book, between the practice of learning by rote gobbets from the authors in school to the practice of regurgitating gobbets in conversation to impress, may well describe the behaviour of a good many English persons of the time but of course cannot (and Kahn does not pretend that it can) account for the significance of classical learning for English Renaissance culture as a whole.

What it can do is indicate a background of patchy acquaintance with Roman writing and history that historians of the Renaissance can guess was quite widespread and therefore quite likely to be something on which a popular playwright could capitalise. It suggests that a frame of reference existed with which the playwright could work. Kahn quotes with approval Karen Newman's description of Renaissance drama as enjoying a 'liminal' (Latin *limina*, threshold) position, neither wholly popular nor wholly elite but enjoyed by both ends of the social spectrum,[10] and Phyllis Rackin's comment that the drama was 'a radically different discursive field' from humanistic scholarship or historiography.[11]

The position of the theatre was, it is true, an interesting one. Companies of players were organised as joint-stock companies but were also often associated with aristocratic patronage and even royal patronage (although this did not always or even often mean much in terms of income). The London theatres were located outside the City to escape its jurisdiction but close enough to entertain its citizens, and the plays and players were often the object of contempt, dislike and even persecution.[12] Kahn sees the plays and players as occupying a marginal position and enjoying a peculiar fluidity of social and political definition.[13]

Kahn contrasts the Roman plays with the English historical plays, arguing that no comparable history was available to Shakespeare for his Roman works, although not demonstrating that his concern was to do with Roman history what he had done and was to do with English history: she quotes Rackin's opinion that the English history play was 'largely Shakespeare's creation'[14] and comments that 'the Roman play was not Shakespeare's creation', on the basis of Clifford Ronan's catalogue of forty-three vernacular 'Roman' plays between 1585 and 1635.[15] This forgets how controversial the category 'Roman' play has been even when debate is restricted to Shakespeare's work. Kahn settles on a sensible definition: 'I would define Roman plays as those whose plots and characters are based on Roman history and legend ... and set in Rome.'[16] However, she wants to include *The Rape of Lucrece* in her survey, and that is not a play at all.

Kahn offers an analogy between the provision of models for emulation from Roman history and legend and the emulation the humanist teacher was supposed to inspire in his charges, drawing on Richard Halpern's application of Althusser's theory of interpellation to the period.[17] She then points to the pageant of the nine worthies in *Love's Labours Lost* as offering a view of a possibility of 'the kind of satirical detachment [such shows] could provoke, perhaps drawing on class resentment in those who lacked access to the humanistic studies',[18] citing Costard the clown who translates Pompeius Magnus as Pompey the Big. There is a comparison to be made here with Mistress Quickly's misreadings of the elements of William Page's grammar lesson, to which Kahn referred earlier.

Kahn describes Plutarch's *Lives* as 'a treasury of exemplars', arguing that it embodied 'an ethically orientated sense of *romanitas* [Romanness]' and quoting Hunter's description of this as 'a set of virtues, thought of as characterizing Roman civilisation – soldierly, severe, self-controlled, self-disciplined ... transmitted to the Tudors, as to the rest of Europe, in a series of images of virtue held up as models or secular *mirabilia* [wonders]'.[19]

However, Shakespeare's approach to Rome differs from that of his contemporaries: 'He takes Rome more seriously and sees its heroes more critically than others do'.[20] Shakespeare's Rome is more particularised and more consistent than that of George Chapman (*c.* 1560–1634) or

Thomas Heywood (1573–1641) or Lodge, and Jonson is concerned to present exemplars. Shakespeare creates a world:

■ Skilfully deploying details culled from Livy [Titus Livius, Roman histor-ian, 59 BC–AD 17] or Plutarch, he evokes the workings of a republic or an empire, making them intelligible to the subjects of a monarchy.[21] □

Most importantly, in Kahn's view, 'Shakespeare made the gender-specific dimensions of exemplars dramatically interesting' by showing them to be 'ideological constructions coterminous with the meaning of Rome itself'. This is an important point. The virtues after which char-acters strive or in the light of which they judge their failures are not merely the characteristics of particular persons whose conduct is to be emulated but the ideological lynchpins of Roman civilisation; they are not naturally emergent but socially constructed; not innate but induced. In a patriarchal society, in which the state sees itself modelled on the family, at the head of which is the *paterfamilias* (father of the family), in which female chastity is to be jealously guarded (women are to be constrained or ideologically conditioned to constrain themselves, as well as literally protected from men's attentions), the virtues that tend to the maintenance of such an order are, unsurprisingly, those most cherished. This, in itself, is not to say very much. It is harder to imagine a society in which virtues are officially promoted that tend to the disorder of that society than it is to imagine the opposite. However, Kahn is not merely saying that Roman virtues tended to maintain the order of Rome: but that such an order is maintained at the expense of some of its members and their interests. This situation is in conflict with some of its deepest impulses, and not merely because virtue is always in a struggle with the temptation to vice, but because virtues may find themselves conflicting with other virtues.

It is not new to claim that societies maintain their existence at the expense of the desires of some of their members. The control and discip-line of the members of a society are matched by self-control and self-discipline on their part in pursuit of a higher good than self-gratification. Arguments concerned with the concept of ideology tend, however, to argue that the higher good is an illusion and that the expense is borne by a class systematically discriminated against. Such systematic discrimin-ation, it is held, cannot be sustained without incurring the penalty of run-ning into contradictions among the ideas upon which the society bases its claim to be in pursuit of a higher good. Developments in feminist theory in the late twentieth century have argued that the apparent, temporary and illusory, stability enjoyed by a society sustained by such ideological constructions is brought about through 'processes of differentiation and distinction, requiring the suppression of ambiguities and opposite elements' in order to maintain stability:[22]

■ Like any discursive construction of gender difference, then, *virtus* proves to be at odds with itself, and its contradictions give these texts their complexity and energy.[23] □

Kahn specifies three 'foci' of Shakespeare's 'problematic of Roman virtue': warriors, wounds, and women, which become the subtitle of her book. Warrior leads straight into a consideration of 'emulation': the eager imitation that becomes rivalry, competition, struggle and eventual defeat and destruction:

■ Emulation figures and enacts the differences *within* the masculine; thus it fractures a seemingly unified *virtus*. □

Kahn relates this to the Renaissance humanist use of the figure of emulation to describe the process of education, and argues that 'the Roman works touch a cultural nerve and articulate contemporary anxieties about English "manly virtue" '.[24] I think this is to play down excessively the extent to which the writers to whom she refers (such as Sir Thomas Elyot, ?1499–1546) were conscious that the educational contest, with oneself or with others, was modelled on or figured after this more dangerous form of emulation, and the jump to 'anxieties about English "manly virtue" ' needs more demonstration than it receives at this point, but the parallel is interesting.

Kahn quotes with approval Bruce Smith's interpretation of Plutarch's position in sixteenth-century England:

■ For most sixteenth-century readers the very act of reading North's translation of Plutarch was an exercise in homosociality ... Noble men's lives are the *subject* of North's book, in more ways than one. Inspiring his readers to emulate 'the speciall acts of the best persons, of the famosest nations of the world ...' is North's very purpose.[25] □

She comments: 'Thus North's readers not only read about emulation but also participated in it'. She goes on to construe Plutarch's purpose as being to incite a competitive spirit between Greeks and Romans:

■ By pairing Greek with Roman exemplars and then comparing the members of eighteen out of twenty-three pairs, Plutarch implicitly sets up rivalries between Greeks and Romans, setting one against another.[26] □

She then says:

■ Shakespeare echoes this dyadic structure by pairing his Roman heroes with rivals: Tarquin and Collatine, Saturninus and Bassianus, Brutus and Cassius, Coriolanus and Aufidius, Antony and Octavius.[27] □

However, Plutarch does not 'implicitly [set] up rivalries between Greeks and Romans': his explicit purpose is to show comparability between the two civilisations, both of which he admired for different but complementary qualities. We may choose to enter into a spirit of competition for reasons of our own and attempt to incite a sense of rivalry, but we should not attempt to enlist Plutarch's support in this endeavour: he may have provided grounds for us but that is not the same thing at all as inciting the spirit we have introduced. Nor does Shakespeare echo this 'dyadic structure' in particular more than any other pairing: his paired figures, as Kahn's list emphasises, are all Romans.

Kahn then explains the subtitle of her text, *Warriors, Wounds and Women*. Invoking feminist 'critiques or appropriations' of the work of Sigmund Freud (1856–1939)[28], Kahn claims that the wound operates as a fetish:

■ The wound attests to a (feminine) vulnerability but at the same time, serves as a cultural marker of manly virtue; like a fetish, it both declares and disavows the feminine.[29] □

Her conclusion and central argument is that:

■ Poised, as it were, between 'warriors' (men locked in agonistic structures of rivalry), and 'women', the wound in these texts is always a site of anxiety and indeterminacy; a point at which it is possible to identify an ideology of gender difference in process. □

Central to this argument is an insistence that emulation is itself an internally disrupted category, signifying at once an identification of the emulator with the emulated and a potentially catastrophic competitive struggle on the part of the emulator to exceed the achievement of the emulated.[30] The 'ideology of gender difference' identified by Kahn 'is built on the binary oppositions of male to female, public to private, *forum* [marketplace] to *domus* [house, home]'.[31] Kahn quotes Shoshana Felman's formulation, claiming to be able to show in Shakespeare's texts how the feminine is not 'outside the masculine, its reassuring canny *opposite*', but 'inside the masculine, its uncanny *difference from itself*'.[32]

In attempting to specify and pin down categories such as masculine and feminine, cultures produce sterile, one-sided stabilities that they defend anxiously, ever watchful to fend off and close down any tendency towards change and indeterminacy, insisting that the complex is simple and the mixed pure. A similar tendency to stabilise class structures to keep people in their places has been observed by Marxists. The tendency to simplify may be observed of Octavius in his disapproval of Antony's seduction by Egyptian culture in the person of Cleopatra.

Kahn's perspective may be summarised as a blend of highly theoretical positions, drawn from Louis Althusser's conception of ideology, for example, and a more pragmatic reasonableness, such as is revealed in the following remark:

> ■ Through exemplars such as the noble Romans whom Shakespeare took as his heroes, humanism made Romanness as manly virtue a widely known ideal of masculinity. When Shakespeare 'translated' that ideal to the public theatre, he opened it up for critical scrutiny by a socially diverse audience that had long been encouraged to consider Rome as a mirror of England.[33] □

This is unexceptionable. A 'socially diverse audience' might well be expected to appreciate such pictures as it was given in many different ways and a canny playwright might be expected to take advantage of this and exploit the ironies and ambiguities in such pictures that such differing interpretation would throw up.

Kahn describes the play as possibly 'Shakespeare's last Roman experiment', based on David Bevington giving 1608 as the latest possible date for *Antony and Cleopatra* and dating *Coriolanus* in 1608, as well as on the basis of allusions and some stylistic features,[34] and says that it is at least 'his most daring and original':

> ■ An attempt to transmute Roman matter and style into a glittering if unstable new alloy of mettle and mutability, a Rome drawn to, and repelled by, and finally fused with what is Other to it.[35] □

She notes Leslie Thomson's observation of the contrast between 'romantic matter' and 'realistic manner', and Michael Neill's identification of 'hyperbole' as the play's structural principle, a tendency always to reach too high and tip over into bathos. She quotes with approval Janet Adelman's description of the play as 'resolutely tragic-comic ... a tragic experience embedded in a comic structure'[36].

Kahn comments that many critics have seen the play in terms of sets of oppositions: Rome and Egypt, 'war and love, public and private, duty and pleasure, reason and sensuality, male and female' that 'form the framework within which the play means'. What 'the play means' within this framework is 'a Roman warrior seduced by an Egyptian queen'. However, although such an opposition can truly be discerned in the play, simply restating it, Kahn argues, prevents us from looking at it critically.

Kahn refers to critics who have gone so far as to dispute that there is an opposition at all and cites Jonathan Dollimore, who argues that 'sexual desire is not that which transcends politics and power, but the vehicle of politics and power',[37] and Linda Charnes, who claims that it is 'an act of misrecognition' to hold that Antony and Cleopatra succeed in transcending the world of politics.[38] Kahn argues that even when critics do not take sides in this opposition, it acquires the status of a truth of nature; that 'Rome' and 'Egypt' become, as it were, principles, like love and duty, for example, and that, in consequence, Antony's Romanness 'is implicitly unified and coherent', and Cleopatra's Egyptianness is 'an external threat to it'.[39] This means that we are discouraged from looking at 'Romanness' and 'Egyptianness' as sides of the same coin, as it were, mutually defining, or aspects of each other; rather we tend to see them as independent of each other and self-contained.

Kahn's whole argument depends upon the proposition that gender ideologies are, as it were, splittings-off of characteristics that are only theoretically separable, and systematic, indeed socially institutionalised, identifications of these characteristics with human beings who are male or female.[40] This social construction of gender identities is susceptible to analysis and demonstration: it can be taken apart so that we can see how it was put together and, if we can take it apart theoretically, we can hope at least to reconstruct it on a new basis, if it is not possible to avoid constructions altogether.

Kahn claims that the tendency to focus on the morality play, as it were, offered by a concentration on these polar opposites, has obscured an equally important relationship, that between Antony and Octavius. These two are locked in a battle of emulation and as such constitute 'a difference within *virtus* and within Rome'. 'Within' because what so often seems to be being discussed as a principle is in fact a set of characteristics that are not held together by a natural harmony but by virtue of political expediency and because of the necessity of maintaining a social structure. Kahn argues that the Latin literary heritage on which Shakespeare drew was heavily influenced by the 'Augustans', Virgil, Ovid, Horace, who owed their position to Octavius, to whom the Senate granted the title Augustus (the exalted) in 27 BC, along with the power to rule Rome's civil, military, political and religious affairs, in effect appointing him emperor. Kahn cites Lucy Hughes-Hallett who claims that 'Cleopatra was Rome's enemy, and we in the West are Rome's heirs'.[41] Kahn goes further, claiming that Octavius used Cleopatra's image as Rome's 'Other' – oriental, female, sensual – as a propaganda weapon in his struggle to defeat Antony as a rival and to establish himself as the undisputed sole ruler of the empire, and that Shakespeare:

■ Fell heir to a legacy of representation on which the Latin curriculum and the *studia humanitatis* [study of humanity] of the Renaissance were founded, a legacy organized by and centring on the mythic construction of Octavius Caesar as the destined victor in a prolonged power struggle who instituted the *pax romana* [Roman peace, that is, peace brought about by and protected by Rome, in other words, the Roman Empire] that ushered in the Christian era.[42] □

This is a large claim and it should be quickly observed that although Octavius might be credited with the inspiration of the first half of this picture of historical development, the Fathers of the Christian Church have something to do with its completion. It is true that Virgil is keen to represent Rome's history as shaped towards his own era but the shaping towards Shakespeare's era took a bit longer and was conducted by men and women whose interests were served by Octavius's ambitions but whose own ambitions went a little further.

The play, in Kahn's view, is directed towards the suicide attempt that gives Antony his fatal wound, a wound that, in keeping with the theory encapsulated in her subtitle, strands Antony at the end between 'warrior', what he was, and 'woman', not only Cleopatra herself but also what Antony was already becoming, in Rome's view, and what he must now become completely.

Kahn cites others who have written on male bonding in the Roman plays,[43] arguing that Antony and Octavius are paired as Coriolanus and Aufidius are paired, as Brutus and Cassius are paired, although on a different basis: 'they mirror each other in a blinding desire for *imperium* [empire]'.[44] She imputes significance to the soothsayer's remarks, suggesting that the prophecy makes the contest between them seem fated and she comments on the hapless intermediaries (Lepidus, Octavia) who drive them asunder as much as they weld them together. Octavia is especially significant, as Claire Kinney notes: 'The mediating female is gradually obliterated; Rome's central relationship is between male rivals'.[45] Kahn comments: 'the female term being suppressed while the male one is doubled'.[46]

However, in the relationship with Cleopatra, Antony finds himself caught up in a vicious circle:

■ Antony's attraction to Cleopatra, rather than simply feminizing him in the service of her lust (as the Romans believe), in fact enters into the dynamics of rivalry. His surrenders to her wily charms, combined with her perceived betrayals, impel him to reassert his masculinity and his Roman identity precisely through his emulous bond with Caesar.[47] □

Kahn follows Linda Fitz in arguing that Shakespeare's version of the battle of Actium serves to 'mitigate Cleopatra's culpability'.[48] She goes further to claim that Shakespeare dramatises the entire process by which Cleopatra is made to appear to be to blame, citing Ania Loomba's perception that Shakespeare does not simply present a stereotypical version of Cleopatra 'but depicts it as constructed by various male perspectives in the play'.[49] She insists, with Fitz, that scene 3.7 shows us Antony determining to fight at sea to accept Caesar's dare to him to do exactly that. Cleopatra merely endorses a decision Antony has already made. This reading of the scene is not impossible but depends upon our interpreting Antony's remark that Caesar 'dares us to't' (3.7.29) more literally than might be prudent and ignores the by-play between Cleopatra and Antony that immediately precedes the remark. Antony enters at 3.7.19 with Canidius, both already in conversation. Antony is clearly made anxious by Caesar's swift progress and he comments on it to Cleopatra, who responds 'Celerity is never more admir'd/Than by the negligent'. Now Cleopatra has just been arguing with Enobarbus that she has as good a right to be personally present in the forthcoming battle as any man and Antony's response to her remark

■ A good rebuke
   That might become the best of men
   To taunt at slackness. □

may indicate that her purpose has been to appear suitably manly and that it has been achieved. However we take her remark, its immediate effect is to determine his resolve to fight at sea. His next words are 'Canidius, we/Will fight with him by sea' and Cleopatra responds, 'By sea, what else?' This does not seem to be a sensible decision; furthermore, it does not arise out of a discussion but appears to be quite unconsidered, a sudden whim. In fact, one obvious interpretation of the moment is that Cleopatra's remark has unfavourably compared Antony's capacity for swift and decisive action with Octavius's and he is stung into a rash decision to impress her.

The Romans clearly blame Cleopatra, as in the conversation between Scarus and Enobarbus immediately after the battle in 3.10, but that simply confirms the view that Fitz and Loomba take, which Kahn is developing. However, Caesar's 'dare' is in fact not explicit, but implicit, and only brought out, we might think, by Cleopatra comparing his speed to what appears to be, by way of contrast perhaps, Antony dragging his feet. If this was meant to show how manly she could be, it does certainly also provoke Antony's defensive pride, in this case to a ruinous error of judgement. Had he remained cool, it is by no means clear that he would still have taken Caesar's speedy progress as an implicit challenge, and there is no indication before Cleopatra speaks that he has done so.

The question of Cleopatra's flight is also vexing: Kahn wants to hold that a sufficient explanation is that Cleopatra simply was not manly enough for the battle, but she admits that when Antony insists that she knew he would follow, Cleopatra does not deny this. Kahn concludes that the picture persists that a woman who covets political power will deprive men of their power, both political and sexual. In fact, running through Kahn's discussion is the belief that the play is about Antony's struggle for his identity. She quotes approvingly Madelon Gohlke and

Richard Wheeler who both argue that Antony's identity is in crisis: Wheeler arguing that Antony represents a typically Shakespearean picture of a hero torn between the desire to merge with another and the anxious recoil into separateness; Gohlke seeing Antony as an example of the paradoxical masculine view (that she calls a 'fantasy') that femininity is weakness but that women are powerful, further seeing this view as a prime motive behind the masculine dominance that is designed to work against such a view taking shape. Neill sees him as a victim of an artificially stable Roman identity; Dollimore as an almost quixotic figure, a picture of a kind of *virtus* outmoded by the emergence of empire with its political realism. Janet Adelman and Peter Erickson interpret Antony's 'o'erflow[ing] the measure' as an identification with female bounty, or at least an acceptance of and submission to it; Cynthia Marshall regards him as caught between the image he has of himself and his actual performance in reality.[50]

These critics' views converge well with Kahn's purpose: to view Antony as a construction, just as Cleopatra and Octavius are constructions, of a dominant gender ideology that 'interpellates' (Louis Althusser's term) men and women into being the people they feel they have to become. Her analysis of the whipping of Thidias (3.13) is a good example of her method. This scene is a low point for Antony. He seeks to recover his self-esteem and the esteem of others by a futile gesture, a challenge to Octavius to single combat. This may suggest that the 'dare' he seems to have seen in Octavius's swift advance – whether or not his seeing this was prompted by Cleopatra – still rankles, and when Octavius's messenger offers to kiss Cleopatra's hand, his jealous fury slips the leash. Kahn sees this scene as an attempt by Antony to restore his image and status as a man and a revelation of his fury at Cleopatra that she has 'leveled him with Caesar's servant':[51]

■ Though both the rhetoric and the spectacle of Thidias's whipping are mere show – symbolic surrogates for the sexual and political leverage Antony has lost – the scene serves to demystify Antony's 'loss of self', the melting of his charisma, through dramatizing the gendered physical modes by which a Roman hero actively carves out his place in the hierarchy of power and status. □

It is not a new perception that Antony shows himself up poorly in this scene: after all, the event is what decides Enobarbus to leave him and the next scene starts with Octavius's contemptuous rejection of the challenge 'the old ruffian' has presented. What Kahn offers is a theoretical framework within which to see this that does not so much throw new light on the scene as offer another way of describing what is going on in it.

By far the longest and most interesting section of the essay is a discussion of Antony's suicide, which argues that far from being offered to us as a mishandled and failed attempt, his suicide fits precisely the model afforded by Cato (Marius Porcius Cato, 95–46 BC, who supported Pompey against Caesar and killed himself in Africa on learning of Caesar's victory over Pompey at Thapsus) and much admired (although complicated by Christian teaching against suicide) throughout the Renaissance.

Kahn insists that Antony's commitment to his rivalry with Octavius is constant, while his commitment to Cleopatra rises and falls as his fortunes rise and fall, and she says that Cleopatra's pretence that she has committed suicide is a device to win back his love from this ruinous rivalry. Thus Antony:

■ Rewrites the female scenario of duplicity in the service of love that is encoded in the Lichas image into a male scenario of honour reclaimed through death.[52] □

Lichas is the messenger who brought Hercules the shirt of Nessus from Deianira, who believes that Nessus has dipped the shirt in a love potion, hoping to regain Hercules' love through this ruse. When the shirt bursts into flames, Hercules, enraged, throws Lichas up to the moon. Antony likens himself to Hercules in his speech at 4.12.43–7.[53] The suicide event, from the preparation through to the monument scene, Kahn reads in terms of the ideology of *virtus*. Much is made of the name of Antony's companion, Eros, enabling Kahn to describe the scene as 'an affair between men',[54] which is not incorrect, but hints at more than it can demonstrate.[55] Kahn goes along with Antony's descriptions of his reasons for seeking death, accepting his account that it is his means of avoiding humiliation at Caesar's hands, and interpreting the event as an attempt to reclaim the honour he has lost through his flight from Actium.

Kahn quotes Helms approvingly, agreeing that Cleopatra's death renders her sexuality (with its power to feminise men) safe at last. Helms speaks of 'an achieved rite of passage' from sexual free agent (or loose cannon) to wife and Kahn confirms this view.[56] It is not impossible to argue though that the claim to have become at last Antony's wife is a poignant irony. Such a view is not incompatible with Kahn's quite different way of discussing the ending of the play. In Kahn's view (which might be thought of as an anthropological approach; the approach taken by an investigator from one culture towards a quite different culture), the symbolic rite of marriage (symbolised itself, in this instance) contains Cleopatra's 'erotic potency' and brings to a close the otherwise 'endless cycle of satisfaction and arousal'.

Ania Loomba offers an interesting way of seeing the play. She argues that:

■ Three centuries of critical opinion, from Samuel Johnson onwards, has been preoccupied with 'overcoming' the heterogeneous nature of both the form and the content of Shakespeare's *Antony and Cleopatra*: the focus has variously been on its disjointed structure, mingling of tragic and comic, flux in character; its divisions between private and public, male and female, high and low life; on what Danby[57] has called the 'dialectic' of the text. However a correlation of these various binaries – the thematic oppositions, the broken structure, its treatment of fluid gender and racial identity – has yet to be attempted.[58] □

This Loomba attempts by noting that:

■ The issues of imperial expansion, political power and sexual domination are dramatically compressed into spatial and geographical shifts and metaphors.[59] □

She describes these movements as 'almost cinematic', noting that power 'is at once something concrete – land, kingdoms, wealth – and something relatively abstract – emotions, ideology and sexuality', insisting that theatrical space 'is not just an inert arena but interacts with the text's treatment of social and psychological space'.[60] Loomba reminds us how frequently the boundaries between domains and different spaces are transgressed or ignored: how expansionist and inclusive the vision of the lovers can be, quoting Cleopatra: 'I'll set a bourn how far to be beloved' and Antony's response: 'Then must thou needs find out new heaven, new earth' (1.1.16–17).

In the play, 'objective space is always invested with political or emotional connotations'[61] and Antony's movements between Rome and Egypt and between Octavia and Cleopatra are a doomed attempt to occupy two contradictory sets of both public and private spaces simultaneously. Interestingly, Loomba sees the decision to fight at sea in terms of an emblematic choice between 'the Roman element, land, or Cleopatra's medium, water'. Loomba regards Cleopatra as 'unique among the independent women in Renaissance drama, for she appears to command her own spaces';[62] nevertheless, this command is threatened politically by Rome and in gender terms by the 'contradictions of heterosexual love' (the transfer of power from the woman as beloved to the man as husband). Importantly, Loomba notes that:

■ However slippery, inconstant and variable Cleopatra may be, however she may threaten the boundaries between male and female, political and private worlds, she remains geographically stationary.[63] □

Loomba believes that Cleopatra cannot reconcile the private and public worlds, being unable to dominate in both simultaneously: 'She can either function within the private life of a man, or enter politics as an honorary man and chaste woman, like Elizabeth [1533–1603; reigned 1558–1603]'.[64] Whether this is because she cannot, in principle, accomplish this double dominance, or because the narrative shows that she in fact does not, is not made clear.

Whereas 'the last act appears to "resolve" the various tensions of the play', Cleopatra is only able to achieve resolution after Antony has died and the poetry, which 'has been seen as sublime', shows 'the politics of sublimation, rather than a transcendence of politics'. Further, she seems to abandon Egypt for Rome, adopting 'the high Roman fashion' but also, most importantly perhaps, 'if these moves reflect Cleopatra's contradictions, they are also strategic and constitute the unruly woman's last performances':[65]

■ Her suicide clouds her political defeat with mystic glamour and a show of autonomy. Her own body is the last 'space' to be wrested from Roman control. The asp will bring her 'liberty' in the absence of real territory. The maternal image of the snake at her breast tames her own earlier identification with the serpent, replacing the deadly Eastern inscrutability with a comprehensible version of the Madonna.[66] □

Further still, though, as Loomba points out:

■ Of course *both* are patriarchal constructions of women. The first demonises the alien woman while the second seeks to domesticise her.[67] □

These resolutions Loomba calls 'false resolutions' and points out that the movements she describes as 'cinematic' come to an end and are replaced by 'the conventional "climax" and the stock devices of formal drama, as patriarchal roles and divisions are apparently reinstated'.[68]

■ The narrative of masculinity and imperialism regains control but Cleopatra's final performance, which certainly exposes her own vulnerability, not only cheats Caesar but denies any final and authoritative textual closure.[69] □

Such clearly identified theoretical positions have the tremendous advantage of making the reader aware that he or she must pursue the argument beyond an opinion concerning the play outwards to the wider encircling arguments concerning such matters as gender and ideology. It is equally true of all critics that a theoretical background must be taken into account: the Augustan background to Dr Johnson's work; the considerations Leavis wants to bring to bear; the idealism that lies behind Coleridge's thinking and so on. What is different in at least some of these cases is that the wider arguments are not as explicitly presented as they are by Kahn and Loomba and the critics whose work is the subject of the final chapter of this Guide.

CHAPTER NINE

Postmodernists: *Antony and Cleopatra*: 'A child o' the time'?

T he critics of *Antony and Cleopatra* discussed in this chapter may be thought of as 'postmodernist' in the general sense that they are not 'modernist', just as the 'modernists' may be thought of as 'modernists' in the sense that they are not Edwardians or Victorians. Chronological divisions must be approximate: methodological categorisations are unreliable. The critics discussed here do share some concerns: they have a broadly common understanding of the nature and significance of language and they are suspicious of the views of society, history and the self of many of the critics whose work precedes theirs. These critics came to prominence in the 1980s but there are interesting precursors; one is Linda Fitz, whose 1977 essay breezily summarises a critical tradition in a light-hearted tone that should not deceive as to the seriousness of the intent.[1]

Fitz points out the many occasions on which Cleopatra has been accused of inconsistency, inconstancy, of manipulating Antony to his detriment, and, on the other hand, those many occasions on which she has been held up as quintessential Woman, and celebrated for the 'infinite variety' she shows in her exploitation of 'feminine wiles'. Fitz suggests that in the last Act we are shown a Cleopatra recognising her inconstancy and striving to overcome it, and that her exploitation of feminine wiles is a desperate effort to shore up with charm what age is robbing her of: youth and beauty. The first half of the essay surveys some of these and other errors of 'sexist' criticism, while the second half sketches out a case for seeing Cleopatra as the protagonist. This case is put tentatively (Fitz claims only to be trying the experiment, not staking a claim for a case) but it is put interestingly. The problem with seeing *Antony and Cleopatra* as a tragedy, and as Antony's tragedy, is what to make of the last Act, which is Cleopatra's. One answer is to make the last Act a sort of extended confirmation of the climax reached at the end of Act 4. Fitz quotes critics such as Daniel Stempel, who argues that the theme of the play is 'the safety of the state' and that the threat is only removed when Octavius shows himself immune to Cleopatra's charms and she kills herself.[2] Robert Fitch puts a slightly different spin on it, seeing the last

Act as a 'stark confrontation of pleasure and power in the figures of Cleopatra and Octavius'.[3] Julian Markels says that Cleopatra 'now learns the lesson of Antony's life' and confirms by her suicide his 'achieved balance of public and private values'.[4] Middleton Murry saw Cleopatra's finest moment as 'the mysterious transfusion of his royal spirit into the mind and heart of his fickle queen'.[5] Peter Alexander allows Cleopatra the opportunity to 'vindicate her right to his devotion',[6] and Michael Lloyd says that the play's structure is faulty 'if we see Antony's tragedy as the centrepiece of the play'.[7]

Fitz points out that Cleopatra is present throughout the play, has the final act to herself and dies at the end, and she invokes 'a forgotten article' by Lucie Simpson, who wrote that the play 'might have been called *Cleopatra* as appropriately as *Hamlet* is called *Hamlet* or *Othello Othello*'.[8] Fitz proceeds to examine the departures that Shakespeare makes from Plutarch, claiming that the effect of these departures is 'almost always to mitigate Cleopatra's culpability'.[9] Fitz argues, for example, as Kahn does,[10] that Actium is Antony's fault in Shakespeare and Cleopatra's in Plutarch; Fitz believes, more importantly perhaps, that Plutarch represents Cleopatra's death brusquely, reducing her 'to a babbling, self-mutilating neurotic',[11] and that Shakespeare, by contrast, 'allows her to die with dignity and even triumph'. Plutarch, she claims, 'reports simply, "Her death was very sudden". The great dying speeches of Cleopatra are Shakespeare's addition.' In fact, Plutarch allows Cleopatra to recover her spirits when Octavius visits her, so much as to show some of her old fire when Seleucus embarrasses her in front of Octavius, as Octavius thinks, and she makes a very fine speech before preparing herself for her final banquet, at which 'a contrieman' appears, bringing a basket of figs containing the asps, concealed from Octavius's soldiers' inspection. Plutarch in fact makes it clear that Cleopatra has resolved to die by her own hand and makes it even more clear that the Seleucus scene is a deception on her part of Octavius and it is part of the plan to do away with herself that culminates in the arrival of the 'contrieman'. He comments of Octavius: 'so he tooke his leave of her, supposing he had deceived her, but in deede he was deceived himself'.[12] Plutarch's comment 'Her death was very sodaine' is a poignant comment, not a dismissal. Shakespeare's speeches are better still but they are not without precedent in Plutarch.

The strength in Fitz's argument is in her pointing out that if we set aside Antony as the hero for the moment, we set aside the awkward question raised by Bradley: how can there be a true tragedy, in the Shakespearean sense, without an inner struggle in the hero? Bradley cannot find that struggle and has to consign the play to a lesser status.[13] Cleopatra, Fitz notes, does struggle: against her theatrical tendencies, against her inconstancy. She claims that the 'composition of *Antony and*

Cleopatra followed closely upon that of *King Lear*', although that is far from clear,[14] and she goes on to suggest a thematic link:

> ■ Surely after watching what Lear was and what Lear became, we should not be too ready to damn what Cleopatra has been while ignoring what she becomes.[15] □

The point about Cleopatra is a true point and well made; the 'evidence' is quite unnecessary. We do not have to think about *King Lear* or exploit the uncertainties about dating the composition of plays to make it.

Fitz claims that Riemer comes close to seeing Cleopatra as the play's hero and then veers off, in Fitz's view inexplicably, arguing that her thoughts and feelings are not the play's and are not shared by the audience.[16] Fitz says that such inability to understand Cleopatra 'owes much to the notion that women in general are impossible for men to understand'. This is not unfair, although, as something of a generalisation, it is probably undemonstrable. Furthermore, Riemer is certainly not arguing that Cleopatra's thoughts and feelings cannot be understood; he is arguing that they are not the play's and are not, by and large, shared by the audience.

Here the comparison with *King Lear* is useful: at the end of the play, Lear is not just a selfish old man who has realised too late where his good really lies; he has become a picture of the universal human experience of tragic incomprehension. He has done so because he is taken through a carefully controlled process of transformation lasting more than half the play. Cleopatra, by contrast, remains almost to the last moment what she has been throughout the play, reaching towards a grandeur that must remain ambiguous for the audience as it appears so late on.

Fitz's closing points are sharp and deserve consideration: Cleopatra's variety, she says, is not infinite; she is 'complex but not inscrutable'.[17] She needs to be 'demythologized'. Fitz has done this: the ageing Cleopatra seeks to win and hold Antony by what strike many critics (and here Fitz is just right) as, in Johnson's phrase, 'the feminine arts, some of which are too low'.[18] This may be seen as poignant rather than objectionable, as Fitz encourages us to do. Whether she has the massiveness she needs to become the hero is something of which Fitz herself is uncertain, and at one point Fitz invokes indeterminacy of genre to come to her aid. She says that if we decide that the play is a history and not a tragedy, then the question of the tragic hero does not arise. This is true but it is also, as she acknowledges, what drove Bradley to think less of the play.

Graham Holderness, Bryan Loughrey and Andrew Murphy's useful collection of excerpts, *Shakespeare: The Roman Plays* (1996), contains essays on *Antony and Cleopatra* by Jonathan Dollimore, Janet Adelman and Leonard Tennenhouse, as well as a handy introductory survey of the development of criticism in the last part of the twentieth and the beginning of the twenty-first century.

In Renaissance studies, the editors argue, a new development emerged in the 1980s, partly as a reaction against the poststructuralist tendencies that had had so profound an influence up to that point. This new perspective in the USA called itself 'new historicism', while in Britain a similar movement, calling itself 'cultural materialism', emerged. Where poststructuralism had derived very much from the 'deconstructionist' critique of structuralism pioneered by Jacques Derrida (1930–2004), and was thus concerned with language, with what could and could not be said – eager to show that many texts, even all texts, could not mean what they set out to mean – these two new movements began from different starting points. Although not denying some of the most basic positions held by critics whose practice might conveniently be called 'poststructuralist', these new movements were characterised by a renewed concern with the historical context of the works they studied. However, the two movements are quite distinct. Cultural materialism derives from the revision by Raymond Williams (1921–88) of some aspects of Marxist theory and is consciously, even self-consciously, committed to social improvement by political means (although this will mean different things to different writers), while new historicism, deriving more from the work of Michel Foucault (1926–84), tends to be gloomy about the prospects for significant improvement.[19]

Leonard Tennenhouse's comments are excerpted from his book *Power on Display* (1986)[20] and discuss the manner in which Cleopatra is represented as powerful, as a monarch. Tennenhouse's interest is in the collusion and contrast between theatre and court as a form of theatre in setting up as well as putting into question such representations.

Tennenhouse compares the play to more modern romances in which the love story is presented as a possible utopian alternative to a world determined by power. He believes that while a modern reader would eagerly embrace the utopian alternative, an early seventeenth-century theatregoer would have been put off by the political implications. Tennenhouse reminds us of Antony's redefinition of 'nobleness' at 1.1.36–7 ('the nobleness of life/Is to do thus'), pointing out that a clear implication is that 'nobleness' here has nothing to do with 'blood' in the sense of heritage and represents what he calls 'a semiotic apocalypse'.[21] He describes this as a challenge offered by Antony in the name of 'Nature' to 'Culture'; the distinctions that national cultures make are overthrown by a natural attraction between two people. However, the play shows, and Tennenhouse holds that any early seventeenth-century theatregoer would have gone along with this, that there are no apolitical acts in this world or at least that Antony cannot resign from the political world. It should be pointed out here that this may well be described as the mainspring of what gives the play a claim to the status of tragedy: the doomed attempt to substitute a life of passion for a life of public responsibility. It might also be pointed out that the modern reader imagined here, eagerly embracing the utopian alternative, must be extremely naive to believe that such an alternative exists. In short, the contrast between the two imagined readers is unrealistic.

The new element introduced into discussion by this play is, according to Tennenhouse, that while usually the aristocratic female is seen as a legitimate access route to the body politic, Cleopatra is an aristocratic female with 'the power to pollute'.[22] Tennenhouse draws an analogy between Shakespeare's representation of Cleopatra and the description of the 'grotesque – or popular – body' in Renaissance culture in the work of Mikhail Bakhtin (1895–1975). Bakhtin's discussion of *Gargantua and Pantagruel* (1533–5) by François Rabelais (*c.* 1495–1553) allows him to develop a theory of the place of carnival in medieval and early Renaissance society that has been an influential contribution to theoretical positions such as Tennenhouse's.[23] Carnival, in Bakhtin's view, only apparently threatens to overthrow aristocratic power; the feasts of fools, of misrule and so on in fact only serve to confirm the rightful authority of the lords and ladies who their antics parody. Tennenhouse claims that Enobarbus's description tends this way:

- Age cannot wither her, nor custom stale
  Her infinite variety. Other women cloy
  The appetites they feed, but she makes hungry
  Where most she satisfies; for vilest things
  Become themselves in her, that the holy priests
  Bless her when she is riggish. ☐   (2.2.234–9)

He comments that 'a body that incorporates the basest things represents the very antithesis of aristocratic power'. This is true, but Enobarbus is complimenting her upon her capacity to turn 'vilest things' into things that are becoming, and he is exaggerating. Hyperbole is not uncommon in *Antony and Cleopatra*: in fact Michael Neill claims that hyperbole is the play's basic rhetorical and structural principle.[24] Enobarbus's words *may* be taken literally but they do not have to be and it may be wrong to do so.

Tennenhouse's view turns out to be not that far removed from a familiar moralistic condemnation of the effect of Cleopatra upon Antony, although it is mobilised in the service of a theory of the representation in the theatre of the actual power relations of the members of the body politic of the time:

- His sexual bond to Cleopatra strips Antony of his military judgement, deprives him of prowess in battle, and deceives him into committing suicide. ☐

His view of Cleopatra's suicide has the virtue of originality:

■ Having denied her the privilege of committing suicide in the Roman manner, he dresses her as Queen of Egypt, surrounds her with her eunuch and ladies in waiting, and then kills her off with an Egyptian viper. This elaborate scene of punishment purges the world of all that is not Roman.[25] □

However, there is another side to this, because Elizabethan power was firmly based upon the very kind of figure Cleopatra is, which Tennenhouse calls 'autochthonous'. This lexical choice is made, perhaps, because 'indigenous' is a paler alternative to the Athenians' claim to have sprung from the very ground on which they lived. Tennenhouse means us to see Cleopatra as so wholly identified with Egypt as to be almost an *avatar* (incarnation) of Egypt. This is not wrong. It is also not wrong to recognise that Elizabeth I identified herself in such a manner with England. However, to say that Cleopatra is a sort of swansong for the Elizabethan principle of monarchy may seem to strain the comparison.

The editors of *Shakespeare: The Roman Plays* themselves acknowledge that Janet Adelman's feminist criticism, which is closely dependent upon psychoanalytical models, is not, strictly speaking, either new historicist or cultural materialist, and this acknowledgement ought to remind us that criticism is not justified by its belonging to particular tendencies but by the insights it affords its readers. In this case, Adelman's concentration on the interiority of Shakespeare's characters contrasts with and complements Tennenhouse's concern with externality, with the public staging of power. Adelman's book, *Suffocating Mothers* (1992), is an exploration of images of maternal figures in Shakespeare. She approaches *Antony and Cleopatra*, however, interested in the construction of masculine identity, especially Antony's.[26]

Adelman claims that 'scarcity' is the sign of the eradication of the female from Rome and with it, 'natural abundance'.[27] Octavius in particular and Rome in general have raised scarcity to the level of a principle, banishing the female, and fecundity. She takes the two portraits of Antony (Octavius's at 1.1.56–71 and Cleopatra's at 5.2.76–92) and charts Antony's progress between the two as emblems of his transfiguration. Adelman strikingly identifies Antony as the 'primary absent object of desire' for the play's major characters, acknowledging the strangeness of the perception precisely because Enobarbus's Cydnus barge speech seems to place Cleopatra in that position. However, as she points out, Octavius imagines him in his absence and so does Cleopatra, and Enobarbus dies addressing him in his absence. Most decisively of all perhaps, Antony addresses his own growing absence to others and himself just before he invites Eros to despatch him.

This staging of an idealised masculinity gives more to the theatre as a creative agency than Kahn's descriptions do, and, it might be said, it also has a more positive tendency, since Adelman wants to claim that Cleopatra's vision reimagines and transforms Antony's masculinity in terms of bounty instead of scarcity. Adelman wants to see this 'rebirth' of masculinity as a defining moment in Shakespeare's career, ending a period reaching back to Old Hamlet. In Adelman's view, from *Hamlet* on, the figure of the mother renders all sexual relationships and the formation of all masculine identities problematic. Old Hamlet was the last father who could control the mother. From that point, tragic masculinity is caught in a tension between the disembodied father and the only too embodied mother until its reimagining in a reuniting with the female in Cleopatra's vision of Antony. In spite of the sympathy he can show for them, Shakespeare tends, from *Hamlet* onwards, to use women characters for men to project their infantile fantasies onto, fantasies of loss and betrayal, original vice and corruption. The female body becomes a stage on which these fantasies are played out; the virgins transformed into the whores their persecutors always knew them to be and on whose bodies terrible vengeances are worked out or what Adelman calls 'revirginations' are attempted.

There is no reason one should assent to such a view: it just offers an interpretation one might find attractive. There is no reason one should agree with Kahn's view either, as it is exactly the same. Interpretations may be dismissed because they seem to exceed the facts on display in a work or because some of those facts cannot be brought into line with it, but not otherwise. However, they cannot be proved either. There are no grounds for imagining Shakespeare's theatrical career to be determined by his own inner journey but neither are there any grounds for denying this. When Adelman sees *The Winter's Tale* as evidence of and celebration of 'manifold recoveries',[28] we are in the position of anyone looking at a work of art and trying to decide whether it offers grounds for hope or reasons for despair or nothing at all.

Octavius's portrait strikes Adelman as showing 'awe, longing, and envy' and this allows her to see Octavius in the position of a son. Adelman extends this analysis to include Octavius's relationship with 'his own father, Julius Caesar, and on Antony's role in the Oedipal dynamic between them'.[29] Octavius refers to Julius Caesar at 3.3.6 as 'my father', although Julius Caesar was in fact his great-uncle but adopted him as his heir shortly before his assassination.

Adelman's complex account of Octavius's relationship with Antony (or rather, with his image of Antony) can be summarised by saying that he is driven to idealise Antony, to recover the father lost in Julius Caesar, and also to denigrate his image, to subdue and possess him. She sees Octavius's speech on hearing of Antony's death as a reduction. She sees, for example, Octavius's description of Antony as 'The arm of mine own body' (5.1.45) as Octavius turning Antony into 'the arm of his own gigantic body',[30] in a fantasy of his gigantic stature absorbing and reducing Antony. This sort of image can be usefully connected with Bakhtin's reflections on the grotesque body with which Tennenhouse is working.[31] Adelman reads Rome's version of events as an inevitable process by which Rome (as imagined by Octavius) must set its father figures on pedestals and then destroy them to create the scarcity by which it defines itself. This is a compelling myth.

For Cleopatra's reconstruction of Antony, Adelman reaches for the translation of Plutarch's 'Of Isis and Osiris'(*The Philosophy, Commonly Called the Morals, of Plutarch*, 1603) by Philemon Holland (1552–1637). Although many critics have assumed or argued that Shakespeare at least knew of this essay, there is little evidence.[32] Adelman does provide some. She argues that Shakespeare's use of the word 'habiliments' to describe Cleopatra's dressing as the goddess Isis (3.6.17) is persuasive, as North uses 'apparell' in his description of this incident but Holland speaks of the 'habilliments' of the goddess Isis. Adelman points out that the word occurs five times in Shakespeare. Her identification of Cleopatra with Isis and Octavius with Typhon, Osiris's envious brother who repeatedly pursues and kills Osiris only to find Isis patiently reconstructing him, is near enough to be plausible but remote enough to be no more than plausible, much like her construction of the myth of Octavius.

Where Adelman is convincing is in her account of Act 4 scene 4 to Act 5 scene 8, in which she shows that Antony, far from being weakened by sexual encounter, is strengthened by Cleopatra; literally armed by her he returns victorious. This triumphant moment is, however, immediately followed by the disaster of Actium. The same ambivalence haunts Adelman's most daring interpretative manoeuvre: seeing Antony's entry into Cleopatra's monument, his entry into the feminised space into which she has herself withdrawn, as a return to the womb, a re-entry into the mother's body, a reclamation of a rejected space – a space sexualised and rejected through a revulsion from it. Adelman describes the dream of return as 'the dangerous dream at the heart of masculine selfhood' and recognises that Antony can only enter into the highly charged space having been fatally wounded. The play identifies individual selfhood with a fear of the fluid, and Rome and Egypt are signally identified with the two conditions opposed in this formula: Rome with distinctions, boundaries, identities and definitions, the dry and the hard; Egypt with all that is watery, slimy, slippery, indistinct, moist and soft.[33] Antony's *braggadocio* (boastful) remark at 1.1.33, 'Let Rome in Tiber melt!' is an exceptionally clear depiction of his position at an early stage of the play, although at that time he surely does not suspect it.

Adelman must read much of Act 4 scene 14 against the grain, as it were, insisting that Antony's phrases are 'langorous', at one point going so far as to say that Antony gives up his armour, his 'bruised pieces' (4.14.42) 'willingly, as though he has finally gotten what he has wanted all along'.[34] 'Reluctantly' will do as well as 'willingly' and 'as though he has finally gotten what he has wanted all along' is overegging the pudding. It is to supply a motive in order to justify an interpretation. Adelman has already introduced into the discussion the 'ambivalence' of the mother–infant bond in the recognition that the sexual relationships that hark back to the mother–infant bond are overcast by this same ambivalence.[35] It is this ambivalence that for her informs the scene and determines Antony's responses. Cleopatra's portrait allows Shakespeare

■ to imagine a fully masculine selfhood that can overflow its own rigid boundaries, a masculinity become enormous in its capacity to share in the female mystery of an endlessly regenerating source of supply, growing the more it is reaped.[36] □

This is, Adelman concludes, a major imaginative achievement.[37]

A final note might be that it is perhaps surprising to find a feminist essay paying relatively little attention to Cleopatra. Adelman's own explanation is that she finds herself agreeing with Linda Bamber's argument that Cleopatra is not allowed the full privileges of selfhood in comparison with Antony.[38]

Dollimore's interest is in power in general and its representations and justifications. He is particularly concerned with the representations of honour and martial prowess in *Antony and Cleopatra* and *Coriolanus* as plays written at a time of, he claims, an unprecedented decline in the power, both political and military, and the prestige of the titular aristocracy. His argument is that such changes in the balance of power in a society throw light on the means by which power has justified itself and enable their exposure as false. This is in line with the Althusserian view taken by Coppélia Kahn and discussed in Chapter 8.

Dollimore cites both C.L. Barber and Mervyn James to support his view that changes in the conduct of war, the professionalisation of the military and an increasing reliance on state armies led to a decline in the importance of the concept of honour as a martial ideal.[39] The replacement of the concept of honour by a concept of policy is the main theme of his essay. In this view, Antony represents for the audience the fast-fading concept of honour or *virtus* and Octavius represents the replacing concept of policy.

The concept of *virtus* is well expressed, in Dollimore's view, by Coriolanus: 'As if a man were author of himself' (5.3.36). At the same time, Dollimore argues, the plays show how each man, Antony and Coriolanus, is in fact a construction of his reputation, and, far from being autonomous, is dependent upon that reputation and the conditions that encouraged its growth. As they act as though they were independent of the power structures on which they actually depend, they risk the disintegration of their reputation and their identities, personal as well as political, as the two are so closely bound together (indeed, one may add, as both men have mistaken the one for the other).

Dollimore disagrees with Eugene Waith's assertion that Antony displays heroism rather than heroic achievement in the latter part of the play.[40] According to Dollimore, the quality can never be independent of the event of achievement, as it is only imputed on the basis of the event and only has life for the duration of the event (or in the remembering of it, it might be added). Dollimore insists that it is no mere 'anti-Romantic moralism' that leads him to reject a view of the play, such as Wilson Knight's, which holds that it 'translineates man to divine likeness'.[41] In fact, he wishes to go beyond the dualism expressed by Derek Traversi between 'a tragedy of lyrical inspiration, justifying love by presenting it as triumphant over death, or … a remorseless exposure of human frailties, a presentation of spiritual possibilities dissipated through a senseless surrender to passion'.[42]

Nor is Dollimore blind to the play's poetry: he only wants to remind the reader that the language of desire, 'far from transcending the power relations which structure this society, is wholly in-formed by them'.[43] This is an example of what the editors speak of as the indebtedness of cultural materialism (in this case) to some of the insights of post-structuralism. Because transcendence, for example, must be spoken of in terms of what it purports to transcend, we can have no idea of transcendence unless we have an idea of what is to be transcended. However, if we have no idea of what is transcended – and if the effort were successful, we should not, as we should have passed beyond it – we should no longer have any idea of transcendence. Every idea is in thrall to its opposite: dependent upon it for its very existence; locked in an endless struggle with it. This struggle takes the shape of one side of the dualism being emphasised at the expense of the other; so, for example, 'man' defined against 'woman' denigrates and demonises as 'other' its opposite, in terms of which it is necessarily defined and from which it can never free itself. This is the process traced by Kahn and Adelman.

Dollimore reads the progress of the play as being a narrowing of the basis of Antony's power from world politics to sexual anxiety and he sees the anxiety, as does Kahn, focused as much if not more on Octavius than on Cleopatra. He regards the bungled suicide attempt as a further demonstration of the slippage of power out of Antony's hands and comments 'even as he is trying to transcend defeat by avowing a tragic dignity in death, [he] suffers the indignity of being dragged up the monument'.[44]

The tension between what Dollimore calls 'realpolitik' and the idealisation of *virtus* called for by the conventions of the representation of the justification of power in this world is the means by which this diminution takes place. The challenge to a sword fight is a key moment, as Enobarbus recognises:

> ■ Yes, like enough! High-battled Caesar will
> Unstate his happiness, and be stag'd to the show
> Against a sworder! □   (3.13.29–31)

Octavius is amazed:

> ■ He calls me boy, and chides me as he had power
> To beat me out of Egypt. My messenger
> He hath whipp'd with rods, dares me to personal combat,
> Caesar to Antony: let the old ruffian know,
> I have many other ways to die; meantime
> Laugh at his challenge. □   (4.1.1–6)

Dollimore points out that Enobarbus says later that as he is 'twenty times of better fortune' than Antony, he is 'twenty men to one' (4.2.3–4).

Dollimore is particularly good on Octavius's speech on hearing of Antony's death. He points out the 'bathos' of the interruption, and hence of the ease with which Octavius turns his mind to other matters, and describes the speech as an 'encomium', remarking that it sketches out the official line: Octavius is the victor; he regrets that this has necessitated Antony's death, which he laments as that of a brother (although diminishing Antony to a part of his own body, his arm); he excuses himself by saying that it was all fated. Even Cleopatra's dream of Antony, Dollimore says, reveals a questioning self-doubt in the 'hesitant syntax' of 'But if there be nor ever were one such'. Dollimore asks whether the final image is not of a commemorative statue:

> ■ That material embodiment of a discourse which, like Caesar's encomium, skilfully overlays (without ever quite obscuring) obsolescence with respect.[45] □

Dollimore describes the conflict as being one between 'the residual/dominant and the emergent power relations', a phrase indebted to Raymond Williams and especially to his book *Marxism and Literature* (1977), in which he develops some of the ideas of Antonio Gramsci (1891–1937), particularly Gramsci's analysis of what he (or rather, his translator) calls 'hegemony', by which word Gramsci indicates the operation of dominance in society that one class holds over the rest. Gramsci is interested in the persistence of ideas beyond their time and talks of 'traditional' or 'inherited' ideas and intellectual habits as well as those that grow up with a class that is set to become the dominant class. Williams develops this into a tripartite structure: residual, dominant and emergent. The residual are those ideas, habits and patterns surviving from an earlier phase; the dominant are those currently hegemonic; the emergent are those that will become the dominant in time. Today's dominant is tomorrow's residual in this scheme. This dimension adds poignancy to Antony's position: not only is he a superseded individual but also the structures within which he has arisen and become defined are superseded. He is, in an unusually thorough sense, yesterday's man.

Dollimore pursues the discussion into what he sees as the 'strange relationship set up in the play between honour and policy'. He cites Pompey's speech to Menas after Menas has offered to murder the triumvirate while they are aboard Pompey's galley. Pompey reluctantly refuses, pointing out that what would have been a service had Menas done it, and not told Pompey until after he had done it, would be dishonourable in him (Pompey) to approve prior to its being done (2.7.73–80). Dollimore rightly sees this moment as representative and draws in other, similar moments in the play, such as the discussion between Thidias and Cleopatra in which Thidias states that Caesar would not regard her relationship with Antony as a blot on her honour as she capitulated to Antony out of fear (the implication is that Caesar is ready to collaborate in this version of events); Cleopatra quickly assents: 'He is a god, and knows/What is most right. Mine honour was not yielded,/But conquer'd merely' (3.13.59–62). It is clear, as Dollimore argues, that 'honour' here is being approached in a pragmatic fashion.

Dollimore has already pointed out that Ventidius, when urged to press his advantage and pursue the enemy, so gaining Antony's gratitude, replies that an officer whose successes exceed those of his general is not likely to win favour (3.1.1–27). This attitude and observation Dollimore calls 'realistic' and he aligns this attitude with the word 'policy'. This is part of his general view that realpolitik is a pervasive theme in the play. He has already argued that Antony mistakenly thinks that *virtus* is a personal quality. One consequence of this mistake is that one's personal merits have nothing to do with it; it is a reflection of what is perceived as one's achievement, as Ventidius wryly observes: 'Caesar and Antony have ever won/More in their officer than person' (3.1.16–17).

In Dollimore's perspective, Enobarbus is almost the shadow of this relationship: a man whose actions and speech seem dictated by the kind of policy that keeps you alive on the edges of the circles of power, which is where he is condemned to exist, but whose identity is fatally fractured by the betrayal of loyalty that policy has dictated. Dollimore comments:

■ The extent of people's dependence upon the powerful is something the play never allows us to forget.[46] □

Perhaps the worst effect of power is its distortion of the meaning of moral qualities, such as honour, loyalty or even truth. Dollimore's discussion of the Seleucus scene, although brief, is interesting. Seleucus, caught between two powerful people, resorts to the truth to save himself. Cleopatra has told him to speak the truth, that is, to lie, 'upon his peril' (5.2.142); Seleucus replies, turning the words back on her, that he 'had rather seel my lips, than to my peril/Speak that which is not'. Cleopatra sees this shifting of allegiance (but after all, who now has the power to enforce the 'peril'?) as 'base' (5.2.156), although Caesar approves the stratagem as 'wisdom' (5.2.149). In this context it is difficult to see what moral worth truth has: Cleopatra urges a servant to lie to remain loyal to her; the servant resorts to truth to save himself, acknowledging that Octavius is really in charge now, not because he thinks that truth is superior to loyalty; Octavius, who is in charge, commends Cleopatra's policy in being deceitful. When power speaks, moral values give way. Dollimore finally reminds us that the consequences of the relationships between the three main characters have been, in Octavia's striking phrase, 'As if the world should cleave, and that slain men/Should solder up the rift' (3.4.31–2). These 'slain men' we do not hear much of.

However, the discussion of the play Dollimore offers, although extremely interesting, bears a close resemblance to, for example, MacCallum's. Both critics see a conflict between views of the world, a conflict in which one view is much stronger than the other; MacCallum tends to make a judgement about what he sees; Dollimore claims not to be doing that but rather to be reading the play as a reflection of historical reality, the declining power of the aristocracy. But even if this is the case, two questions need to be discussed: first, we need to know whether it is being claimed that the play reflects historical reality because its author sets out to make it do that, or from some other cause, and, if it is the latter, what is the nature of that other cause? Second, we need to ask whether the play displays an attitude to what it reflects (whether it does this as a consequence of a deliberate act on the part of its author or from some other cause). The question of authorship is itself a vexed one but even if we take the position that the author's intentions are irrelevant, we are still faced with the question of the attitude of the play towards the reality it reflects. In what direction, that is, are our feelings marshalled by the play, whether or not we wish to attribute this marshalling to the author? It is a mark of Dollimore's sensitivity as a critic that he is aware of the urgency of this question, he seeks to answer it and his answer is a good one.

His closing discussion of sexuality and power runs quickly through the sort of imagery in which Antony and Cleopatra freely mix martial and political figures in their evocation to one another and to themselves of their delight in their sexuality. He sees this as showing that 'their sexuality is rooted in a fantasy transfer of power from the public to the private sphere, from the battlefield to the bed'.[47] Not all that unusual a fantasy one might guess. The point is that the romantic view of the play does no more than concur with this fantasy. The deeper point is that:

> ■ His [Antony's] sexuality is informed by the very power relations which he, ambivalently, is prepared to sacrifice for sexual freedom; correspondingly, the heroic *virtus* which he wants to reaffirm in and through Cleopatra is in fact almost entirely a function of the power structure which he, again ambivalently, is prepared to sacrifice for her. □

The fantasy is self-destructive: to achieve it would be to lose what it was based on and from which it is inextricable, power. The 'fantasy transfer of power from the public to the private sphere, from the battlefield to the bed' cannot be effected unless power is enjoyed in the public sphere and on the battlefield, but if the attempt is made to effect the transfer of that power to the private sphere and to the bed, then the power is immediately lost. The romantic view is a mistake. This is an answer to the second question we need to consider: that is, in what direction our feelings are marshalled. In the end it does not much matter whether the power of the aristocracy at the time the play was written was in decline or not: our interest is focused on the lovers' desperate gamble to evade the consequences of their defeat at the hands of their enemy.

Conclusion: 'Infinite variety'?

This Guide has surveyed a range of critical accounts of *Antony and Cleopatra*, and if there has been a discernible thread running through those accounts, it has been an unwillingness to stake a claim for the status of the play unqualified by doubts and reservations (with the notable exception of Coleridge). Jonathan Dollimore's hard but fair view of romantic illusion suggests a possible line of argument that may be taken up in future.

The argument that the romantic view is a mistake is a powerful argument. What it must contend with, and what it makes no attempt to contend with, is the view that Antony is stripped of his power before the last Act is played out and that Cleopatra's final moments are free of illusion. She has seen through the power that attracted her to him in the first place and she addresses herself to him now in the complete absence of that power, wounded and dying and defeated. Such a view is complicated by the threat to her of humiliation but there is no need to make a straightforward choice between the two motives for her suicide. What the play shows is two people who come to realise too late what romantic love might offer them, whose tragedy is to have stumbled upon what might have been fulfilling had they not come upon it too late, at a point in their lives when they had already spent far too long being what they were, which was not much. The tragedy of the play is the tragedy of a self-realisation postponed until it is too late to enjoy it but not too late to glimpse what it might have offered.

If we regard Antony and Cleopatra as two people having pursued aims they found attractive for so long that they became deaf to the calls of anything finer, until it was too late for them to enjoy it when they did hear it, then we may feel no more than that they got what they deserved. If we add to that, however, that it was in themselves and in each other that they finally heard this finer thing, then we have the inner struggle that Bradley felt was lacking. This is the struggle for perfection, although not against an evil so clear as Iago or as the temptations within himself with which Macbeth struggles, but against lassitude and moral weakness in a world so well described by Mungo MacCallum as 'the struggling and contentious throng of worldlings and egoists', in which both Antony and Cleopatra have ruled supreme as the greatest worldlings and egoists of them all. Shakespeare's triumph of dramatic poetry is to make us doubt, at the play's supreme moments, whether these two are not simply speaking the truth.

What does the future hold for criticism of *Antony and Cleopatra*? To a large extent, this will depend upon the development of new theoretical perspectives and it is fruitless to try to predict what they will be. In one sense, too much emphasis may be placed on theory: what may matter is what opinions emerge as a result of its application. If this test is applied, then the critical history of *Antony and Cleopatra* appears remarkably even: what changes is the judgement of the behaviour of either Antony or Cleopatra or both. What separates Dollimore and MacCallum is the reasons each gives for coming to their conclusions and not so much the conclusions themselves. Different critics believe different things about the nature of the world but about the nature of the vision offered by the play there is remarkable unanimity. Only Shaw stands out as determinedly having no truck with such nonsense as romantic illusions about sexual attraction: others may believe different things about the causes and implications of sexual attraction and may judge quite differently the nature of its significance, but there is general agreement that it is significant; that people have illusions about it; and that it is of no use to point out either to them or to ourselves that they are illusions.

Where there is significant room for development is in the question of whether or not the play is a tragedy. Dr Johnson and Bradley both believed that the play was really a history and thus nothing much more could be expected from it, although Bradley at least was very moved by it. Leavis and Mason follow Bradley in this estimate, although neither of them explicitly addressed the generic question. The generic question is indeed in danger of circularity: a genre is only those works defined as belonging to it and to add to or subtract from the works said to belong to the genre is to define the genre differently. Thus Bradley rules out *Romeo and Juliet* from his category of tragedy as 'an early work, and in some respects an immature one', but it is convenient that he should do so, because his definition of tragedy better suits those plays with a single male hero. Perhaps it is better to start with the works and seek to arrive at a definition, but the problem with that is the habits of mind ingrained by close acquaintance with some powerful works. Both Jones and Dollimore offer some notions of how the play may be seen tragically: Jones in terms of conceptions of shape, and Dollimore exploring the structure of a world in which the fantasies of the lovers are doomed. Jones's conception of the shape of the play, likened in the Guide to a whirlpool, coupled with Dollimore's ruthless account of romantic illusion against a backdrop of realpolitik offers grounds for seeing *Antony and Cleopatra* as an integrated work of art. It remains to be seen whether such lines of argument will lead anywhere. In the meantime, it may be enough to reflect that the play, like Cleopatra herself, has seduced and bewildered, and that, perhaps, 'age cannot wither' nor 'custom stale' the 'infinite variety' not only of the play's central female character but also of the play itself.

Notes

CHAPTER ONE: 'LET'S DO IT AFTER THE HIGH ROMAN FASHION': SHAKESPEARE'S CLASSICAL WORLD

1   The translation was published in London in 1592 together with *A discourse of life and death. Written in French by Ph. Mornay* as *Antonius, a tragoedie written also in French by R. Garnier. Both done in English by the Countess of Pembroke.* It was published in a second edition in 1595 as *The tragedie of Antonie. Doone into English by the Countess of Pembroke.* Case has *Antonie* (1595) as the first publication (p. xxxv); later editors (Jones, 1977; Bevington, 1990; Wilders, 1995) have *Antonius* (1592). Case has to point out that even though Daniel's *Cleopatra* appeared in 1594, both its dedication and the postscript to *Antonie*, which reads, 'At Ramsbury. 26. of November, 1590', make clear that the Countess of Pembroke's work precedes Daniel's. Incidentally, *Antonius* (1592) carries a similar postscript: 'At Ramsburie. 26. of Nouember. 1590'.

2   This work and other similar works are discussed by Mungo MacCallum. See Chapter 7.

3   There are other plays on the same set of subjects. See Willard Farnham, *Shakespeare's Tragic Frontier: The World of His Final Tragedies* (Berkeley: University of California Press, 1950) pp. 149–150; A.P. Riemer, *A Reading of Shakespeare's 'Antony and Cleopatra'* (Sydney: Sydney University Press, 1968) pp. 12–14; Marilyn Williamson, *Infinite Variety: Antony and Cleopatra' in Renaissance Drama and Earlier Tradition* (Mystic, CN: Lawrence Verry, 1974) pp. 169–80.

4   See, for example, David Bevington, *Introduction* to *Antony and Cleopatra*, ed. David Bevington, *The New Cambridge Shakespeare* (Cambridge: Cambridge University Press, 1990) pp. 2–3.

5   T.S. Eliot, 'The Metaphysical Poets', in *Selected Essays* (London: Faber, 1951) p. 288.

6   J. Upton, *Critical Observations on Shakespeare* (1746); P. Whalley, *An Inquiry into the Learning of Shakespeare with Remarks on Several Passages of his Plays* (1748).

7   B. Vickers, *Shakespeare: The Critical Heritage*, 6 vols (London: Routledge & Kegan Paul, 1979) vol. 5, p. 76.

8   E. Malone, *William Shakespeare, Poems and Plays* … with the corrections and illustrations of various commentators … edited, after Mr Malone's death by James Boswell the Younger, 21 vols (London, 1821).

9   K. Walker, ed., *John Dryden*, The Oxford Authors (Oxford: Oxford University Press, 1987) p. 110.

10   Cited in E.K. Chambers, *Shakespeare: A Study of Facts and Problems*, 2 vols (Oxford: Clarendon Press, 1930) vol. II, p. 211.

11   Vickers (1979) vol. 2, p. 199.

12   Vickers (1979) vol. 1, pp. 341–2.

13   *Of Dramatic Poesy*. See K. Walker (1987).

14   The first blast of the trumpet in this campaign was Robert Greene's attack on the 'upstart Crow' whom he nicknamed 'Shakescene'. See S. McMillin, 'Professional Playwrighting', in David Scott Kastan (ed.) *A Shakespeare Companion* (Oxford: Blackwell, 1999) pp. 232–4 for a useful discussion of Greene's attack and its context in class rivalry and education.

15   J. Fiske, 'Forty Years of Bacon-Shakespeare Folly', *The Atlantic Monthly*, 80 (1897) pp. 635–52. See also J.M. Robertson, *The Baconian Heresy: A Confutation* (London, 1913); 'The

Learning of Shakespeare', *The University Magazine and Free Review*, X (1898) pp. 166–80; *Montaigne and Shakespeare and Other Essays on Cognate Questions* (London, 1897, 1909); 'The Originality of Shakespeare', *The University Magazine and Free Review*, X (1898) pp. 577–608.

16   J. Dover Wilson, 'Shakespeare's "Small Latin" – How Much?', *Shakespeare Survey*, X (1957) pp. 12–26.

17   T.W. Baldwin, *William Shakespeare's Small Latine and Lesse Greeke* (Illinois University Press, 1944).

18   J.A.K. Thomson, *Shakespeare and the Classics* (London: Allen & Unwin, 1952) p. 153.

19   Dover Wilson (1957) p. 21.

20   See, for example, M. Dobson, *The Making of the National Poet: Shakespeare, Adaptation and Authorship* (Oxford: Oxford University Press, 1995).

21   'British' becomes increasingly commonly used after James I had had himself proclaimed 'King of Great Britain' in 1604.

22   J.W. Velz, *Shakespeare and the Classical Tradition: A Critical Guide to Commentary, 1660–1960* (Minnesota: University of Minnesota Press, 1968) p. 30.

23   Velz (1968) p. 3; entry on Frederick S. Boas, 'Aspects of Classical Legend and History in Shakespeare', *Proceedings of the British Academy*, 29 (1943) pp. 107–32.

24   See F.J. Furnivall, 'What Did Shakespeare Learn at School', *Athenaeum*, 2554 (1876) p. 464, for example, and J.S. Smart, *Shakespeare: Truth and Tradition* (London, 1928).

25   See, for example, M. van Doren, *Shakespeare* (New York, 1939) and A. Harman, 'How Great was Shakespeare's Debt to Montaigne?', *PMLA*, LVII (1942) pp. 988–1008 for dissenting voices. The 'Seneca' debate may be consulted *passim*: John W. Cunliffe, *The Influence of Seneca on Elizabethan Tragedy* (London, 1893); T.S. Eliot, 'Seneca in Elizabethan Translation' (1927) and 'Shakespeare and the Stoicism of Seneca' (1927) in *Selected Essays*; H. Baker, *Induction to Tragedy: A Study in a Development of Form in 'Gorboduc', 'The Spanish Tragedy' and 'Titus Andronicus'* (LSU Press, 1939); C. Mendell, *Our Seneca* (Yale University Press, 1941); H.W. Wells, 'Senecan Influence on Elizabethan Tragedy: A Re-Estimation', *South Atlantic Bulletin*, XIX (1944) pp. 71–84; P. Ure, 'On Some Differences Between Senecan and Elizabethan Tragedy', *Durham University Journal*, X (1948) pp. 17–23. R.S. Miola has pursued both these issues recently, in *Shakespeare and Classical Comedy: The Influence of Plautus and Terence* (Oxford: Oxford University Press, 1994) and *Shakespeare's Reading* (New York: Oxford University Press, 2000).

26   Velz (1968) p. 122. The tone of hostility was also adopted by Dover Wilson it must be said: speaking of those writers who were arguing for a 'classical' Shakespeare, he wrote: 'the most ambitious and certainly the most voluminous of them all is Baldwin of Illinois' (p. 15).

27   Velz (1968) p. 122.

28   Velz (1968) p. 112, commenting on J.A.K. Thomson, '*Studies in Elizabethan Drama* by Percy Simpson', *Review of English Studies*, VII (1956) pp. 424–7.

29   T.W. Baldwin, *Shakspere's Five-Act Structure: Shakspere's Early Plays on the Background of Renaissance Theories of Five-Act Structure from 1470* (Illinois UP, 1947).

30   Velz (1968) pp. 126–7.

31   Velz (1968) p. 127.

32   Velz (1968) p. 127.

33   See Chapters 8 and 9.

CHAPTER TWO: SHAKESPEARE'S WORLD WELL LOST? THEATRE IN ENGLAND DURING THE INTERREGNUM AND AFTER

1   The first 'private' theatre was James Burbage's second venture (he had built the theatre at Shoreditch in 1576, the first of the 'public' theatres, shortly afterwards joined by its neighbour, the Curtain): the purchase and conversion of part of what had been the Blackfriars' monastery in 1596. The 'private' playhouses were roofed in and were more

exclusive than the 'public' playhouses, such as the Globe (1599), because more expensive to get into but were not in a stricter sense private, that is, requiring membership. This is the sort of theatre for which Dryden and the others were writing in the Restoration period (after 1660). The first theatres of Charles II's reign were converted tennis courts. See, for example, A. Nicoll, *British Drama*, 5th edn (London: Harrap, 1962) pp. 96–7, 138–9; A. Gurr, 'Shakespeare's Playhouses', in D.S. Kastan (ed.) *A Shakespeare Companion* (Oxford: Blackwell, 1999) pp. 362–76.

2 The Cockpit, one of the 'private' theatres, had originally opened in 1617. It had been immediately destroyed by rioters. On its first reopening, it became known as the Phoenix. It was to become the first Theatre Royal to stand at the Drury Lane site.

3 Nicoll (1962) p. 137.

4 Nicoll (1962) p. 143.

5 *Restoration Tragedies*, ed. J. Sutherland (Oxford: Oxford University Press, 1977) p. 18.

6 B. Jonson, *The Complete Poems*, ed. G. Parfitt (Harmondsworth: Penguin, 1988) pp. 446–9.

7 I take this illustration from B. Vickers, *English Renaissance Literary Criticism* (Oxford: Clarendon Press, 1999) p. 24. His discussion of *imitatio* on pages 22–39 is exemplary. See also W. Jackson Bate, *The Burden of the Past and the English Poet* (Cambridge, MA: Harvard University Press, 1970) and H. Bloom, *The Anxiety of Influence*, 2nd edn (Oxford: Oxford University Press, 1997) for developments of this theme.

8 K. Walker (ed.) *John Dryden* (Oxford: Oxford University Press, 1987) p. 160.

9 Walker (1987) p. 162.

10 Walker (1987) p. 163.

11 Walker (1987) p. 163.

12 Walker (1987) p. 163.

13 J. Sutherland (ed.) *Restoration Tragedies* (Oxford: Oxford University Press, 1977) p. 11.

14 Sutherland (1977) p. 11.

15 See, for example, A. Nicoll (1962) or P. Hartnoll, *A Concise History of the Theatre* (London: Thames & Hudson, 1968).

16 Sutherland (1977) p. 12.

17 Sutherland (1977) p. 12.

18 Sutherland (1977) pp. 12–13.

19 Sutherland (1977) p. 12.

20 See, for example, M. Berman, *All That Is Solid Melts Into Air: The Experience of Modernity* (London: Verso, 1983) and B. Anderson, *Imagined Communities: Reflections on the Origins and Spread of Nationalism* (London: Verso, 1983).

21 Chedreux was a fashionable wig-maker of the period.

22 Sutherland (1977) p. 13.

23 Sutherland (1977) p. 13.

24 Rochester had been friendly with Dryden but became annoyed with him, to the extent of believing, or pretending to believe, that an anonymous satire against him published in 1679 had been written by Dryden and hiring, on this pretext, men to waylay and attack Dryden who was then an ill and elderly man. J.H. Wilson has taken issue with the view that Rochester was responsible for the attack: see 'Rochester, Dryden, and the Rose-Street Affair', *Review of English Studies*, 15 (1939) pp. 294–301. Dryden's *Preface* was written in March 1678 and is a response to the poem composed in 1675–6 (see D.M. Vieth, *Attribution in Restoration Poetry: A Study of Rochester's 'Poems' of 1680*, Yale Studies in English 153 (New Haven: Yale University Press, 1963).

25 Sutherland (1977) p. 14.

26 *The Letters of John Dryden*, ed. C.E. Ward (Chapel Hill, NC: 1942) p. 64.

27 Sutherland (1977) p. 18.

28 F.R. Leavis, *The Living Principle: 'English' as a Discipline of Thought* (London: Chatto & Windus, 1975) p. 144.

29 Leavis (1975) p. 144.
30 W. Wordsworth, *The Complete Poetical Works*, ed. T. Hutchinson, rev. E. de Selincourt (Oxford: Oxford University Press, 1950) p. 737.
31 A. Samson, *F.R. Leavis* (Toronto: University of Toronto Press,1992) has some useful remarks on the relationship between Leavis's work and Martin Heidegger's.
32 F.R. Leavis, *Nor Shall My Sword* (London: Chatto & Windus, 1972) p. 62.
33 'The knowledge both of the Poet and the Man of science is pleasure; but the knowledge of the one cleaves to us as a necessary part of our existence, our natural and inalienable inheritance; the other is a personal and individual acquisition, slow to come to us, and by no habitual and direct sympathy connecting us with our fellow-beings. The Man of science seeks truth as a remote and unknown benefactor; he cherishes and loves it in his solitude: the Poet, singing a song in which all human beings can join with him, rejoices in truth as our visible friend and hourly companion. Poetry is the breath and finer spirit of all knowledge; it is the impassioned expression which is in the countenance of all Science.' Preface to *Lyrical Ballads, Poetical Works*, p. 738. This passage can be placed alongside Coleridge's objection that, without Imagination, the world consists merely of objects 'fixed and dead' (*Biographia Literaria*, London: J.M. Dent, 1965).
34 W. Wordsworth, The *Prelude*, III, 62–3.
35 Leavis (1975) p. 52.
36 Leavis (1975) p. 34.
37 Leavis (1972) p. 56.
38 'Wordsworth' in *Essays in Criticism:* second series, ed. S.R. Littlewood (London: Macmillan, 1951) pp. 73–96.
39 Leavis (1975) pp. 144–5.
40 Leavis (1975) p. 146.
41 Leavis (1975) p. 147.
42 Leavis (1975) p. 151.
43 Leavis (1975) p. 151.
44 See N. Potter, ed., *Shakespeare: 'Othello': A Reader's Guide to Essential Criticism* (Basingstoke: Palgrave Macmillan, 2000) pp. 120–31, for an account of this discussion.
45 *Antony and Cleopatra*, ed. M. R. Ridley (London: Methuen, 1965) p. 99n.
46 Leavis (1975) p. 154.
47 Leavis (1975) p. 151.
48 Leavis (1975) p. 98.
49 I think of Johnson's curt dismissal of Othello's agonised 'I must weep,/But they are cruel tears. This sorrow's heavenly;/It strikes where it doth love (5.2.20–22) that he glosses thus: 'This tenderness, with which I lament the punishment I must inflict, is a holy passion'. He comments: 'I wish these two lines could be honestly ejected. It is the fate of Shakespeare to counteract his own pathos'. It is an instructive critical exercise to compare Johnson's gloss with Othello's words.
50 Leavis (1975) p. 99.
51 Leavis (1975) p. 99.
52 B. Vickers, *Shakespeare: The Critical Heritage* (London: Routledge & Kegan Paul, 1979) vol. 2, p. 199.
53 Vickers (1979) vol. 1, pp. 341–2.

CHAPTER THREE: DRYDEN'S RE-VISION OF *ANTONY AND CLEOPATRA*

1 These 'unities' were deduced by Ludovico Castelvetro from Aristotle's essay *On Poetry*, which he translated into Italian (1570), and were copied by other translators, including Thomas Rymer, who translated René Rapin's *Réflexion sur la poëtique* (1674) into English. Rymer is better known as the castigator of *Othello*. See, for example, N. Potter (ed.) *Shakespeare: Othello: A Reader's Guide to Essential Criticism* (Basingstoke: Palgrave Macmillan, 2001) Ch. 1.

2   See *Restoration Tragedies*, ed. J. Sutherland (Oxford: Oxford University Press, 1977). I have followed Sutherland's use and given the Act numbers in roman numerals.
3   F.R. Leavis, *The Living, Principle* (London: Chatto & Windus, 1975) p. 154.
4   See *Restoration Tragedies*, ed. Sutherland (1977) pp. ix–x, for a similar view.
5   *A New Variorum Edition of Shakespeare*, edited by H.H. Furness, *The Tragedie of Antonie and Cleopatra* (Philadelphia: Lippincott, 1907) p. xvi. Furness provides Sir Walter Scott's Introductory Remarks on *All for Love* in an appendix (p. 473). Scott admitted preferring Dryden's version of the Cydnus barge scene, 'chiefly upon the beauty of the language and imagery, which is flowery without diffusiveness, and rapturous without hyperbole' (p. 475). He did say that he felt 'almost afraid to avow' the preference.
6   See G. Winchester Stone Jr., 'Garrick's Presentation of *Antony and Cleopatra*', *Review of English Studies* 13 (1937) pp. 20–38.
7   W. Hazlitt, *A View of the English Stage* (London: 1818) p. 27.
8   See, for example, G.C.D. Odell, *Shakespeare from Betterton to Irving*, 2 vols (New York: Constable, 1920).

CHAPTER FOUR: ROMANTICS TO VICTORIANS: 'THIS ENCHANTING QUEEN'

1   *Lectures on Dramatic Literature*, 1809–11. See J.R. Brown, ed., *Shakespeare: 'Antony and Cleopatra'* (Basingstoke: Macmillan, 1968) p. 27. Hereafter, Brown (1968).
2   Brown (1968) p. 27.
3   Brown (1968) p. 27.
4   Brown (1968) p. 27.
5   Brown (1968) pp. 27–8.
6   Brown (1968) p. 28.
7   Brown (1968) p. 29.
8   Brown (1968) pp. 28–9.
9   Brown (1968) p. 29.
10   Brown (1968) p. 29.
11   Brown (1968) p. 30.
12   Brown (1968) p. 31.
13   Brown (1968) p. 32.
14   Brown (1968) p. 33.
15   Byron implicitly condemns Shakespeare in his Preface to *Sardanapulus* in which he observes, without making any exceptions, that he has observed or approached the unities, 'conceiving that with any very distant departure from them, there may be poetry, but can be no drama'. *Poetical Works*, ed. F. Page; new edn corr. J. Jump (Oxford: Oxford University Press, 1970) p. 453.
16   Brown (1968) p. 34.
17   Brown (1968) p. 34.
18   Brown (1968) p. 35.
19   Brown (1968) p. 36.
20   Brown (1968) pp. 37–8.
21   See *Antony and Cleopatra*, ed. M.R. Ridley (London: Methuen, 1965) p. xlv. Ridley describes a passage he quotes from Mrs Jameson's essay, but does not attribute to her, as an example of 'the meaningless verbiage of befuddled bewilderment'.
22   Brown (1968) p. 38.
23   Brown (1968) p. 39.
24   Brown (1968) p. 40.
25   Brown (1968) p. 41.
26   Brown (1968) pp. 41–2.
27   Brown (1968) p. 42.
28   Brown (1968) p. 42–3.

29   Brown (1968) pp. 43–4.
30   Brown (1968) p. 44.
31   Brown (1968) p. 43.
32   Brown (1968) p. 44.
33   Brown (1968) pp. 45–6.
34   Brown (1968) p. 45.
35   Brown (1968) p. 46.
36   M.W. MacCallum, *Shakespeare's Roman Plays and their Background* (London: Macmillan, 1910) pp. 307–8.
37   Brown (1968) p. 65.
38   A.C. Bradley, *Shakespearean Tragedy* (Harmondsworth: Penguin, 1991) p. 21.
39   Bradley (1991) p. 28.
40   Bradley (1991) p. 38.
41   Bradley (1991) p. 51.
42   Bradley (1991) pp. 24–5.
43   Brown (1968) pp. 67–9.
44   Brown (1968) p. 70.
45   Brown (1968) p. 71.
46   *Antony and Cleopatra*, ed. M.R. Ridley (London: Methuen, 1965) p. 256.
47   Brown (1968) p. 85, n 2.
48   Brown (1968) p. 72.
49   Brown (1968) p. 73.
50   Brown (1968) p. 74.
51   Brown (1968) p. 84.
52   Bradley's quotation from Coleridge may be compared with the passage as it appears in, for example, *Coleridge on Shakespeare*, ed. T. Hawkes, introd. A. Harbage (Harmondsworth: Penguin, 1969) p. 269, in which the phrase is 'giant strength'. 'Angelic strength' becomes so eloquent in Bradley's hands one almost wishes Coleridge had written it. H.A. Mason certainly assumes that he had, and follows Bradley; so does M. MacCallum. Bradley did not have the benefit of T.M. Raysor's edition of 1930 (revised, 2 vols, London: J.M. Dent, 1960).
53   Brown (1968) p. 64.
54   Brown (1968) pp. 64–5.
55   Brown (1968) p. 75.
56   Brown (1968) p.83.
57   Brown (1968) p. 77.
58   George Bernard Shaw, *Three Plays for Puritans* (Harmondsworth: Penguin, 1946) pp. xviii–xix.
59   Shaw (1946) pp. xx–xxi.
60   Shaw (1946) p. xxi.
61   Shaw (1946) p. xxi.
62   Shaw (1946) pp. xxi–xxii.
63   Shaw (1946) p. xxxix.

CHAPTER FIVE: MODERNISTS: 'NO MORE BUT E'EN A WOMAN'

1   *Lectures on Dramatic Literature*, 1809–11. See J.R. Brown, ed., *Shakespeare: 'Antony and Cleopatra'* (Basingstoke: Macmillan, 1968) p. 27. Hereafter, Brown (1968) p. 89.
2   Brown (1968) p. 90.
3   Brown (1968) p. 91.
4   Brown (1968) p. 97.
5   Brown (1968) p. 105.
6   Brown (1968) p. 106.
7   Brown (1968) p. 114.

8 Brown (1968) p. 115.
9 Brown (1968) pp. 117–8.
10 Brown (1968) p. 119.
11 Brown (1968) p. 120.
12 Brown (1968) pp. 120–1.
13 Brown (1968) p. 122.
14 Brown (1968) p. 128.
15 Brown (1968) p. 132.
16 Brown (1968) p. 133.
17 Brown (1968) p. 129.
18 Brown (1968) p. 130.
19 Brown (1968) p. 17.
20 Brown (1968) pp. 83–4.
21 Brown (1968) p. 208.
22 Brown (1968) p. 209.
23 Brown (1968) pp. 208–9.
24 Brown (1968) p. 209.
25 G. Wilson Knight, *The Imperial Theme: Further Interpretations of Shakespeare's Tragedies Including the Roman Plays* (Oxford: Oxford University Press, 1931).
26 Brown (1968) p. 213.
27 Brown (1968) p. 214.
28 Brown (1968) p. 173.
29 A.C. Bradley, *Shakespearean Tragedy* (Harmondsworth: Penguin, 1991) p. 177.
30 Brown (1968) p. 176.
31 Brown (1968) p. 144.
32 Brown (1968) p. 150.
33 Brown (1968) p. 151.
34 Brown (1968) p. 153.
35 Brown (1968) p. 156.
36 Quoted by Franklin M. Dickey in Brown (1968) p. 157, n1.

CHAPTER SIX: THE EDITIONS: 'THE VARYING SHORE O' THE WORLD'

1 M. Bradbrook, 'Fifty Years of the Criticism of Shakespeare's Style: A Retrospect', *Shakespeare Survey*, 7 (1954) 1–11.
2 A.C. Bradley, *Oxford Lectures on Poetry* (1909) p. 307, note C.
3 *Antony and Cleopatra*, ed. M.R. Ridley (London: Methuen, 1965) p. xxix.
4 Ridley (1965) p. xxix
5 Ridley (1965) p. xxx.
6 Ridley (1965) pp. xxx–xxxi.
7 Ridley (1965) p. xxxi.
8 Ridley (1965) p. xxx.
9 Ridley (1965) p. xxxi–ii.
10 Ridley (1965) p. xxxii.
11 Ridley (1965) pp. xxxiii–xxxiv.
12 See, for example, N. Potter, ed., *Shakespeare: Othello: A Reader's Guide to Essential Criticism* (Basingstoke: Macmillan, 2000) p. 99.
13 Ridley (1965) pp. xxviii–xxix.
14 Ridley (1965) p. xxxiv.
15 Ridley (1965) pp. xxxv–xxxvi.
16 Ridley (1965) pp. xliii–xliv.
17 Ridley (1965) p. xliv.
18 Ridley (1965) p. xliv.

19 Ridley (1965) p. xl.
20 *A New Variorum Edition of Shakespeare,* edited by H.H. Furness, *The Tragedie of Antonie, and Cleopatra* (Philadelphia: Lippincott, 1907) p. 352n.
21 Ridley (1965) p. 276.
22 Ridley (1965) p. xli.
23 Ridley (1965) p. xl.
24 Ridley (1965) p. xli.
25 Ridley (1965) p. xlvi.
26 Ridley (1965) p. xlvi.
27 Ridley (1965) p. xlvi.
28 Ridley (1965) p. xliii.
29 Ridley (1965) p. xlv.
30 Ridley (1965) p. xlvii.
31 Ridley (1965) p. xlvii.
32 Ridley (1965) p. xlvii.
33 Ridley (1965) p. xlvii.
34 Another point on which they disagree is the degree to which Shakespeare's craftsmanship is engaged in the play. Case believes the play a hurried composition (Ridley, 1965, p. xxxv) while Ridley (1965) claims that 'there is no carelessness about it' (Ridley, 1965, p. xliii).
35 Ridley (1965) p. xlix.
36 See, for example, Potter (2000) p. 130.
37 *Antony and Cleopatra,* ed. B. Everett (New York: New American Library of World Literature, 1964) pp. xxxii–xxxiii.
38 Everett (1964) p. xxiii.
39 Everett (1964) p. xxxiv.
40 Everett (1964) p. xxxv.
41 Everett (1964) p. xxxvi.
42 I am not sure that there is any evidence in the play to the effect that Octavius acknowledges this himself, however.
43 Everett (1964) p. xxiii.
44 E. Schanzer, *The Problem Plays of Shakespeare: A Study of 'Julius Caesar', 'Measure for Measure', and 'Antony and Cleopatra'* (New York: Schoken, 1963).
45 Everett (1964) p. xxii.
46 Everett (1964) pp. xxii–iv.
47 Everett (1964) p. xxvii.
48 Everett (1964) p. xxviii.
49 Everett (1964) p. xxix.
50 Everett (1964) p. xxx.
51 Everett (1964) p. xxxi.
52 Everett (1964) pp. xxxi–ii.
53 Everett (1964) p. xxxii.
54 B. Vickers, ed., *Shakespeare: The Critical Heritage* (London: Routledge & Kegan Paul, 1979) vol. V, p. 148.
55 Vickers (1979) p. 62.
56 Vickers (1979).
57 Everett (1964) p. xxxii. See *Antony and Cleopatra,* ed. D. Bevington (Cambridge: Cambridge University Press, 1990) pp. 8–13 for a useful introductory discussion of Renaissance iconography relating to Mars and Venus as well as to Hercules and Omphale.
58 *Antony and Cleopatra,* ed. E. Jones (Harmondsworth: Penguin, 1977) pp. 31–2.
59 Jones (1977) p. 27.
60 Such as Thomas Rymer sneeringly compares *Othello* with in his notorious *A Short View of Tragedy,* 1695. See Potter (2000).
61 Jones (1977) p. 11.

62   Jones (1977) pp. 21–2.
63   Jones (1977) p. 30.
64   Jones (1977) pp. 35–6.
65   Jones (1977) pp. 28–29.
66   Jones (1977) p. 28.
67   Jones (1977) p. 31.
68   Jones (1977) p. 31.
69   Jones (1977) p. 31.
70   Jones (1977) p. 32.
71   Jones (1977) p. 33.
72   Jones (1977) p. 37.
73   S. Wells and G. Taylor note that the Prologue to *Romeo and Juliet* is structured as a sonnet and that their love is first declared in a sonnet. See *William Shakespeare: The Complete Works* (Oxford: Oxford University Press, 1988) p. 335.
74   Bevington (1990) p. 25.
75   Bevington (1990) p. 16.
76   S. Barnet, 'Recognition and Reversal in *Antony and Cleopatra*', *Shakespeare Quarterly*, 8 (1957) pp. 331–4; R. Nevo, *Tragic Form in Shakespeare* (Princeton, NJ: Princeton University Press, 1972).
77   M. Mack, 'The Jacobean Shakespeare: Some Observations on the Construction of the Tragedies', in J. Russell Brown and B. Harris, eds, *Jacobean Shakespeare* (1960) pp. 11–41.
78   Bevington (1990) p. 7.
79   Bevington (1990) p. 8.
80   N. Frye, *Fools of Time* (Toronto: University of Toronto Press, 1967) pp. 49, 59, 71–3.
81   Bevington (1990) p. 12.
82   Bevington (1990) p. 13.
83   Bevington (1990) p. 13. Richard Wagner's opera, *Tristan und Isolde* (1865) tells the story of the doomed passion of an Irish princess and a Cornish knight. The notion of 'love-as-death' or *Liebestod* was first applied by Liszt to the final pages of the work depicting Isolde's death.
84   Bevington (1990) p. 22.
85   Bevington (1990) p. 26.
86   Bevington (1990) p. 27.
87   Bevington (1990) p. 39.
88   See also M. Lamb, *'Antony and Cleopatra' on the English Stage* (Toronto: University of Toronto Press, 1980).
89   *Antony and Cleopatra*, ed. J. Wilders (London: Routledge, 1995) p. xvii.
90   Wilders (1995) p. 28.
91   Wilders (1995) p. 29.
92   Wilders (1995) pp. 28–9.
93   Wilders (1995) p. 37.
94   See Chapter 1.
95   Wilders (1995) pp. 39–40.
96   Wilders (1995) p. 40.
97   Wilders (1995) p. 41
98   Wilders (1995) p. 42
99   Schanzer (1963).
100   Wilders (1995) p. 45.
101   Wilders (1995) p. 47.
102   Wilders (1995) p. 48.
103   Wilders (1995) p. 49. Arnold's remark may be found in 'The Study of Poetry' in *Essays in Criticism*, second series (1888).
104   Wilders (1995) p. 50.

105   M.W. MacCallum in *Shakespeare's Roman Plays and their Background* (London: Macmillan, 1910) pp. 648–52.

106   See J. Dover Wilson, ed., *Antony and Cleopatra* (Cambridge: Cambridge University Press, 1950) p. x; E. Schanzer, 'Antony and Cleopatra and the Countess of Pembroke's *Antonius*', *Notes and Queries*, CCI (1956) pp. 152–4; G. Bullough, *Narrative and Dramatic Sources of Shakespeare* (New York: Columbia University Press, 1964) pp. 228–31.

107   Schanzer, (1963) p. 151.

108   Wilders (1995) p. 62.

109   Wilders (1995) p. 63.

110   J. Adelman, The *Common Liar: An Essay on 'Antony and Cleopatra'* (New Haven: Yale University Press, 1973) p. 91; B.J. Bono, *Literary Transvaluation: From Vergilian Epic to Shakespearean Tragicomedy* (Berkeley: University of California Press, 1984) p. 176; R.B. Waddington, 'What Venus Did with Mars', *Shakespeare Survey*, 2 (1966) pp. 210–27. Cf. *Venus and Adonis*, ll. 97–114.

111   Wilders (1995) p. 64.

112   Adelman (1973) pp. 81–3; Bevington (1990) pp. 9–10.

113   Waddington (1966) pp. 210–27.

114   See Schanzer (1963); J. Coates, '"The Choice of Hercules" in *Antony and Cleopatra*', *Shakespeare Studies* (1978) pp. 45–52; Bevington (1990) p. 9.

115   See Schanzer (1963) pp. 158–9; R.A. Brower, *Hero and Saint: Shakespeare and the Greco-Roman Heroic Tradition* (1971) pp. 350–2; Adelman (1973) pp. 68–74.

116   See Adelman (1973) pp. 177–83; M. Spevack, ed., *Antony and Cleopatra* (New York: MLA, 1990) pp. 603–4.

117   See Bono (1984) pp. 199–219; Bevington (1990) p. 11; J. Adelman, *Suffocating Mothers: Fantasies of Maternal Origin in Shakespeare's Plays* (New York: Routledge, 1992) p. 184.

118   Wilders (1995) p. 67.

CHAPTER SEVEN: THE ROMANNESS OF THE ROMAN PLAYS (1)

1   J.W. Velz, 'The Ancient World in Shakespeare: Authenticity or Anachronism: A Retrospect', *Shakespeare Survey* 31, 1978, 1–12.

2   Velz (1978) p. 2.

3   Velz (1978) pp. 1–2.

4   Velz (1978) p. 2.

5   F.R. Leavis offers an interesting discussion of this question in his 'The Logic of Christian Discrimination', *The Common Pursuit* (London: Hogarth, 1952).

6   M.W. MacCallum, *Shakespeare's Roman Plays and their Background* (London: Macmillan, 1910) pp. 71–2.

7   M. Doran, '"High Events as These": The Language of Hyperbole in *Antony and Cleopatra*', *Shakespeare's Dramatic Language: Essays by Madeleine Doran* (Madison: University of Wisconsin Press, 1976).

8   Velz (1978) p. 3.

9   T.J.B. Spencer, 'Shakespeare and the Elizabethan Romans', *Shakespeare Survey*, 10 (1957) pp. 27–38.

10   J.L. Simmons, *Shakespeare's Pagan World: The Roman Tragedies* (Charlottesville, VA: University of Virginia Press, 1973).

11   P.A. Cantor, *Shakespeare's Rome: Republic and Empire* (Ithaca, NY: Cornell University Press, 1976).

12   R.A Brower, *Hero and Saint: Shakespeare and the Graeco-Roman Heroic Tradition* (Oxford: Oxford University Press, 1971); M. Boone Kennedy, *The Oration in Shakespeare* (Chapel Hill, NC: University of North Carolina Press, 1942).

13   S.L. Bethell, *Shakespeare and the Popular Imagination* (London, 1944) pp.144–7; J. Markels, *The Pillar of the World: 'Antony and Cleopatra' in Shakespeare's Development*

(Columbus, OH: Ohio State University Press, 1968), especially Chapter 6, 'The Protean Language of the Man-made World'.

14   Velz (1978) p. 12.

15   M.W. MacCallum (1910) p. vii.

16   McCallum takes this to be Richard Bower, master of the Chapel Royal at Windsor in 1599. A reference to what may be the plague might suggest 1563 as a year of production (McCallum, pp. 2–3).

17   MacCallum (1910) p. 10.

18   MacCallum (1910) p. 49.

19   MacCallum (1910) p. 58.

20   MacCallum (1910) p. 59.

21   MacCallum (1910) p. 61.

22   MacCallum (1910) p. 71.

23   MacCallum (1910) p. 71–2.

24   MacCallum (1910) p. 73.

25   MacCallum (1910) p. 74.

26   MacCallum (1910) p. 75.

27   MacCallum (1910) p. 78.

28   MacCallum (1910) p. 79.

29   MacCallum (1910) p. 81.

30   MacCallum (1910) p. 84.

31   MacCallum (1910) pp. 84–5.

32   MacCallum (1910) p. 85.

33   S. Wells and G. Taylor, *The Oxford Shakespeare* (Oxford: Oxford University Press, 1988) p. xlviii.

34   K. Walker, ed., *John Dryden*, The Oxford Authors (Oxford: Oxford University Press, 1987) p. 110.

35   MacCallum (1910) p. 90.

36   MacCallum (1910) p. 91.

37   MacCallum (1910) p. 93.

38   MacCallum (1910) p. 119.

39   MacCallum (1910) p. 163.

40   MacCallum (1910) p. 332.

41   MacCallum (1910) p. 337.

42   MacCallum (1910) p. 340.

43   MacCallum (1910) pp. 342–3.

44   MacCallum (1910) p. 345.

45   MacCallum (1910) p. 348.

46   MacCallum (1910) p. 349.

47   MacCallum (1910) p. 356.

48   MacCallum (1910) p. 357.

49   MacCallum (1910) p. 358.

50   MacCallum (1910) p. 401.

51   MacCallum (1910) p. 413.

52   MacCallum (1910) p. 421.

53   MacCallum (1910) p. 425.

54   MacCallum (1910) p. 413.

55   MacCallum (1910) p. 426.

56   See Chapter 2.

57   *Antony and Cleopatra*, ed. M.R. Ridley (London: Methuen, 1965) p. 275.

58   MacCallum (1910) p. 434.

59   MacCallum (1910) p. 439.

60   MacCallum (1910) p. 440.

61   *A New Variorum Edition of Shakespeare*, ed. H.H. Furness, *The Tragedie of Antonie, and Cleopatra* (Philadelphia: Lippincott, 1907) p. 494.

62   MacCallum (1910) p. 443.

63   I do not mean to imply here that I believe that there is a Shakespearean world 'in itself': I mean the world of the play as MacCallum's responses reveal it to be. My point is that he cannot accept the implications of his insights.

64   MacCallum (1910) p. 453.

65   M. Charney, *Shakespeare's Roman Plays: The Function of the Imagery in the Drama* (Cambridge, MA: Harvard University Press, 1961).

66   D. Traversi, *Shakespeare: The Roman Plays* (Stanford: Stanford University Press, 1963).

67   Brower (1971).

68   G. Wilson Knight, *The Imperial Theme: Further Interpretations of Shakespeare's Tragedies Including the Roman Plays* (Oxford: Oxford University Press, 1931).

69   Cantor (1976).

70   J.E. Phillips, *The State in Shakespeare's Greek and Roman Plays* (New York: Columbia University Press, 1940, reprinted New York: Octagon, 1972).

71   G.K. Paster, *The Idea of the City in the Age of Shakespeare* (Athens: Georgia University Press, 1985).

72   A. Leggatt, *Shakespeare's Political Drama: The History of the Roman Plays* (London: Routledge, 1988).

73   M. Platt, *Rome and Romans According to Shakespeare*, Salzburg Studies in English Literature, JDS, no. 51, Salzburg Institut für Englische Sprache und Literatur, 1983.

74   P.N. Siegel, *Shakespeare's English and Roman History Plays: A Marxist Approach* (London: Associated University Presses, 1986).

75   V. Thomas, *Shakespeare's Roman Worlds* (London: Routledge, 1989).

76   Simmons (1973).

77   R. Walker, 'The Northern Star: An Essay on the Roman Plays', *Shakespeare Quarterly* 2 (1951) p. 287.

78   R.S. Miola, *Shakespeare's Rome* (Cambridge: Cambridge University Press, 1983).

79   Miola (1983) p. 15.

80   Miola (1983) p. 16.

81   Miola (1983) p. 17.

82   E. Schanzer, *Problem Plays* cites *Aeneid* IV and Chaucer's *Legend of Good Women* and Marlowe's *Dido Queen of Carthage* (pp. 159–61); J. Adelman, *Common Liar* (1973), also.

83   Miola, *Shakespeare's Rome*, p. 127.

84   In this at least he has Brower's support, who argues in *Hero and Saint* (1971) p. 351, that *Antony and Cleopatra* is an 'imaginative sequel' to the *Aeneid*, and J. Adelman's, who in *The Common Liar* (1973) detects further parallels and echoes between the two works (pp. 71 ff.).

85   Miola (1983) p. 134.

86   Miola (1983) p. 144.

87   Quoted in Furness (1907) p. 287.

88   Markels (1968) p. 168.

89   Miola (1983) p. 147.

90   Miola notes that Charney (1961) makes a similar point on pp.125–33.

91   Miola (1983) p. 150.

92   Miola (1983) p. 151.

93   Adelman (1973) pp. 61–4.

94   Miola (1983) p. 156.

95   S. Orgel, *The Jonsonian Masque* (Cambridge, MA: Harvard University Press, 1965) p. 79.

96   See for example H. Felperin, *Shakespearean Representation: Mimesis and Modernity in Elizabethan Tragedy* (Princeton: Princeton University Press, 1977) pp. 107–12; S.R. Homan, 'Divided Response and the Imagination in *Antony and Cleopatra*', *Philological Quarterly*, 49

(1970) pp. 460–8; Markels (1968); N. Rabkin, *Shakespeare and the Common Understanding* (New York: Free Press, 1967) pp. 184–8; B.T. Spencer, 'Antony and Cleopatra and the Paradoxical Metaphor', *Shakespeare Quarterly*, 9 (1958) pp. 373–8; S.A. Shapiro, '"The Varying Shore of the World": Ambivalence in *Antony and Cleopatra'*, *Modern Language Quarterly*, 27 (1966) pp. 18–32; Traversi (1963) pp. 79–203.
97   Miola (1983) p. 161.
98   Moral readings may be found in, for example: D.G. Cunningham, 'The Characterization of Shakespeare's Cleopatra', *Shakespeare Quarterly*, 6 (1955) pp. 9–17; F.M. Dickey, *Not Wisely But Too Well: Shakespeare's Love Tragedies* (San Marino, CA: Huntington Library, 1957) pp. 144–202; J. Leeds Barroll, 'Shakespeare and Roman History', *Modern Language Review*, 53 (1958) pp. 327–43; R.E. Fitch, 'No Greater Crack?', *Shakespeare Quarterly*, 19 (1968) pp. 3–17; Simmons (1973) pp. 109–63; Platt (1976) pp. 246 ff.; A. Fichter, '"Antony and Cleopatra": "The Time of Universal Peace"', *Shakespeare Survey*, 33 (1980) pp. 99–11. Political readings may be found in, for example: D. Stempel, 'The Transmigration of the Crocodile', *Shakespeare Quarterly*, 20 (1969) pp. 59–72; Phillips (1940, 1972) pp. 188–205; P.L. Rose, 'The Politics of *Antony and Cleopatra'*, *Shakespeare Quarterly*, 20 (1969) pp. 379–89.
99   Miola (1983) p. 162.

CHAPTER EIGHT: THE ROMANNESS OF THE ROMAN PLAYS (2)

1   C. Kahn, *Roman Shakespeare: Warriors, Wounds and Women* (London: Routledge, 1997) p. 1.
2   Kahn (1997) p. 1. Here Kahn acknowledges a debt to J. Butler's criticism of G. Rubin, 'The Traffic in Women: Notes on the "Political Economy" of Sex', in R. Reiter, ed., *Toward an Anthropology of Women* (New York: Monthly Review, 1975) pp. 157–210, in J. Butler's *Gender Trouble: Feminism and the Subversion of Identity* (London: Routledge, 1990).
3   See Butler (1990).
4   Kahn (1997) p. 2.
5   See 'Word, Dialogue and Novel' (1969) trans. A. Jardine, T. Gora and L.S. Roudiez in T. Moi, ed., *The Kristeva Reader* (Oxford: Blackwell, 1986).
6   G.K. Hunter, 'A Roman Thought: Renaissance Attitudes to History Exemplified in Shakespeare and Jonson', in B.S. Lee, ed., *An English Miscellany: Presented to W.S. Mackie* (New York: Oxford University Press, 1977) p. 95.
7   See, for example, H.A. MacDougall, *Racial Myth in English History: Trojans, Teutons, and Anglo-Saxons* (Hanover, NH: University Press of New England, 1982).
8   A. Grafton and L. Jardine, *From Humanism to the Humanities: Education and the Liberal Arts in 15th and 16th Century Europe* (Cambridge, MA: Harvard University Press, 1986); T.W. Baldwin, *William Shakespeare's Small Latine and Lesse Greeke* (Urbana, IL: University of Illinois Press, 1944) 2 vols.
9   Kahn (1997) p. 6.
10   K. Newman, 'Renaissance Family Politics and Shakespeare's *The Taming of the Shrew'*, *English Literary Renaissance* 16,1 (1986) pp. 86–100.
11   P. Rackin, *Stages of History: Shakespeare's English Chronicles* (Ithaca: Cornell University Press, 1990) p. 21.
12   See, for example, *A Companion to Shakespeare*, ed. D. Scott Kastan (Oxford: Blackwell, 1999), especially R. Dutton, 'Licensing and Censorihp', pp. 377–91; S. McMillin, 'Professional Playwrighting', pp. 225–38; W. Ingram, 'The Economics of Playing', pp. 313–27.
13   See S. Mullaney, *The Place of the Stage: License, Play and Power in Renaissance England* (Chicago: University of Chicago Press, 1988); L.A. Montrose, '"The Purpose of Playing": Reflections on a Shakespearean Anthropology', *Helios* 7, 2 (1980) pp. 51–74.
14   Rackin (1990) p. 31.
15   C. Ronan, *'Antike Roman': Power Symbology and the Roman Play in Early Modern England, 1585–1635* (Athens, GA: University of Georgia Press, 1995).

16   Kahn (1997) p. 11.
17   R. Halpern, *The Poetics of Primitive Accumulation: English Renaissance Culture and the Genealogy of Capital* (Ithaca: Cornell University Press, 1991).
18   Kahn (1997) p. 13.
19   G.K. Hunter, 'A Roman Thought: Renaissance Attitudes to History Exemplified in Shakespeare and Jonson', in B.S Lee, ed., *An English Miscellany: Presented to W.S. Mackie* (New York: Oxford University Press, 1977) p. 94.
20   Kahn (1997) p. 14.
21   MacCallum argues that Shakespeare had no appreciation especially of Roman republican theory and could only offer analogies with the history of his own and his contemporaries' immediate experience. See Chapter 7.
22   J.W. Scott, 'Gender: A Useful Category of Historical Analysis', in *Gender and the Politics of History* (New York: Columbia University, 1988) p. 38.
23   Kahn (1997) p. 15.
24   Kahn (1997) p. 16.
25   B. Smith, *Homosexual Desire in Shakespeare's England: A Cultural Poetics* (Chicago: Chicago University Press, 1991) pp. 56–7.
26   Kahn (1997) pp. 16–17.
27   Kahn (1997) p. 17.
28   Kahn specifically cites N. Schor, 'Female Fetishism: The Case of George Sand', in S.R. Suleiman (ed.) *The Female Body in Western Culture: Contemporary Perspectives* (Cambridge, MA: Harvard University Press, 1986) pp. 363–72; C. Bernheimer, 'Freudianism and Decadence: Salome's Severed Heads', in E. Apter and W. Pietz, *Fetishism as Cultural Discourse* (Ithaca: Cornell University Press, 1993) pp. 62–83; M. Garber, 'Fetish Envy', *October* 54 (1990) pp. 45–56.
29   Kahn (1997) p. 18.
30   Kahn cites W.A. Rebhorn, 'The Crisis of Aristocracy in *Julius Caesar*', *Renaissance Quarterly* 43, 1 (1990) pp. 75–111, who argues that 'In Renaissance rhetorical and educational theory, emulation is classified as a form of imitation, an identification with one's model at the same time as one attempts surpass it' and interprets this as suggesting that emulation can imply 'a form of brotherhood or comradeship or even love' but also 'is a competitive urge that necessarily involves struggle, but which can also, when taken to an extreme, entail feelings of hatred and envy or jealousy'. This is reasonably put. However, to say that something may become something else is not to say that it is really something else all along. Emulation may turn into rivalry but it is not itself rivalry.
31   Kahn (1997) p. 19.
32   S. Felman, 'Re-reading Femininity', *Yale French Studies* 62 (1981) pp. 19–44.
33   Kahn (1997) p. 20.
34   See D. Bevington, ed., *Antony and Cleopatra* (Cambridge: Cambridge University Press, 1990). Wells and Taylor claim that echoes of the play in Barnabe Barnes's *The Devil's Charter*, acted by Shakespeare's company in February 1607, suggest that *Antony and Cleopatra* was written no later than 1606, 'and stylistic evidence supports that date': *Coriolanus* they place 'around 1608'(*William Shakespeare: The Complete Works*, ed. S. Wells and G. Taylor, Oxford: Oxford University Press, 1988). R.H. Case argued for 1606/7 and ruled out 1608 (see p. 71 *supra*).
35   Kahn (1997) p. 110.
36   L. Thomson, '*Antony and Cleopatra*, Act 4, Scene 16: "A Heavy Sight"', *Shakespeare Survey* 41 (1988) pp. 77–90, pp. 77–8; M. Neill, 'A Note on the Staging of 4.16 and 5.2', in *The Tragedy of Antony and Cleopatra*, ed. M. Neill (Oxford: Oxford University Press, 1994) p. 68; J. Adelman, *The Common Liar: An Essay on Antony and Cleopatra* (New Haven: Yale University Press, 1973).
37   J. Dollimore, 'Shakespeare, Cultural Materialism, Feminism and Marxist Humanism', *New Literary History: A Journal of Theory and Interpretation* 21, 3 (1990) pp. 471–93, p. 486.

38   L. Charnes, 'What's Love Got to Do With it? Reading the Liberal Humanist Romance in Shakespeare's *Antony and Cleopatra*', *Textual Practice* 6, 1 (1992) pp. 1–16, p. 7.

39   Kahn (1997) p. 111.

40   J. Butler (1990) warns us not to assume a straightforward order of priority in which given biological sex distinctions are translated via cultural practice into gender identities. I do not proceed further with this discussion as it is not directly germane to Kahn's discussion of *Antony and Cleopatra* but it is most important not to assume that *any* identification is 'prior' to cultural practice.

41   L. Hughes-Hallett, *Cleopatra: Histories, Dreams and Distortions* (London: Bloomsbury, 1990) p. 4.

42   Kahn (1997) p. 112.

43   C. Kinney, 'The Queen's Two Bodies and the Divided Emperor: Some Problems of Identity in *Antony and Cleopatra*', in A.M. Haselkorn and B.S. Travitsky (eds) *The Renaissance Englishwoman in Print: Counterbalancing the Canon* (Amherst: University of Massachusetts Press, 1990) pp. 177–86; E. Kosofsky Sedgwick, *Between Men: English Literature and Male Homosocial Desire* (New York: Columbia University Press, 1985).

44   Kahn (1997) p. 113.

45   Kinney (1990) p. 180.

46   Kahn (1997) p. 115.

47   Kahn (1997) p. 116.

48   L.T. Fitz, 'Egyptian Queens and Male Reviewers', *Shakespeare Quarterly* 28, 3 (1977) pp. 297–316, p. 310.

49   A. Loomba, *Gender, Race, Renaissance Drama*, 2nd edn (Oxford: Oxford University Press, 1992) p. 75.

50   R.P. Wheeler, '"Since first we were dissevered": Trust and Autonomy in Shakespearean Tragedy and Romance' in M. Schwartz and C. Kahn, eds, *Representing Shakespeare: New Psychoanalytic Essays* (Baltimore: Johns Hopkins University Press, 1980); M. Gohlke, '"I wooed thee with my sword": Shakespeare's Tragic Paradigms', in Schwartz and Kahn (1980); M. Neill, 'A Note on the Staging of 4.16 and 5.2', in *The Tragedy of Antony and Cleopatra*, ed. M. Neill (Oxford: Oxford University Press, 1994); J. Dollimore, '*Antony and Cleopatra* (c. 1607): *Virtus* Under Erasure' in *Radical Tragedy: Religion, Ideology and Power in the Drama of Shakespeare and His Contemporaries* (Manchester: Manchester University Press, 1984); P. Erickson, *Patriarchal Structures in Shakespeare's Drama* (Los Angeles: University of California Press, 1985); J. Adelman, *Suffocating Mothers: Fantasies of Maternal Origin in Shakespeare's Plays* (New York: Routledge, 1992).

51   Kahn (1997) p. 120.

52   Kahn (1997) p. 130.

53   See E.M. Waith, *The Herculean Hero in Marlowe, Chapman, Shakespeare and Dryden* (London: Chatto & Windus, 1962) pp. 115–21, for a discussion of Antony's Herculean rage.

54   Kahn (1997) p. 131.

55   Kahn misses an opportunity when she later, quite correctly, describes Cleopatra's suicide as 'exclusively a female enterprise'. This contrast is not so fully pointed up without Antony's being an equally exclusively male enterprise. Perhaps this was the contrast in which Shakespeare the dramatist was interested, as it does offer a poignant pattern of the lovers isolated from one another and accompanied exclusively by members of their own sex.

56   L. Helms, '"The High Roman Fashion": Sacrifice, Suicide and the Shakespearean Stage', *PMLA* 107, 3 (1992) pp. 554–65, p. 559.

57   J.F. Danby, 'The Shakespearian Dialectic: An Aspect of *Antony and Cleopatra*', *Poets on Fortune's Hill* (Faber: London, 1952).

58   Loomba (1992) p. 124.

59   Loomba (1992) p. 125.

60   Loomba (1992) p. 125.

61   Loomba (1992) p. 126.

62   Loomba (1992) p. 127.
63   Loomba (1992) p. 128.
64   Loomba (1992) p. 128.
65   Loomba (1992) p. 128–90.
66   Loomba (1992) p. 129.
67   Loomba (1992) p. 129.
68   Loomba (1992) p. 130.
69   Loomba (1992) p. 130.

CHAPTER NINE: POSTMODERNISTS: *ANTONY AND CLEOPATRA*: 'A CHILD O' THE TIME'?

1   L.T. Fitz, 'Egyptian Queens and Male Reviewers', *Shakespeare Quarterly* 28, 3 (1977) pp. 297–316.
2   D. Stempel, 'The Transmigration of the Crocodile', *Shakespeare Quarterly* 7 (1956) pp. 59–72, p. 63.
3   R.E. Fitch, 'No Greater Crack?', *Shakespeare Quarterly* 19 (1968) pp. 3–17, p. 6.
4   J. Markels, *The Pillar of the World: 'Antony and Cleopatra' in Shakespeare's Development* (Columbus, OH: Ohio State University Press, 1968) p. 140.
5   J. Middleton Murry, *Shakespeare* (London: Jonathan Cape, 1936) p. 377.
6   P. Alexander, *Shakespeare's Life and Art* (London: J. Nisbet, 1939) p. 178.
7   M. Lloyd, 'Cleopatra as Isis', *Shakespeare Survey* 12 (1959) pp. 88–94, p. 94.
8   L. Simpson, 'Shakespeare's "Cleopatra"', *Fortnightly Review*, 129 (1928) pp. 332–42, p. 332. The essay was reprinted in *The Secondary Heroes of Shakespeare and Other Essays* (1951). Fitz gives the article reference as 'NS 123' (March 1928).
9   Fitz (1977) p. 310.
10   See Chapter 9 above.
11   Fitz (1977) p. 313.
12   *Antony and Cleopatra*, ed. M.R. Ridley (London: Methuen, 1965) p. 276.
13   A.C. Bradley, *Oxford Lectures on Poetry* (London: Macmillan, 1909) pp. 286–7.
14   *King Lear* is at least as early as 26 December 1606, when it was performed at court before James VI and I (according to the entry in the Stationers' Register on 26 November 1607), and may have been composed in late 1605. For *Antony and Cleopatra*, R.H. Case argued for a date earlier than 1608, although the entry in the Stationers' Register is for 20 May 1608 (*Arden Shakespeare*, 1906); S. Wells and G. Taylor go further, claiming that it was composed 'no later than 1606' (*Oxford Shakespeare*, 1988). Kahn follows Bevington's argument in favour of 1608 as the latest possible date. It seems likely that these plays were written close together.
15   Fitz (1977) p. 315.
16   A.P. Riemer, *A Reading of Shakespeare's 'Antony and Cleopatra'* (Sydney: University of Sydney Press, 1968) p. 100.
17   Fitz (1977) p. 316.
18   Quoted by Case, *Antony and Cleopatra*, ed. M.R. Ridley (London: Methuen, 1965) p. xxxii.
19   See D. Macey, ed., *The Penguin Dictionary of Critical Theory* (Harmondsworth: Penguin, 2000) for brief definitions and further reading.
20   L. Tennenhouse, *Power on Display: The Politics of Shakespeare's Genres* (London: Methuen, 1986).
21   G. Holderness, B. Loughrey and A. Murphy, eds, *Shakespeare: The Roman Plays* (London: Longman, 1996) pp. 66–71.
22   Holderness et al. (1996) p. 68.
23   See D. Macey, ed. (2000).
24   M. Neill, ed., *The Tragedy of Antony and Cleopatra* (Oxford: Oxford University Press, 1994) p. 68.

25   Holderness et al. (1996) p. 70.

26   There is an impressive literature on Antony's masculinity as a new kind of, or development of, masculinity. See R.J. Dorius, 'Shakespeare's Dramatic Modes and *Antony and Cleopatra*', *Literatur als Kritik des Lebens* (Heidelberg: Quelle und Meyer, 1975) pp. 91–3; P. Erickson, *Patriarchal Structures in Shakespeare's Drama* (Berkeley: University of California Press, 1985) pp. 131–4; J.J. Greene, '*Antony and Cleopatra*: The Birth and Death of Androgyny', *University of Hartford Studies in Literature* 19 (1987) pp. 25–44; R. Ornstein, 'The Ethic of the Imagination: Love and Art in "Antony and Cleopatra"', *Later Shakespeare*, Stratford-upon-Avon Studies 8 (London: Edward Arnold, 1966); R.B. Waddington, 'Antony and Cleopatra: "What Venus did with Mars"', *Shakespeare Studies* 2 (1963) pp. 223; E.M. Waith, 'Manhood and Valour in Two Shakespearean Tragedies', *English Literary History* 17 (1950) pp. 268–73. C. Thomas Neely, *Broken Nuptials in Shakespeare's Plays* (New Haven, CT: Yale University Press, 1985) argues that Antony, enlarging masculinity by incorporating female elements, confirms it.

27   Holderness et al. (1996) p. 71.

28   Holderness et al. (1996) p. 73.

29   Holderness et al. (1996) p. 74.

30   Holderness et al. (1996) p. 79.

31   It is worth noting that Cleopatra also imagines Antony's body as gigantic: 'his rear'd arm/Crested the world (V.ii.82–3)'.

32   H. Fisch, '"Antony and Cleopatra": The Limits of Mythology', *Shakespeare Survey* 23 (1970) pp. 61; M. Lloyd, 'Cleopatra as Isis', *Shakespeare Survey* 12 (1959) pp. 91–4; B. Bono, *Literary Transvaluation From Vergilian Epic to Shakespearean Tragicomedy* (Berkeley: University of California Press, 1984) pp 199–213.

33   Adelman wryly notes that this set of connections is well established in the critical literature. She cites: Ornstein, 'The Ethic of the Imagination', p. 36; Adelman, *Common Liar*, pp. 127–31; M. Payne, 'Erotic Irony and Polarity in *Antony and Cleopatra*', *Shakespeare Quarterly* 24 (1973) pp. 266–9; Dorius, 'Shakespeare's Dramatic Modes, p. 93; C. Brown Kuriyama, 'The Mother of the World: A Psychoanalytic Interpretation of Shakespeare's *Antony and Cleopatra*', *English Literary Renaissance* 7 (1977) pp. 324–51, p. 338; S. Snyder, 'Patterns of Motion in *Antony and Cleopatra*, *Shakespeare Survey* 33 (1980) pp. 115–21. See also D. Bevington's introduction to his edition of *Antony and Cleopatra* (Cambridge: Cambridge University Press, 1990) p. 26 for a useful summary.

34   Holderness et al. (1996) p. 85.

35   S.A. Shapiro has explored ambivalence in *Antony and Cleopatra*: 'The Varying Shore of the World: Ambivalence in *Antony and Cleopatra*', *Modern Language Quarterly* 27 (1966) pp. 18–32.

36   Holderness et al. (1996) pp. 85–6.

37   I do not think that the question can be given an answer as clear-cut as I think that Adelman does; I would place more emphasis still than she does on the fact that they both must die to enter this imaginative space, which means, of course, that it is eliminated in the moment of its achievement, although I certainly go along with her estimation of the power of Cleopatra's portrait of Antony.

38   L. Bamber, *Comic Women, Tragic Men: A Study of Gender and Genre in Shakespeare* (Stanford, California: Stanford University Press, 1982) esp. pp. 55–9, 66–9.

39   C.L. Barber, *The Idea of Honour in the English Drama 1591–1700* (Göteborg, 1957); M. Jones, *English Politics and the Concept of Honour 1485–1642* (Oxford: Past and Present Society, 1978).

40   E. M. Waith, *The Herculean Hero in Marlowe, Chapman, Shakespeare and Dryden* (London: Chatto & Windus, 1962) p. 118.

41   G. Wilson Knight, *The Imperial Theme: Further Interpretations of Shakespeare's Tragedies Including the Roman Plays* (London: Methuen, 1965) p. 217.

42   D. Traversi, *An Approach to Shakespeare*, II (London: Hollis & Carter, 1968) p. 208.

43 Holderness et al. (1996) p. 96.
44 Holderness et al. (1996) p. 100.
45 Holderness et al. (1996) p. 102.
46 Holderness et al. (1996) p. 103.
47 Holderness et al. (1996) p. 105.

Select Bibliography

Researching for this Guide, I collected over six hundred titles, not all of which had direct relevance to *Antony and Cleopatra*, but a good few of which did. Shakespeare has had more written about him than any other English writer, and more than many put together. Background reading will necessarily be selective. Starting with an essay that interests you, or pursuing a topic (*Antony and Cleopatra* psychoanalytically interpreted perhaps, following Janet Adelman; or *Antony and Cleopatra* as a political play, looking at J.E. Phillips or Paul Siegel), you will quickly come across other references in those essays and will be able to pursue your own path from that point. These recommendations are starting points.

The periodicals *Shakespeare Quarterly* and *Shakespeare Survey* should be consulted for reviews as well as for substantive articles.

STUDIES BEFORE 1970

Barnet, Sylvan, 'Recognition and Reversal in *Antony and Cleopatra*', *Shakespeare Quarterly*, 8 (1957) pp. 331–4

Barroll, J. Leeds, 'Shakespeare and Roman History', *Modern Language Review*, 53 (1958) pp. 327–43

Bethell, S.L., *Shakespeare and the Popular Imagination* (London: P.S. King, 1944)

Bradley, A.C., *Oxford Lectures on Poetry* (London: MacMillan, 1909)

Charney, M., *Shakespeare's Roman Plays: The Function of the Imagery in the Drama* (Cambridge, MA: Harvard University Press, 1961)

Cunningham, Dolora G., 'The Characterization of Shakespeare's Cleopatra', *Shakespeare Quarterly*, 6 (1955) pp. 9–17

Danby, John F., 'The Shakespearian Dialectic: An Aspect of *Antony and Cleopatra*', in *Poets on Fortune's Hill* (London: Faber, 1952)

Dickey, Franklin M., *Not Wisely But Too Well: Shakespeare's Love Tragedies* (San Marino, CA: Huntington Library, 1957)

Farnham, Willard, *Shakespeare's Tragic Frontier: The World of His Final Tragedies* (Berkeley: University of California Press, 1950)

Fitch, Robert E., 'No Greater Crack?', *Shakespeare Quarterly*, 19 (1968) pp. 3–17

Frye, Northrop, *Fools of Time* (Toronto: University of Toronto Press, 1967)

Knight, G. Wilson, *The Imperial Theme: Further Interpretations of Shakespeare's Tragedies Including the Roman Plays* (Oxford: Oxford University Press, 1931)

Lloyd, Michael, 'Cleopatra as Isis', *Shakespeare Studies*, 12 (1959) pp. 88–94

MacCallum, Mungo W., *Shakespeare's Roman Plays and their Background* (London: Macmillan, 1910)

Ornstein, Robert, 'The Ethic of the Imagination: Love and Art in "Antony and Cleopatra"', *Later Shakespeare*, Stratford-upon-Avon Studies 8 (London: Edward Arnold, 1966)

Rabkin, Norman, *Shakespeare and the Common Understanding* (New York: Free Press, 1967)

Riemer, A.P., *A Reading of Shakespeare's 'Antony and Cleopatra'* (Sydney: Sydney University Press, 1968)

Rose, Paul Lawrence, 'The Politics of Antony and Cleopatra', *Shakespeare Quarterly*, 20 (1969) pp. 379–89

Schanzer, Ernest, *The Problem Plays of Shakespeare: A Study of 'Julius Caesar', 'Measure for Measure', and 'Antony and Cleopatra'* (New York: Schocken, 1963)

Shapiro, Stephen A., ' "The Varying Shore of the World": Ambivalence in *Antony and Cleopatra'*, *Modern Language Quarterly*, 27 (1966) pp. 18–32

Simpson, Lucie, 'Shakespeare's "Cleopatra" ', *Fortnightly Review*, 129 (1928) pp. 332–42 (reprinted in *The Secondary Heroes of Shakespeare and Other Essays*, London, 1951)

Spencer, Benjamin T., '*Antony and Cleopatra* and the Paradoxical Metaphor', *Shakespeare Quarterly*, 9 (1958) pp. 373–8

Spencer, T.J.B., 'Shakespeare and the Elizabethan Romans', *Shakespeare Survey*, 10 (1957) pp. 27–38

Stempel, Daniel, 'The Transmigration of the Crocodile', *Shakespeare Quarterly*, 20 (1969) pp. 59–72

Stone, George Winchester Jr., 'Garrick's Presentation of *Antony and Cleopatra'*, *Review of English Studies*, 13 (1937) pp. 20–38

Traversi, D., *Shakespeare: The Roman Plays* (Stanford: Stanford University Press, 1963)

Traversi, Derek, *An Approach to Shakespeare* (London: Hollis & Carter, 1968)

Van Doren, Mark, *Shakespeare* (New York: Doubleday, 1939)

Waddington, Raymond B., 'What Venus Did with Mars', *Shakespeare Survey*, 2 (1966) pp. 210–27

Waith, Eugene M., *The Herculean Hero in Marlowe, Chapman, Shakespeare and Dryden* (London: Chatto & Windus, 1962)

Walker, Roy, 'The Northern Star: An Essay on the Roman Plays', *Shakespeare Quarterly*, 2 (1951) p. 287

LATER STUDIES

Adelman, Janet, *The Common Liar: An Essay on 'Antony and Cleopatra'* (New Haven: Yale University Press, 1973)

Adelman, Janet, *Suffocating Mothers: Fantasies of Maternal Origin in Shakespeare's Plays* (New York: Routledge, 1992)

Bamber, Linda, *Comic Women, Tragic Men: A Study of Gender and Genre in Shakespeare* (Stanford, CA: Stanford University Press, 1982)

Bate, Jonathan, *Shakespeare and Ovid* (Oxford: Clarendon Press, 1994)

Bono, Barbara J., *Literary Transvaluation: From Vergilian Epic to Shakespearean Tragicomedy* (Berkeley: University of California Press, 1984)

Brower, Reuben A., *Hero and Saint: Shakespeare and the Greco-Roman Heroic Tradition* (New York: Oxford University Press, 1971)

Cantor, Paul A., *Shakespeare's Rome: Republic and Empire* (Ithaca, NY: Cornell University Press, 1976).

Charnes, Linda, 'What's Love Got to Do With it? Reading the Liberal Humanist Romance in Shakespeare's *Antony and Cleopatra'*, *Textual Practice* 6, 1 (1992) pp. 1–16

Coates, John, ' "The Choice of Hercules" in *Antony and Cleopatra'*, *Shakespeare Studies* (1978) pp. 45–52

Doran, Madeleine, ' "High Events as These": The Language of Hyperbole in *Antony and Cleopatra'*, *Shakespeare's Dramatic Language: Essays by Madeleine Doran* (Madison: University of Wisconsin Press, 1976)

Erickson, Peter, *Patriarchal Structures in Shakespeare's Drama* (Berkeley: University of California Press, 1985)

Felperin, Howard, *Shakespearean Representation: Mimesis and Modernity in Elizabethan Tragedy* (Princeton: Princeton University Press, 1977)

Fichter, Andrew, '*Antony and Cleopatra*: "The Time of Universal Peace" ', *Shakespeare Survey*, 33 (1980) pp. 99–111

Fisch, Harold, '*Antony and Cleopatra*: The Limits of Mythology', *Shakespeare Survey*, 23 (1970) pp. 59–67

Fitz, Linda T., 'Egyptian Queens and Male Reviewers', *Shakespeare Quarterly*, 28, 3 (1977) pp. 297–316

Greene, James J., '*Antony and Cleopatra*: The Birth and Death of Androgyny', *University of Hartford Studies in Literature*, 19 (1987) pp. 25–44

Helms, L., ' "The High Roman Fashion": Sacrifice, Suicide and the Shakespearean Stage', *PMLA*, 107, 3 (1992) pp. 554–65

Holderness, Graham, Bryan Loughrey and Andrew Murphy, eds, *Shakespeare: The Roman Plays* (London: Longman, 1996)

Homan, Sidney R., 'Divided Response and the Imagination in *Antony and Cleopatra*', *Philological Quarterly*, 49 (1970) pp. 460–8

Kahn, Coppélia, *Roman Shakespeare: Warriors, Wounds and Women* (London: Routledge, 1997)

Kinney, C., 'The Queen's Two Bodies and the Divided Emperor: Some Problems of Identity in *Antony and Cleopatra*', in A.M. Haselkorn and B.S. Travitsky (eds) *The Renaissance Englishwoman in Print: Counterbalancing the Canon* (Amherst: University of Massachusetts Press, 1990) pp. 177–86

Kuriyama, Constance Brown, 'The Mother of the World: A Psychoanalytic Interpretation of Shakespeare's *Antony and Cleopatra*', *English Literary Renaissance*, 7 (1977) pp. 324–51

Lamb, Margaret, '*Antony and Cleopatra*' on the English Stage (Toronto: University of Toronto Press, 1980)

Leggatt, Alexander, *Shakespeare's Political Drama: The History of the Roman Plays* (London: Routledge, 1988)

Loomba, Ania, *Gender, Race, Renaissance Drama* (Manchester: Manchester University Press, 1989)

Markels, Julian, *The Pillar of the World: 'Antony and Cleopatra' in Shakespeare's Development* (Columbus, OH: Ohio State University Press, 1968)

Miola, Robert S., *Shakespeare's Rome* (Cambridge: Cambridge University Press, 1983)

Neill, Michael, 'A Note on the Staging of 4.16 and 5.2', in *The Tragedy of Antony and Cleopatra*, ed. Michael Neill (Oxford: Oxford University Press, 1994) p. 68

Neely, Carol Thomas, *Broken Nuptials in Shakespeare's Plays* (New Haven, CT: Yale University Press, 1985)

Nevo, Ruth, *Tragic Form in Shakespeare* (Princeton, NJ: Princeton University Press, 1972)

Paster, G.K., *The Idea of the City in the Age of Shakespeare* (Athens: Georgia University Press, 1985)

Payne, Michael, 'Erotic Irony and Polarity in *Antony and Cleopatra*', *Shakespeare Quarterly* 24 (1973) pp. 266–9

Phillips, J.E. Jr., *The State in Shakespeare's Greek and Roman Plays* (1940; rpt. New York: Octagon, 1972)

Platt, M., *Rome and Romans According to Shakespeare*, Salzburg Studies in English Literature, JDS, no. 51 (Salzburg Institut für Englische Sprache und Literatur, 1983)

Siegel, Paul N., *Shakespeare's English and Roman History Plays: A Marxist Approach* (London: Associated University Presses, 1986)

Simmons, J.L., *Shakespeare's Pagan World: The Roman Tragedies* (Charlottesville, VA: University of Virginia Press, 1973).

Snyder, Susan, 'Patterns of Motion in *Antony and Cleopatra*', *Shakespeare Survey*, 33 (1980) pp. 115–21

Tennenhouse, Leonard, *Power on Display: The Politics of Shakespeare's Genres* (London: Methuen, 1986)

Thomas, V., *Shakespeare's Roman Worlds* (London: Routledge, 1989)

Thomson, Leslie, '*Antony and Cleopatra*, Act 4, Scene 16: "A Heavy Sight" ', *Shakespeare Survey*, 41 (1988) pp. 77–90

Velz, John W., 'The Ancient World in Shakespeare: Authenticity or Anachronism: A Retrospect', *Shakespeare Survey*, 31 (1978) pp. 1–12

Index